Questions about the authenticity and authority of sunna have long been of central importance to the study of Islam, especially to those concerned with Islamic law. In this fascinating study, Daniel Brown traces the emergence of modern debates over sunna, focusing in particular on Egypt and Pakistan where these controversies have raged most fiercely, and assesses the implications of new approaches to the law on contemporary movements of Islamic revival. Using the case of modern Islam as a starting-point, the author considers how adherents of any great tradition deal with change and explores the impact of modernity on attitudes towards religious authority generally. This important book makes a major contribution to the understanding of contemporary Islam, and will be of interest to scholars of the Middle East and South Asia, as well as to those specifically concerned with the teaching and implementation of Islamic law.

Cambridge Middle East Studies

Rethinking tradition in modern Islamic thought

Cambridge Middle East Studies has been established to publish books on the nineteenth- and twentieth-century Middle East and North Africa. The aim of the series is to provide new and original interpretations of aspects of Middle Eastern societies and their histories. To achieve disciplinary diversity, books will be solicited from authors writing in a wide range of fields including history, sociology, anthropology, political science and political economy. The emphasis will be on producing books offering an original approach along theoretical and empirical lines. The series is intended for students and academics, but the more accessible and wide-ranging studies will also appeal to the interested general reader.

1 Parvin Paidar, *Women and the political process in twentieth-century Iran*
2 Israel Gershoni and James Jankowski, *Redefining the Egyptian nation, 1930–1945*
3 Annelies Moors, *Women, property and Islam: Palestinian experiences, 1920–1990*
4 Paul Kingston, *Britain and the politics of modernization in the Middle East, 1945–1958*

Rethinking tradition in modern Islamic thought

Daniel W. Brown
Mount Holyoke College

CAMBRIDGE
UNIVERSITY PRESS

Published by the Press Syndicate of the University of Cambridge
The Pitt Building, Trumpington Street, Cambridge CB2 1RP
40 West 20th Street, New York, NY 10011-4211, USA
10 Stamford Road, Oakleigh, Melbourne 3166, Australia

First published 1996

Printed in Great Britain at the University Press, Cambridge

A catalogue record for this book is available from the British Library

Library of Congress cataloguing in publication data

ISBN 0 521 570778 hardback

SE

To Carol

Contents

Preface

This study owes its inspiration to Fazlur Rahman who was both a keen scholar of modern Islamic thought and himself a major contributor to the rethinking of the Islamic tradition that is the focus of this book. His personal concern for questions related to sunna first alerted me to the importance of the topic for modern Muslims, and readers familiar with Fazlur Rahman's work will recognize the imprint of his scholarship here. His death in 1988 was a loss to all those concerned with the study of Islam and a special loss to his students.

I am likewise indebted to friends, colleagues, and family who encouraged me to carry the project forward. Thanks especially to Wadad Kadi, Charles Adams, and William Graham who all gave generously of their advice and time at various stages of my work. I am grateful to the many people who helped me in the course of research visits to Pakistan and Egypt: Peter and Erica Dodd and the staff of United States Educational Foundation in Pakistan, Dr. Zafar Ishaq Ansari and the faculty and staff of the Islamic Research Institute in Islamabad, Aḥmad Ramaḍān of the Library of Congress office in Cairo, and Dr. Muḥammad Sirāj and other faculty and staff of the Dār al-ʿUlūm at Cairo University. Thanks also to my colleagues in the Department of Religion at Mount Holyoke College for their encouragement.

The field research that enabled me to proceed with this project would have been impossible without generous funding from a Fulbright Grant for research in Pakistan and a Fulbright–Hayes dissertation fellowship for research in both Pakistan and Egypt. The writing of the dissertation was supported by a grant from the Charlotte Newcombe Foundation.

My final note of thanks must go to my family, whose love, support, and encouragement made this work possible. My parents, Ralph and Polly Brown, not only supported much of my education but passed on to me and to all their children their own love for Pakistan, their adopted home. My children, Sarah, Ruth Anne, and Stephen, grew with this project; they were a frequent source of refreshment from the weariness of study. Thanks, finally, to Carol, my wife, friend, and fellow-traveler who took on this project with me and deserves much of the credit for its completion.

Introduction: the prism of modernity

Since the middle of the nineteenth century, Muslim thinkers have faced numerous and repeated challenges to classical Islamic ideas about religious authority. Upheavals in the Muslim world have stimulated widespread reexamination of the classical sources of Islamic law as Muslims have struggled to preserve, adapt, or redefine their social and legal norms in the face of changed conditions. A central issue in this ongoing struggle has been the question of the nature, status, and authority of the sunna, the normative example of the Prophet Muḥammad. Because of Muḥammad's status as messenger of God, his words and actions are accepted by most Muslims as a source of religious and legal authority second only to the Qurʾān. Indeed, the Qurʾān itself repeatedly commands its readers to obey Allāh *and* His messenger. The *imitatio Muḥammadi* thus became the standard for ethical behavior among Muslims, forming the basis for Islamic law and setting the standard for even the most mundane activities – the order in which fingernails should be cut or the proper length of the beard. During the twentieth century, however, the position of sunna has been threatened in a variety of ways as Muslim thinkers have searched for a solid basis for the revival of Islam. The problem of sunna has become the most important dimension of a modern Muslim crisis of religious authority, occupying a central place in Muslim religious discourse.

Understanding the Muslim struggle to define the position of sunna is critical if we are to understand fully the experience of modern Muslims, but the topic also has universal relevance for our understanding of how adherents to the great religious traditions have faced the challenges posed by modernity. The way that modern Muslims have faced their own crisis of religious authority, centered on sunna, suggests insights into a larger problem in the study of religion, that is, the relationship between tradition and modernity and the related question of how participants in a great tradition deal with change. Our central subject, then, is tradition – not tradition according to current scholarly fashion, but tradition in an old-fashioned sense: a deposit of knowledge or truth, originating with a past authority, and handed down within a religious community.[1] In Islamic thought, tradition in this sense is embodied in the sunna of the Prophet, preserved by his followers and faithfully handed down within the Muslim community. For most Muslims, sunna is a symbol of the link with the Prophetic era, the representation of the Prophet in the here and now, a concrete embodiment of the need that Muslims have felt in every generation for continuity with an ideal past.

In seeking to understand modern Muslim discussions of sunna and what they tell us about tradition and modernity, we must take on a tendency, evident in many treatments of modern Muslim intellectual history, to view the development of Muslim ideas in heuristic terms. Modern Islamic thought, according to the paradigm adopted by many orientalists, is in a transitional phase in which Muslim thinkers must come to terms with the inexorable forces of modernity, rationalism, and liberalism emanating from the West. According to this paradigm, exemplified in Wilfred Cantwell Smith's classic *Islam in Modern History*, modern controversies among Muslims, such as the debates over sunna described in this study, should be viewed as skirmishes in an ongoing battle between tradition and modernity, revelation and reason, liberalism and reaction.

Such an approach presumes a clearcut dichotomy between tradition and modernity, a presumption which is deeply rooted in Enlightenment thought, but which deserves reexamination. For Enlightenment thinkers, reason was a searchlight, piercing the darkness of tradition, breaking through a fog of ignorance to illuminate the truth. The pioneers of the Enlightenment might be excused for dramatizing the clash of reason and tradition or reason and revelation so starkly: they were engaged in a battle for liberty of thought, in which their lives were sometimes at stake. But in so portraying the conflict of reason and tradition, Enlightenment thinkers perhaps failed to recognize the degree to which they were, themselves, rooted in the traditions from which they claimed to have escaped.

Against the Enlightenment tradition, which is still pervasive in western academic culture, I would suggest that tradition is not an enemy of change, but the very stuff that is subject to change. Tradition both changes and may be used to justify change; it can, in fact, be revolutionary.[2] The history of Islamic thought provides numerous examples of how the intellectual tradition of Islam has provided the underpinnings for adaptation, reform, and revolution. The early Kharijite movement, the ʿAbbāsid "revolution," and the reformism of Ibn Taymiyya are early examples of the dynamism of tradition. The "Islamic" revolution in Iran, the strength of Sunni revivalism in the Arab world, and the emergence of

Islamic feminism are some widely divergent examples of more recent movements that look to tradition to justify change.

At the same time, it is also evident that tradition is frequently appealed to as a way of defending against perceived innovation, as a way of preserving threatened values. Alternative uses of tradition are thus a major battleground; there is fierce competition to control the process by which the content of tradition is defined, and for modern Muslims, sunna has become the bitterest point of conflict. Thus, the modern problem of sunna arises out of conflict among Muslims over the definition and content of the authentic tradition, and over the method by which that tradition is to be defined.

If modernity and tradition should not be viewed as diametrically opposed to one another, how are we to understand their relationship? I would suggest a reversal of the Enlightenment metaphor. Rather than viewing modernity as a source of light, dispelling the darkness of tradition, we should instead imagine tradition as a beam of light, refracted by the prism of modernity. A tradition emerges from the prism of modernity as a multi-colored spectrum of responses. Some responses will show the effects of modernity much more dramatically than others, but none will be entirely untouched. At the same time, each color of the spectrum, each different response, is clearly rooted in the tradition. All responses to modernity from a religious tradition, and even those that seem to have left the tradition altogether behind, maintain a certain continuity with the tradition, just as each band of the spectrum is present in the light entering a prism.

Numerous issues of concern to modern Muslims might be used to illustrate this pattern. Modern debates over women's rights and status, for example, provide a vivid illustration of the dramatically divergent uses to which the tradition can be put. So-called neo-muʿtazilism, the revival of certain aspects of Muʿtazilite theology to justify a rationalist method, offers another example. But no case can provide a better illustration of the relationship of tradition and modernity in Islam than the very symbol and anchor of the tradition, the sunna itself, for as I will argue here, sunna is the fulcrum on which the central debates over religious authority turn.

The major contention of this work, then, is that modern Muslims, along with participants in all great human traditions, are engaged in an ongoing process of *rethinking* the traditions in which they participate. Some, of course, deny any connection with the tradition, and others deny that their activity can be called "rethinking," preferring to see it as the revival or preservation of some ideal and unchanging model. Nonetheless, even the most radical opponents of tradition are not departing from the tradition, but molding it and seeking to lay claim to the authenticity it bestows. Likewise, even the most conservative defenders of tradition cannot help but reshape the very tradition that they seek to preserve unchanged.

Methodology

The understanding of the relationship of tradition and modernity that I have proposed has important implications for our approach to the history of ideas. In the study of modern Muslim intellectual history – indeed, all intellectual history – the attention of scholars is quite naturally drawn to currents of thought that would seem to be new, innovative, holding promise for change. Our attention is riveted especially on ideas that may seem to be the peculiar product of modernity and seem to arise from a struggle to reconcile tradition with the pressures of the modern world. But this tendency is both a product of our own cultural biases and a vestige of the Enlightenment idea of progress. Too often such an approach projects the wishful thinking of the scholar onto his subject; we tend to focus upon ideas and figures that meet with our approval, neglecting broader, but less attractive, currents of thought. Change is not always uni-directional, nor does it always come in packages that seem attractive to academics. The Iranian revolution and the resurgence of fundamentalist and evangelical Protestantism in the United States are cases in point. Both developments came as a surprise to many scholars, and some continue to believe, or hope, that these are merely potholes on the otherwise smooth highway of secularization.

The danger of emphasizing the attractive, the new, or the progressive correlates closely with certain difficult methodological choices faced by anyone engaged in tracing the history of ideas. Among the most important of these is the choice between emphasizing outstanding individuals and emphasizing general trends or "schools of thought." Albert Hourani astutely identified the dangers in both approaches.[3] If we stress the impact of outstanding individuals, we must be certain that the figures chosen are truly influential and truly representative of significant trends in thought. Perhaps the greatest danger inherent in such an approach is of focusing on thinkers whose ideas meet with our approval; we judge someone significant because his or her ideas are attractive. Yet the second method, emphasizing schools of thought rather than individuals, risks a blurring of distinctions between individuals and the false imposition of unity on diverse ideas.

In this work I have chosen the second approach. If we are concerned, as we must be, with the *influence* of ideas and not just with the ideas themselves, then we risk less by choosing to analyze general trends in thought rather than individuals. Indeed, the problem of sunna cannot, in my judgment, be adequately addressed by viewing a few outstanding writers in isolation. Although individual thinkers figure prominently in my analysis, I take them as representative of broader trends or viewpoints. Our concern must be not merely to understand the work of such individuals, but to examine the intellectual climate out of which their ideas grew and the responses their ideas have elicited. In other words, we must heed the reactions of those who may be far from first-rate thinkers, but whose opinions are nevertheless important indicators of the spread of ideas.

In choosing my sources, I have applied a simple test: if a published statement draws a measurable response, it is important; if it passes largely unnoticed, it is not. In effect, then, I have gauged the importance of a work in proportion to the level of controversy it has elicited. Consequently, the major sources for this study are mostly connected with a handful of controversies over sunna in Egypt and Pakistan.

The method I have adopted to analyze modern writings on sunna and the controversial literature that has grown up around them has been to extract from these writings the most important (i.e., most frequently recurring) themes, to establish the context and background of these themes in classical Islamic scholarship, and to analyze modern positions on the topic. In other words, I have attempted to map out the most prominent issues, the *topoi,* around which discussions of sunna have been concentrated, and to analyze the main positions established on these issues by modern Muslims. This approach holds certain disadvantages. It cannot, for instance, do justice to the historical or social context in which each approach to sunna has emerged. Moreover, by isolating sunna as an independent issue it may obscure the interconnectedness of the ideas of an individual or group. A topical approach also has great advantages, however. Such an approach closely reflects the way that Muslims themselves have approached the problem of sunna and it accurately mirrors the structure of their own discussions. In this way it has been my intent to portray modern discussions of sunna as part of an ongoing conversation among Muslim intellectuals centered on a common quest for a vision of society which is at once true to the tradition and relevant to the contemporary situation.

1 The relevance of the past: classical conceptions of Prophetic authority

Modern debates about religious authority are shaped by what Muslims see when they look back at the early history of Islam. Consequently, these modern debates must not be approached in a historical vacuum, as if they represent completely new and unprecedented challenges to traditional ideas about religious authority. In some respects the discussions I will describe are indeed new and a product of modern circumstances, but in other respects they look surprisingly like discussions that took place during the formative phase of Islamic legal thought. The content of Muslim tradition was a matter of controversy long before the reemergence of these questions in the nineteenth century. In fact, hardly an element of the classical consensus about Prophetic authority became established without serious contest.

Controversies over sunna, both ancient and modern, should be viewed as an essential corollary of efforts by Muslims to adapt doctrine to changed circumstances. Because of the stature of sunna as a symbol of the authority of Muḥammad and as a source of continuity with the past, no doctrinal dispute, no legal controversy, no exegetical discussion can be carried on without reference to it. Even for those who seek to reject its authority, sunna has proved too important to ignore. Consequently, early Muslims produced their own spectrum of approaches to sunna, a spectrum remarkably similar to the modern one. Herein lies the connection between ancient and modern debates over sunna, and the significance of the ancient debates to this study.

The classical consensus

Most classical theories of sunna incorporated three essential elements. In classical manuals of Islamic law, the term sunna refers to the authoritative example set by Muḥammad and recorded in traditions (ḥadīth; *akhbār*) about his words, his actions, his acquiescence to the words or actions of others, and his personal characteristics (*ṣifāt*).[1] Thus the first defining element of the doctrine of sunna in its mature form is the exclusive identification of the term with Muḥammad; sunna is by definition *sunnat al-nabī*, the sunna of the Prophet. The second element of the classical theory of sunna is the complete identification of sunna with ḥadīth reports traced to Muḥammad and judged to be authentic; sunna is coextensive with the set of authenticated traditions.[2] A third and final defining characteristic of sunna is its status as revelation (*waḥy*). Sunna, according to classical doctrine, was revealed by God through the agency of the Prophet just as was the Qur'ān.[3] Both sunna and Qur'ān spring from a single source, and the distinction between them is of form only, not of substance. The difference between the two classes of revelations is in how they are used and in the certainty with which they are known. The Qur'ān is revelation that is used in ritual recitation (*tilāwa*), while the sunna is not recited (*ghayr matlū*). In the case of the Qur'ān both text and meaning are of divine origin and can be relied upon with complete certainty, but for sunna the wording of the text is merely conjectural and only the reliability of the sense is guaranteed.

The main building blocks of a classical consensus on sunna were in place during the career of Muḥammad b. Idrīs al-Shāfiʿī (d. 204 A.H.). Moreover, it seems that al-Shāfiʿī was himself chiefly responsible for integrating these building blocks into a coherent system of jurisprudence by effectively championing the adoption of his method as the only legitimate approach to sunna. His great effort, and one in which he was largely successful, was to argue for the exclusive identification of "sunna" with specific precedents set by Muḥammad, that is, with authentic traditions traced back to the Prophet himself. Those who opposed him on this point were the adherents of the early regional "schools" of jurisprudence – in the Ḥijāz, in Iraq, and in Syria – who held to less rigorous definitions of sunna. They incorporated in their definition of sunna not only Prophetic ḥadīth, but also various other sources of precedent, including the example of the Prophet's Companions, the rulings of the Caliphs, and the practice that had gained general acceptance among the jurists of that school. It was against this flexible notion of sunna as the cumulative *accepted practice* of the early schools of jurisprudence, what Schacht calls the "living tradition" of the schools, that al-Shāfiʿī directed the greater part of his polemics.[4]

Evidence of al-Shāfiʿī's success in championing the identification of sunna with Prophetic ḥadīth and in establishing the superiority of this sunna over other sources of precedent is clear: after Shāfiʿī we seldom find the term sunna used for anything other than the sunna of the Prophet.[5] But al-Shāfiʿī's defense of the position of authentic Prophetic ḥadīth as the sole legitimate source of sunna was only a part of his effort to create a system of jurisprudence centered on a coherent approach to the sources of Islamic law. Delineating the relationship between the various sources, especially the relationship of Qurʾān and sunna, was central to his project. On this question al-Shāfiʿī forcefully argued the thesis that the sunna stands on an equal footing with the Qurʾān in authority for "the command of the Prophet is the command of God."[6]

The fact that al-Shāfiʿī had to engage in polemics on such issues – the exclusive identification of sunna with specific precedents of Muḥammad or the revealed nature of sunna – provides sufficient evidence of the existence of a spectrum of approaches to sunna prior to and during his career. At least two approaches to sunna were represented among al-Shāfiʿī's contemporaries: one was the approach of the early legal schools with their "living tradition"; another was that of the speculative theologians, the *ahl al-kalām*, who rejected ḥadīth altogether in favor of reliance on the Qurʾān alone. Shāfiʿī engaged in extended polemics with both of these groups.[7] Consequently, we know that a variety of different attitudes to sunna existed and were debated during the career of al-Shāfiʿī. But it is less clear when and how these attitudes emerged in the two centuries separating his career from that of Muḥammad.

Sunna before al-Shāfiʿī

The word sunna predates the rise of Islam and is well attested in pre-Islamic sources. Sunna is derived from a root meaning of the verb *sanna*, "to form, fashion, or shape" and by extension, "to institute, establish, or prescribe." Bravmann has shown that the concrete meaning of *sanna*, "to assign a certain amount of money or goods to someone," was extended in specialized usage to refer to the action by which an individual decrees or establishes something.[8] Consequently, sunna must of necessity refer to a practice decreed or instituted by a particular person or a group of definite persons.[9] Sunna cannot refer simply to the customs of a tribe or group, but must be associated with a specific individual who instituted it.[10]

The pre-Islamic notion of sunna was almost certainly applied to Muḥammad even during his lifetime.[11] It is improbable that a religious and political figure of the reputation and stature of Muḥammad was not consciously emulated by his followers.[12] Moreover the Qurʾān, although it never mentions *sunnat al-nabī,* certainly gives the Prophet special status and authority among Muslims by the oft-repeated command to obey God and His Prophet.[13] "When the Word of God calls the Prophet's character 'exemplary' and 'great,'" argues Rahman, "is it conceivable that the Muslims from the very beginning, should not have accepted [sunna] as a concept?"[14] The absence in the Qurʾān of specific references to the sunna of Muḥammad does suggest that the application of the term sunna to the

Prophet is post-Qurʾānic, but it does not justify the conclusion that the *idea* of the Prophet as exemplar was a late development.[15]

We may conclude, then, that some notion of sunna was applied to Muḥammad and was in circulation at a very early stage, perhaps during his lifetime. But there is none of the rigidity about early understandings of sunna that we find in the classical discussion. Ideas about sunna developed in a context of rapid social and political change, when notions of religious authority were fluid. From the beginning Muḥammad, as messenger of God, was the focus of religious authority. But when the Prophet was no longer with them, Muslims were not of one mind about how Prophetic authority should be mediated. In the early years after Muḥammad's death it is likely that the dominant assumption, which was preserved in Shīʿite ideas of religious authority, was that Muḥammad's authority would be taken up and wielded by charismatic successors. Such a notion of religious authority would render sunna, in its classical formulation, more or less irrelevant. What need is there to preserve the normative example of the Prophet when you have a living embodiment of Prophetic authority? Later Shīʿī theologians did not reject the notion of sunna, but for them the locus of authority and the source of sunna was with the Shīʿī imāms. But for those Muslims who had no charismatic leader to stand in the place of the Prophet, appeals to the practice of the Prophet became decisive. Nevertheless, until after al-Shāfiʿī there was no clear Sunni consensus about how Muḥammad's authority was to be preserved, passed on, and interpreted.

Consequently, early Muslim ideas about sunna differed from classical definitions of sunna in important ways: first, early Muslims did not give Muḥammad's sunna precedence over the sunnas of other prominent Muslims, notably the early Caliphs and his other Companions; second, at this early stage Muslims did not always identify sunna with specific reports about Muḥammad, i.e., ḥadīth reports did not serve as the exclusive vehicle for sunna as they later would; and, finally, early Muslims did not draw the rigid distinctions between the various sources of religious authority, especially between sunna and Qurʾān, that are so carefully delineated by later scholars.

Prophetic sunna and other "sunnas"

The most obvious point of difference between pre- and post-Shāfiʿī notions of sunna has to do with the relationship between the sunna of the Prophet and other "sunnas." Central to al-Shāfiʿī's system was the uniqueness of Muḥammad's sunna over all other sources of authority. For al-Shāfiʿī the only true sunna was Prophetic sunna, *al-sunna al-nabawiyya,* and this he exclusively identified with authenticated Prophetic ḥadīth. In his view traditions from any source other than the Prophet are of no account and carry no weight when measured against Prophetic precedent.[16] The success of al-Shāfiʿī's thesis is well attested in subsequent legal writings; as Juynboll points out, later writers "hardly ever thought of sunna as comprising anything but that of the Prophet."[17]

There is abundant evidence, however, even from al-Shāfiʿī's own writings, that this elevation of the Prophet's sunna was slow to develop, and that in the minds of earlier Muslims the sunna of the Prophet was simply one among several potential sources of religious authority, including the Qurʾān, the sunnas of the Companions, and the sunna of the early Caliphs.[18] The equality of other "sunnas" with the sunna of the Prophet is reflected in traditions used to defend the existing legal doctrines of the early schools of law against attacks from proponents of Prophetic tradition. It is reported, for example, that ʿUmar b. al-Khaṭṭāb, when asked about appointing a successor, replied that he could either follow the Prophet and leave the matter open or follow Abū Bakr and make an appointment; either course of action would be sunna.[19] In another case, ʿAlī reports that Muḥammad and Abū Bakr both applied forty lashes as a penalty for drinking while ʿUmar applied eighty; in the words of the tradition, "All this is sunna."[20] Abū Yūsuf adds: "Our companions are agreed that the punishment for drinking wine is 80 stripes."[21] Yet again ʿUmar, on his deathbed, instructs the Muslims on the sources from which they should seek guidance when he is gone: the Qurʾān, the Muslims who emigrated to Medina with Muḥammad *(muhājirūn)*, those in Medina who welcomed the Muslims *(ansār)*, the people of the desert, and finally the protected communities of Jews and Christians *(ahl al-dhimma)*.[22] After the formalization of Islamic jurisprudence, the absence of sunna from this listing would have been unthinkable; its absence here tells us that even though the idea of Prophetic sunna may have existed from the earliest years of Islam, it had not yet achieved universal acceptance as an indispensable source of religious authority.[23] Whatever the provenance of such traditions, those who circulated and cited them did so in order to assert the equality in theory and, in some instances, the superiority in practice of other sources of authority over traditions from the Prophet.

Prophetic sunna and Prophetic ḥadīth

A second important difference between early Muslim ideas about sunna and those of the classical period concerns the link between the sunna of the Prophet and ḥadīth. The content of sunna in its classical usage is specific: sunna is coextensive with the set of authenticated ḥadīth traced to

Muḥammad. To many early Muslims, by contrast, sunna and ḥadīth remained conceptually independent, and the two concepts did not fully coalesce until after al-Shāfiʿī. We especially notice a dissociation between ḥadīth and sunna in early historical reports, where "sunna" is often used generically signifying nothing more than "acceptable norms" or "custom" and where the sunna of the Prophet, "*al-sunna al-nabawiyya*," seems to connote not a set of specific, identifiable precedents but a general appeal to principles of justice. In al-Ṭabarī's history, for example, where references to sunna are frequent, the term is most often used in a generic sense as the antonym for heretical innovation (*bidʿa*) and without any reference to specific precedents.[24] Ṭabarī talks of the sunna of God, the sunna of the Muslims, the sunna of Abū Bakr and ʿUmar, and, surprisingly infrequently, he mentions the sunna of the Prophet. When "*al-sunna al-nabawiyya*" is explicitly mentioned, it is often in the context of political oaths or slogans used by rebels. Crone and Hinds have shown that the formula "*Kitāb Allāh wa sunnat nabiyyihi*," as it is recorded by al-Ṭabarī, was the rallying cry of every major revolt, regardless of the particular ideology of the rebels. "Sunna" in this formula represents not an appeal to specific precedents set by Muḥammad, but an appeal to a general standard of justice and right conduct of which he is the most powerful symbol.[25]

Early theological epistles offer more evidence of the independence of "sunna" from specific precedent. The *Risāla fi'l-Qadar* of al-Ḥasan al-Baṣrī, for example, allegedly written at the request of ʿAbd al-Malik (65–86 A.H.), mentions the sunna of the Prophet in a very general way but is empty of references to specific cases; and this despite ʿAbd al-Malik's specific request for "a transmitted report (*riwāya*) from any one of the companions of the Prophet of God."[26] That the author of the epistle could mention the sunna of the Prophet, yet fail to cite any specific traditions and expressly admit that the controversy about free will and determinism was a new development, suggests that he viewed sunna not as a collection of concrete precedents, but as a vague principle of religious authority without specific content.[27] The same pattern of vague, formulaic references to sunna and clear dissociation between sunna and ḥadīth can be observed in The *Kitāb al-Irjā'* of al-Ḥasan b. Muḥammad b. al-Ḥanafiyya, the first letter of Ibn Ibād to ʿAbd al-Malik, and the *Risāla* of Abū Ḥanīfa addressed to ʿUthmān al-Battī.[28] Even in instances where sunna clearly has concrete content, referring to specific rules, it often remains conceptually distinct from ḥadīth. A pattern of appealing to sunna or *al-sunna al-nabawiyya* quite independently of ḥadīth reports is evident, for example, in early legal writings and discussions. In fact, the earliest Islamic legal reasoning seems to have been virtually ḥadīth-free;

lawyers may have believed they were treading in the path of the Prophet, but they felt no obligation to back this claim with documentation. It was only gradually, over the course of the second century A.H., that "the infiltration and incorporation of Prophetic *aḥādīth* into Islamic jurisprudence" took place.[29]

The suggestion that the notion of sunna was distinct from the phenomenon of ḥadīth transmission should not be construed to imply that the pattern of ḥadīth transmission was itself a late development. Since Schacht the *terminus ante quem* for the regular use of the *isnād* and the development of a formal system of ḥadīth transmission has been repeatedly revised backwards. Recent research suggests that the earliest ḥadīth reports can be traced back to the first century A.H. and quite probably to the Companions of the Prophet themselves.[30] But if ḥadīth or proto-ḥadīth reports began to circulate in the very earliest years of Islam and if, as we have argued, the notion of Prophetic sunna is also traceable to the time of the Prophet, then what accounts for the independence of the two ideas? The most satisfying hypothesis postulates the existence, from a quite early date, of a class of individuals associated with the promotion of sunna and a second distinct class known for collecting and transmitting specific information about Muḥammad and other prominent Muslims, i.e., a class of ḥadīth transmitters. Sometimes the work of these two groups may have overlapped but, on the whole, as Goldziher first pointed out, early Muslim biographers viewed association with the sunna as something quite distinct from expertise in ḥadīth.[31] Juynboll has elaborated this argument, showing that in early biographical accounts individuals who are associated with sunna are seldom identified as experts in ḥadīth. In fact, they are frequently criticized for careless transmission of ḥadīth or even for outright fabrication of reports.[32] This situation apparently persisted into the period of early legal activity; early *qāḍīs* were not often distinguished by their knowledge of ḥadīth, even though they are usually identified as protagonists of sunna. Thus the notion of sunna and the phenomenon of ḥadīth transmission originated and grew separately, following parallel but largely independent lines of development until after al-Shāfiʿī.

Sunna and Qur'ān

So far we have established that sunna, prior to al-Shāfiʿī, was a principle of authority identified closely but not exclusively with Muḥammad, and that the idea of sunna remained conceptually independent of specific ḥadīth precedents. But what was the relationship between sunna and Qurʾān? Or, to state the problem more broadly: how did early Muslims view the relative status of the Qurʾān, Prophetic sunna, and non-

Prophetic sunna? One thing is clear: early Muslims did not draw sharp distinctions between sources of authority which, in the classical period, became sharply distinguished. During the earliest years of Islam, the Qurʾān, the sunna of the Prophet, and the sunnas of the Companions and early Caliphs were bound together in a largely undifferentiated mass of tradition, all of it marked with the aura of revelation.[33] During a period when this material was being used loosely, unsystematically, and primarily for moral edification, no urgency was attached to the task of defining the precise nature of the sources and their relationship to each other. But in the face of an increasingly complex religious and political environment this unsystematic approach could not last. As conflicts shook the community, the need arose to find firm support for one's own views and ways of undermining the evidence of one's opponents. This required the establishment of a hierarchy of revealed material whereby the evidence one liked could be justified and the evidence of one's opponents could be dismissed. The mass of "revealed" material had to be systematically differentiated. It was out of this contingency that the nascent disciplines of jurisprudence (*uṣūl al-fiqh)*, ḥadīth criticism (*ʿulūm al-ḥadīth*), and abrogation (*al-nāsikh wa'l-mansūkh*) emerged.

This period of turbulence and conflict over the sources of Islamic law is amply testified to in the polemical writings of al-Shāfiʿī. The central issue in these debates was the relative status of various sources of legal authority: the Qurʾān, the sunna of the Prophet, the sunnas of other authorities, and various methods of legal reasoning such as *qiyās* and *istiḥsān*. In the polemical literature of these debates three main groups may be identified: legal pragmatists (*ahl al-raʾy*), speculative theologians (*ahl al-kalām*), and partisans of tradition (*aṣḥāb al-ḥadīth*).

The *ahl al-raʾy* were eclectic in their approach to sources and preferred the accepted practice of their own school above systematic application of a universal theory of legal authority. This was the party of the earliest region-based schools of law and jurisprudence. These schools recognized and made use of Prophetic sunna, but they failed to distinguish it sharply from other sources; sunna was but one source among many. Thus they upheld the conclusions of their own methods of legal reasoning in the face of contradictory ḥadīth. For the *ahl al-raʾy,* coherent application of their own doctrine took precedence over systematic reliance on the Qurʾān or Prophetic sunna.

The *ahl al-kalām* took a more radical line, rejecting the authority of ḥadīth altogether.[34] What we know of their ideas about sunna is drawn primarily from polemical works written against them. We get our first substantial view of their arguments from the writings of al-Shāfiʿī. During al-Shāfiʿī's time the *ahl al-kalām* are portrayed as rejecting almost all ḥadīth reports. For traditions to be accepted by them, the assurance of their accuracy would have to match the reliability of the Qurʾān.[35] They accepted no reports about the accuracy of which there is the smallest doubt and they believed that ḥadīth, being of uncertain veracity, should never be allowed to rule on the Qurʾān.[36] They were, in fact, reluctant to accept any extra-Qurʾānic evidence for legal problems dealt with in the Qurʾān and tended to regard questions not referred to in the Qurʾān as having been left deliberately unregulated by God.[37] Naturally, they were highly critical of both the traditionists' method and the results of their work. Although the traditionists claimed to accept or reject ḥadīth on the basis of the qualities of the transmitter, their method was, in fact, purely arbitrary according to their opponents. As a result of the inadequacy of the traditionists' work the corpus of ḥadīth is filled with contradictory, blasphemous, and absurd traditions.[38]

The *bête noire* of both of these groups, representing the position that finally won the day, was the party of the traditionists, the *aṣḥāb al-ḥadīth.* The traditionists were dedicated to the proposition that traditions from the Prophet represent the only viable basis for sunna – that sunna and authenticated Prophetic ḥadīth are, in fact, coextensive. As ḥadīth professionals, their livelihoods were bound up in the gathering and transmittal of received knowledge, and they naturally considered their own activity to be the authentic representation of the Prophet's legacy and authority. The attitude they represent is probably an early one, extending back to the earliest collectors and transmitters of ḥadīth. The traditionist thesis was powerful, seeming to offer Muslims a concrete, easily definable, and irrefutable link with the Prophet through the medium of ḥadīth. It was difficult, if not impossible, for a Muslim to deny the theoretical authority of truly authentic traditions – to do so would be to question the authority of the Prophet himself.

In fact neither the *ahl al-raʾy* nor the *ahl al-kalām* rejected the authority of the Prophet in theory. They did, however, question whether, as the traditionists held, ḥadīth reports were the best representation of that authority. What gave force to these debates was the fact that each of these groups believed itself to be acting on the legacy of the Prophet; they were not fighting over *whether* to follow the Prophet, but rather over *how* to follow him. The issue between the *ahl al-raʾy* and the traditionists was not over whether the Prophetic example, when clearly manifest, was authoritative; on this point they agreed. What they differed on was whether the legacy of the Prophet was always best represented by ḥadīth precedents. The *ahl al-raʾy* thought that ḥadīth must sometimes be subjected to other overriding principles which better represent the spirit of the Prophet; among these principles they included the continuous practice of the community and general principles of equity. In other words, while agreeing with the traditionists on the importance of sunna, the *ahl al-raʾy* differed over its precise content and meaning.

Similarly, the *ahl al-kalām*, at least as they are portrayed by al-Shāfiʿī and Ibn Qutayba, do not argue that the Prophetic example is not authoritative. They argue rather that ḥadīth does not accurately reflect this example and that the true legacy of the Prophet is to be found elsewhere – first and foremost in following the Qurʾān. As al-Shāfiʿī portrays them the *ahl al-kalām* are concerned primarily with the reliability of the transmission of reports (*aḥādīth; akhbār*); they do not challenge the authority of the Prophet nor do they question the duty of the Muslims to obey him. Shāfiʿī is quick to make use of this admission. If, as his opponents grant, God did command obedience to the Prophet, then he must necessarily have intended particular commands. These rules, set out by Muḥammad in his words and actions, are therefore authoritative for Muslims and they can reach later generations of Muslims only by means of traditions (*akhbār*).[39] At the core of al-Shāfiʿī's argument is a simple proposition: having commanded believers to obey the Prophet, God must certainly have provided the means to do so. As it turned out, the *ahl al-kalām* were unable to withstand the force and logic of the traditionist argument. We find that the later *ahl al-kalām*, the Muʿtazila, while they maintained a degree of skepticism with regard to ḥadīth, bowed increasingly to the pressure of the traditionist arguments in favor of ḥadīth. Jāḥiẓ illustrates the ambivalence felt by many of the Muʿtazila: the sunna would be indisputable, he claims, if only we had sure knowledge of it. Unfortunately flaws in the process of transmission have made the task of recapturing authentic information about the Prophetic sunna impossible. Yet his skepticism does not keep him away from ḥadīth himself. Thus he laments the failure of the early Muslims to establish the authentic sunna as they had the text of the Qurʾān while at the same time he makes free use of ḥadīth to bolster his own arguments.[40]

The classical approach to the relationship between the Qurʾān and the sunna was forged within this polemical environment and the outcome was much affected by these debates. In the doctrinal synthesis that grew out of these controversies two seemingly contradictory tendencies emerge. On the one hand there is a clear concern for establishing the text of the Qurʾān as unique, uncorrupted, and incorruptible: a product of the divine will without taint of human influence or intervention.[41] Yet around the same time we find the increasing articulation of another apparently contradictory doctrine according to which sunna, like the Qurʾān, is also a product of divine revelation; they originate at the same source, and they share the same authoritative status. This belief begins to appear in traditions which define the relationship between sunna and Qurʾān and assert the revealed status of the former. Thus we find it reported that "Gabriel used to descend to the Prophet with sunna just as he descended with the Qurʾān."[42] Whenever Muḥammad received a revelation, he was also delivered a sunna to explain it.[43] The belief reflected in these traditions, that sunna is a product of direct divine revelation, was latent in the outlook of the earliest Muslims, but the formal identification of sunna as *waḥy* is a later development, probably an outgrowth of the second- and third-century controversies over the sources of Islamic law.[44]

This antinomy, that the Qurʾān is unparalleled but that the sunna is nevertheless equal to it in status, was enshrined in the classical formula which defines sunna as unrecited revelation (*waḥy ghayr matlū*) and differentiates it from recited revelation (*waḥy matlū*), which is found only in the Qurʾān. The distinction made here is one of form and not of substance. Sunna is not a different mode of revelation, but it is used differently and transmitted differently.[45] This formula maintains the superiority of the Qurʾān in the realm of ritual and devotion while asserting the equal status of the sunna as a source of legal authority. In the Qurʾān both the words and commands are of divine provenance; in the sunna only the intent of the command is trustworthy, for the text itself is liable to corruption. Shāfiʿī seems to be aware of this formula: "The prophet of God proffered nothing that was not [by the agency of] *waḥy*," he writes, "for *waḥy* includes [both] that which is recited [i.e., the Qurʾān] and also *waḥy* by which the Prophet established sunna."[46] This doctrine is not an important element of his argument, however, and he makes little use of it in his polemics, preferring to support his views by Qurʾānic exegesis. By the time of Ibn Qutayba, however, the doctrine was well established. It was an argument that clearly had utility in the *uṣūl* debates, first as a general defense of the traditionist position, but more particularly as a means of dealing with the vexing problem of abrogation (*naskh*).[47] The application of *naskh* involved the assertion that a particular command found in the Qurʾān or in the sunna had been nullified by God Himself. In the *uṣūl* controversies, a critical question was whether sunna could abrogate a command from the Qurʾān and, similarly, whether the Qurʾān could be interpreted as abrogating an element of sunna. Pre-Shāfiʿī legists seem to have had no problems with this: they accepted abrogation of the Qurʾān by means of the sunna and vice versa, drawing no great distinction between the two sources. But this eclectic approach was threatened by the arguments of the *ahl al-kalām* who took advantage of apparent inconsistencies between the two sources to undermine sunna, arguing that in all such cases the Qurʾān must take precedence. Shāfiʿī, to divert such attacks, rejected both *naskh* of Qurʾān by sunna and *naskh* of sunna by

Qurʾān. After him, as "the threat from the Qurʾān-only party receded," the older, looser attitude toward *naskh* reasserted itself.[48] At this point the utility of the doctrine of the divine provenance of sunna revealed itself, and in subsequent literature we find increasing reference to the revealed nature of sunna as a means of justifying abrogation of Qurʾān by sunna. Ibn Qutayba (d. 276/889) offers an early example. Abrogation of Qurʾān by Qurʾān or Qurʾān by sunna are equally admissible, he says, because sunna, like the Qurʾān, was brought to the Prophet by Gabriel from God; hence, *waḥy* which is Qurʾān can be abrogated by *waḥy* which is not Qurʾān.[49] Al-Ghazālī offers a concise statement of the classical position:

> There is no dispute concerning the view that the Prophet did not abrogate the Qurʾān on his own initiative. He did it in response to inspiration. God does the actual abrogating, operating through the medium of His Prophet. One ought thus to hold that the rulings of the Qurʾān may be abrogated by the Prophet, rather than solely by the Qurʾān. Although the inspiration (*waḥy*) in these cases is not Qurʾānic inspiration, the Word of God is nevertheless one. God does not have two words, one expressed in the Qurʾān style which we are bidden to recite publicly, and called the Qurʾān, while the other word is not Qurʾān. God has but one word which differs in the mode of its expression. On occasions God indicates his Word by the Qurʾān, on others, by words in another style, not publicly recited, and called sunna.[50]

The doctrine of the divine origin of sunna also had utility in other spheres of classical scholarship. It was particularly important, for instance, as a justification for the key role played by sunna in the discipline of Qurʾān interpretation (*tafsīr*). Both ancient and modern authors have argued that sunna is indispensable in the task of Qurʾānic exegesis; it is the practical outworking of the revealed text and the essential commentary on the Qurʾān. The claim that, apart from sunna, the Qurʾān is incomprehensible is not idle: sunna is the only source for information about abrogated and abrogating verses as well as the only guide to the context of Qurʾānic legislation (*asbāb al-nuzūl*). Hence the maxim "the Qurʾān has greater need of the sunna than the sunna of the Qurʾān."[51] The accusation has been made repeatedly in both ancient and modern debates about sunna, with some justification, that those who oppose ḥadīth do so merely to have their own way with the Qurʾān. Raising sunna to a place of virtual equality with the Qurʾān was one means of protecting the organic link between the two sources.

Sunna after al-Shāfiʿī

After the third century A.H. we find hardly a word spoken in opposition to the main tenets of the classical doctrine of sunna. From this point on, until debates over sunna reemerge in the nineteenth century, the nature or justification of sunna are not important issues. We no longer find any confusion between the sunna of the Prophet and other sunnas, nor does the essential reliability of ḥadīth come into question. In theory Prophetic sunna was ascendant, even over the Qurʾān. Hence the maxims "The sunna rules on the Qurʾān, but the Qurʾān does not rule on the sunna" and "The Qurʾān has greater need of the sunna than the sunna of the Qurʾān."

This was, by all appearances, a complete triumph for the *aṣḥāb al-ḥadīth*. In fact, however, their victory was limited. While the traditionist definition of sunna had won the day, the traditionists were not entirely successful in their bid to establish the primacy of ḥadīth in the field of law. Acceptance of the theory was one thing, application in practice quite another. The classical *madhhabs* might have found the doctrine of sunna promoted by al-Shāfiʿī and his traditionist allies irrefutable, but they showed themselves unwilling to abandon their positions on substantive matters.

Where actual legal points were concerned there were still a great many ways to get around the application of a particular tradition without ever challenging the theoretical position of sunna.[52] Recourse could be sought, for example, in the argument that not all that the Prophet had said or done had legal intent. Only the most extreme of the traditionist legists, those of the Ẓāhirī school along with some Ḥanbalites, made imitation of the Prophet in every detail a matter of legal obligation. All of the other schools of law insisted on the need for an interpretive step between a tradition and its legal application: not every tradition that appeared to be a command was in fact a command.[53] Hence the division of commands into legal categories: required, recommended, indifferent, discouraged, and forbidden. Such categorization could be used to mitigate the effect of traditions one did not like and there was, in fact, much difference of opinion among jurists on how certain practices should be categorized. What is more, the jurists generally accepted a distinction between the actions of the Prophet that were related to his religious mission and other actions, declaring the latter to be non-binding. Even such a staunch defender of ḥadīth as Ibn Qutayba maintains this distinction. He divides sunna into (1) that which was brought by Gabriel; (2) that which was instituted by Muḥammad's own *raʾy* and is binding, but subject to revision and; (3) non-binding sunna, bearing no penalty for failure to follow it. This argument too found its way into ḥadīth in the form of the famous date-tree tradition. According to this report, after having given what proved to be faulty advice to some unfortunate Medinan date farmers, Muḥammad said: "I am only human. If I command something related to religion, then obey, but if I order you to do something on the basis of my own opinion (*raʾy*), then I am only a human being."[54]

The jurists also argued that understanding the legal import of an incident from the life of the Prophet required an acquaintance with the surrounding context. We find this attitude enshrined in a number of polemical traditions in which one Companion accuses others of erring, not by transmitting incorrectly, but by disregarding the context and thus coming to an incorrect conclusion. One of the most frequently cited such incidents, and one that recurs repeatedly in modern discussions of the problem of sunna, has ʿĀʾisha refuting the tradition "the dead suffer from the mourning of their relatives over them" by explaining that the report resulted from a careless combining of two unrelated statements. The Prophet, while walking near the grave of a recently deceased Jewish woman said that she was suffering and then added: "Her relatives are mourning over her." Some of his hearers misunderstood his intent and put the two statements together, concluding that the woman was suffering as a result of the mourning of her relatives.[55] The lesson is clear: there is more to the sunna than just accepting traditions at face value.

Of course the main recourse for preserving existing legal doctrine without challenging the theoretical authority of sunna proved to be the science of ḥadīth criticism itself. The jurists learned to play the attribution game, substituting arguments from traditions for other methods of reasoning. Since the sunna of the Prophet was now elevated above all other sources of precedent, there was a powerful motive for the attribution of opinions to Muḥammad which had previously been attributed to a Companion or Successor or simply based on *raʾy*. Hence the phenomenon of the backward growth of *isnāds*. With the establishment of the traditionist definition of sunna the method of choice for refuting the views of an opponent was to discredit his authorities – to tear apart his *isnāds*. Indeed, it can be persuasively argued that it was this sort of competition that gave rise to the ḥadīth criticism in the first place. According to the traditional account, the systematic study of ḥadīth and the scrutiny of *isnāds* resulted from the altruistic response of pious scholars to widespread forgery of traditions. The guardians of tradition are supposed to have begun scrutinizing the character of those who transmitted reports in response to political upheaval, the emergence of new and dangerous heresies and the deaths of those who could claim to have a personal link with the Prophet himself. This standard explanation fails adequately to account for the atmosphere of conflict in which ḥadīth criticism emerged, however. Even the name given to the nascent science, *al-jarḥ wa al-taʿdīl*, wounding and rectifying, belies romantic notions of its origin. Ḥadīth criticism was often employed as a means of waging intellectual battle with one's opponents; the rating of traditions, building good *isnāds* for oneself and questioning the *isnāds* of one's enemies, was a way of combating opposing evidence while justifying one's own positions.[56]

Finally, the orthodox schools of law sealed their position, and placed a shield around existing legal doctrine by means of their doctrine of consensus (*ijmāʿ*). As many scholars have pointed out, *ijmāʿ* provides the logical foundation, although not the formal basis, for the whole system of Islamic law. In the final analysis, even sunna itself may be considered to be validated by *ijmāʿ*. The result was that, for the orthodox *madhhabs*, the substance of the law remained only peripherally affected by the triumph of the traditionist views about sunna. The acceptance of the classical doctrine of sunna simply shifted the locus of debate. In practice the legal doctrine of the various schools of law was shielded from revision and remained largely unaffected by the triumph of the traditionist thesis.

There remained an important exception to this pattern. Among the followers of Ibn Ḥanbal, traditionist ideas remained relatively undiluted. The Ḥanbalīs mounted a prolonged movement of protest against the tendency, prevalent in the other schools, to resist the strict application of ḥadīth. For this reason, as Hodgson points out, Ḥanbalism has been a remarkably creative force in Islamic history:

> Ḥanbalism had never really been primarily a school of *fiqh* at all. It remained a comprehensive and essentially radical movement, which had elaborated its own *fiqh* in accordance with its own principles, but whose leaders were often unwilling to acknowledge the same kind of *taqlīd* as provided the institutional security of the other schools, and rejected the *ijmāʿ* tradition of the living community on principle. *Ijtihād* inquiry remained alive among the Ḥanbalis; each major teacher felt free to start afresh, according to the needs of his own time for reform in a puritan direction.[57]

The vitality of Ḥanbalism illustrates the creative tension that had arisen out of the divergence between the classical theory of sunna and the actual doctrine of the *madhhabs*. The orthodox schools of law had given assent in theory to the importance of ḥadīth while resisting its thorough application in practice. In so doing they made themselves vulnerable to the continued attacks of traditionists who sought to base practice exclusively on ḥadīth, literally understood. As long as practice diverged from ḥadīth the doctrine of sunna provided an authoritative standard against which the moral, religious, and legal status quo could be measured. It was in this context that the notion of reviving the sunna (*iḥyāʾ al-sunna*) took on special significance. Sunna was viewed as a tool for purification and reform and an appeal to sunna allowed all intermediate authorities to be dismissed. It is just such a pattern of sunna-based reform that forms the background for the reemergence of sunna as a problem in the mid-nineteenth century.

2 The emergence of modern challenges to tradition

Since the mid-nineteenth century the nature of Prophetic authority has emerged as a critical issue for Muslim religious thinkers. The nineteenth century was a period when the hegemony of the West and the corresponding political and economic weakness of Muslim societies created intense pressure for reform of Islamic legal and social institutions, both to accommodate western values and to restore the strength of Islam. The pressure for reform in turn created pressure to reexamine the essential foundations of religious authority in Islam. Concerns about Prophetic tradition became central to this reexamination.

Several aspects of the colonial experience encouraged a special preoccupation with Prophetic tradition. The scripturalism of Protestant missionaries certainly influenced the way in which some Muslims viewed the relationship between tradition and scripture, for the nineteenth century was a period of intense Christian missionary activity and interreligious debate, especially in India. The late nineteenth century was also a period when Muslims were faced with a growing challenge from orientalist scholars who were just beginning to take a critical attitude toward the authenticity of Muslim tradition literature. Again, the effect was felt most directly in India, where William Muir and Alois Sprenger became the first western scholars to question whether the ḥadīth literature really reflected the words and deeds of the Prophet, whether its transmission was reliable, and whether the classical methods of sorting reliable traditions from unreliable were valid.

It would be a serious error, however, to conclude that the modern Muslim preoccupation with questions about Prophetic tradition was simply a reaction to colonialism. A pattern of rethinking tradition as a means of adapting to change was set well before Muslims felt the direct impact of western hegemony. The modern preoccupation with issues of Prophetic authority is in continuity with trends already well under way before the specific challenge of Europe was felt. The most important of these trends was the emergence of vital reformist movements in the eighteenth and nineteenth centuries – movements which adopted a critical stance toward the classical legacy, rejected blind adherence to received doctrine *(taqlīd),* and called for the revival of sunna as a basis for Islamic revival and reform. Both in Egypt and in the Subcontinent the tendency to challenge ḥadīth germinated within such movements.

Eighteenth-century reform movements

During the eighteenth century the traditionist idea that sunna should be the primary basis of Islamic law and that the legal status quo could and should be subjected to scrutiny in the light of Prophetic tradition reasserted itself in sometimes dramatic ways in many parts of the Islamic world. This idea was not an original contribution of eighteenth-century reformers; throughout the classical period this traditionist thesis was kept alive within the Ḥanbalī school of law. But eighteenth-century reformers and reform movements gave these ideas new vigor. In so doing, they provided the stock of ideas and established the main categories of response on which nineteenth- and twentieth-century Muslims would draw when faced with new challenges. In particular many eighteenth-century scholars became troubled by what they perceived to be growing signs of social and moral decay around them. They had no difficulty diagnosing the illness: Muslims had strayed from the pure, unadulterated sunna of the Prophet and were being poisoned by dangerous innovation (*bidʿa*) and blind adherence (*taqlīd*) to the teachings of the classical law books and commentaries. Prevailing ṣūfī doctrines and practices were singled out as a particularly dangerous and abhorrent cancer. The cure was to return to the original sources, the Qurʾān and the sunna, in order to regain the spirit of the Prophet. Under the banner of reviving the sunna (*iḥyāʾ al-sunna*) reform-minded *ʿulamāʾ* moved beyond the classical legal compendiums and commentaries and began studying earlier collections of ḥadīth, asserting their right, in varying degrees, to come to their own conclusions based on the Qurʾān and the sunna and to use their reading of these sources as a standard against which to judge the prevailing religious and social mores of their day.[1]

Among the many scholar-activists who came under the influence of these ideas, two in particular, the Indian Shāh Walī Allāh (1702–1762) and the Yemenite Muḥammad al-Shawkānī (1760–1834), have been important for later attitudes toward sunna. Shāh Walī Allāh's career spanned a period during which Muslim political power in the Subcontinent was disintegrating.[2] The breakdown of Mughal authority which accelerated after the death of Aurangzēb in 1708 led to a loss of Muslim power which was to prove irreversible. Shāh Walī Allāh was preoccupied with this disintegration and its effect on the Muslim community in India, and his career may be viewed as an attempt to arrest the process of decline. In the political arena he sought to encourage the revival of a strong central authority and to this end he actively invited the intervention of powerful Muslim leaders, encouraging them to wage *jihād* in order to restore Muslim political dominance. More significantly, in the field of religion, Shāh Walī Allāh sought to arrest a moral decline which corresponded to the political one by restoring and giving new vitality to the intellectual legacy of Islam. Responsibility for the preservation of Islam was divided, in his view, between two caliphates – one external (*ẓāhirī*) one internal (*bāṭinī*). To the external caliphate belongs the responsibility for maintaining administrative and political order and for applying the *Sharīʿa*. The internal caliphate is charged with giving guidance to the religious leaders of the community. It was just such a role that Shāh Walī Allāh took upon himself.[3]

Revival of the study of ḥadīth was at the heart of his program. Early in his career he came under the influence of ḥadīth scholars in the Ḥijāz, where he studied ḥadīth under one of the period's most influential teachers, Shaykh Abū Ṭāhir Muḥammad b. Ibrahīm al-Kurānī al-Kurdī (d. 1733).[4] Shāh Walī Allāh had come to the Ḥijāz already inclined toward traditionist views. His family was connected with the tradition of ḥadīth studies in the Subcontinent which had been established a generation earlier by another scholar with close ties to the Ḥijāz, ʿAbd al-Ḥaqq Dihlawī. But his contact with scholars in Mecca and Medina must certainly have reinforced his view of the science of ḥadīth as the foundational science against which all knowledge must be tested.[5] Moreover, it introduced him to a tradition of ḥadīth scholarship quite different from that of his training in India. The influence of his studies in the Ḥijāz is seen especially in the emphasis he placed on the study of Mālik's *Muwaṭṭaʾ*, elevating it above all other collections of traditions and placing it, along with the canonical collections of Bukhārī and Muslim, in the highest category for reliability. Even Bukhārī and Muslim he considered hardly more than footnotes on the *Muwaṭṭaʾ*, offering additional documentation but little original material. This was a marked divergence from the established pattern of ḥadīth studies in the Subcontinent where the emphasis was on the study of the six canonical collections.

Such an emphasis on the study of early sources of ḥadīth as opposed to reliance on later compilations represents an assertion of independence from classical compilers of ḥadīth. Furthermore, this special emphasis on ḥadīth was accompanied by a generally negative assessment of the results of classical scholarship. Shāh Walī Allāh and other reformers of his time considered themselves competent to study the sources of the classical collections for themselves and in doing so they implied that the classical legal tradition was subject to reevaluation – an attitude which found its chief expression in a general rejection of *taqlīd* and a revival of interest in the use of personal effort to decide a point of law (*ijtihād*). Shāh Walī Allāh was opposed to unthinking adherence to the rulings of the classical schools of law. The legal systems of the four schools must, he insisted, be subordinated to sunna. He thus opposed, in principle, blind adherence to legal doctrine, supported *ijtihād*, and granted to sunna a place of primacy in this process.[6]

Shāh Walī Allāh's approach to ḥadīth, its interpretation, and its relationship to sunna is not unsophisticated, nor does his method differ radically from the approach of the classical jurists. Like them he is well aware of the interpretive gulf separating ḥadīth from its legal application. He accepts the standard distinction between Prophetic actions of Muḥammad and non-Prophetic, the latter representing non-binding precedents in such areas as medicine or agriculture. He agrees with classical legal theory that not all traditions are legally applicable.[7] He is also cognizant of a deeper problem of interpretation: the Companions who themselves recorded the words and actions of the Prophet were not always clear on the significance of the events they witnessed, and their misunderstandings or differences in interpretation are sometimes carried over into ḥadīth reports. As a result the ḥadīth literature itself contains numerous apparent contradictions – contradictions which can only be resolved by scholars who have expertise *both* in ḥadīth studies and in the discipline of jurisprudence.

Shāh Walī Allāh's emphasis on involving the *fuqahā'* (specialists in jurisprudence) in ḥadīth studies has important echoes in the twentieth century. The clarity with which Shāh Walī Allāh perceived these problems of ḥadīth interpretation is connected with a central concern, running through all of his writings, for uncovering the rationale or the effective causes (*ʿilāl*) of *Sharīʿa* rulings. He was especially concerned to link the spirit of the law with its form – to explain how an eternal, changeless divine law must take particular concrete forms which differ according to the customs of the people to whom they are revealed. God's pedagogical method is to reveal His law in a concrete form within the context of a particular people. In the case of Islam, He established the *Sharīʿa* in accordance with Arab customs and then used the Arabs as models for its application, to disperse the law more widely. Hence the importance of sunna as a practical model for behavior – the divine law made manifest, so to speak. By making this argument Shāh Walī Allāh was not advocating the abandonment or modification of *Sharīʿa* rule, although many modern Muslims have chosen to interpret him in this way. On the contrary, his speculation was aimed at *reinforcing* the value of these forms by emphasizing their connection with the universal *Sharīʿa*. Inspired by such ideas, later writers have tried to define Shāh Walī Allāh as a legal relativist, advocating the modification of the particular forms of the *Sharīʿa* in accordance with changes in circumstances. Muḥammad Iqbāl, for example, interpreted Shāh Walī Allāh to mean that particular rules of *Sharīʿa* (*aḥkām*) are "in a sense specific to [a particular] people." Since the observance of these rules is not an end in itself, "they cannot be strictly enforced in the case of future generations."[8] Even when the value of a particular ruling cannot be adequately understood or explained, as in the case of the minimum amount of property (*niṣāb*) liable to *zakāt*, Shāh Walī Allāh insists that Muslims remain bound by the details of the ruling. But if speculation about the rationale of a particular rule cannot invalidate that rule, such reasoning nevertheless plays an essential role in the process of interpretation, i.e., in moving from the text of Qurʾān or ḥadīth to its legal application.

It was the negative aspects of Shāh Walī Allāh's thought, however, particularly his opposition to *taqlīd*, that were emphasized by his successors. In the process of transmission, his ideas, especially his attitude toward ḥadīth, were stripped of their eclectic and latitudinarian aspects. Among his sons, especially Shāh ʿAbd al-ʿAzīz, there was a tendency to emphasize the purificationist side of his thought – a tendency which gained force with each generation culminating in the *jihād* of Sayyid Aḥmad Barēlvī.

Muḥammad b. ʿAlī al-Shawkānī (1760–1834), separated from Shāh Walī Allāh by a generation, displays similar but more extreme views on the questions of *taqlīd* and *ijtihād*.[9] For Shawkānī *ijtihād* is limited only by the ability and knowledge of the *mujtahid*. There are neither different degrees of *ijtihād*, nor are later Muslims at any disadvantage in their ability to engage in it. Shawkānī turns on its head the traditional argument against *ijtihād* – that only earlier generations were close enough to the Prophet to have the requisite knowledge. Rather than becoming more difficult, he insists, *ijtihād* has now become easier than ever because the sources have been collected, organized, and made available on a wide scale. Consequently Shawkānī rejects any special status for the founders of the legal schools. Muslims are bound to follow the Qurʾān and the sunna no matter what the teaching of the imāms or the classical schools of law.[10] The opinions of the imāms are to be followed only if one fully understands how they were arrived at in the first place. Acceptance of their legitimate arguments is allowed, but to accept their teachings uncritically is simply to follow their *raʾy*. This amounts to innovation (*bidʿa*) and is completely forbidden.[11] In this respect Shawkānī's teaching represents a far more radical rejection of the legacy of classical Islam than that of Shāh Walī Allāh. The latter's rejection of *taqlīd* was set within a conservative framework which accepted many of the classical limitations on the *mujtahid*; in practice Shāh Walī Allāh's method amounted to *talfīq*, picking and choosing among the decisions of the law schools those he considered closer to sunna. Shawkānī, by contrast, is willing to reject the whole structure of classical Islam or at least to subject it all to the test of his own reading of the sources.

As with Shāh Walī Allāh, Shawkānī's position on *ijtihād* and *taqlīd* leads to a preoccupation with ḥadīth, and like Shāh Walī Allāh he was viewed by later Muslim scholars primarily as a ḥadīth specialist (*muḥaddith*). Perhaps his most influential work has been his *Nayl al-awṭār*, a critical and exhaustive commentary on *al-Muntaqā min aḥādīth al-aḥkām*, a work on ḥadīth by the Ḥanbalite ʿAbd al-Salām b. Taymiyya (d. 1254).[12] By applying strict standards for the acceptance of ḥadīth, and by calling attention to the presence of weak traditions which had crept into Ibn Taymiyya's work, Shawkānī illustrates the trend toward increased stringency and rigorous scholarship in ḥadīth studies.

The rejection of much of the classical tradition by Shawkānī and by the followers of Shāh Walī Allāh and their use of ḥadīth to critique this tradition represents a significant divergence from the attitude of classical law schools toward sunna.[13] According to the classical theory of jurisprudence, ḥadīth was formally recognized as the only legitimate basis for sunna, but in the actual method of the legists *ijmāʿ* held a higher place.[14] In other words, the real basis for practice was represented by the dominant doctrines of the classical legal schools and these doctrines rested primarily upon the foundation of *ijmāʿ* rather than on sunna, for it was by *ijmāʿ* that decisions about the authenticity of sunna itself, and its interpretation, were validated. By upholding the supremacy of ḥadīth in practice as well as in theory, and by reinvigorating the study of ḥadīth literature, Shāh Walī Allāh, al-Shawkānī, and their successors challenged this system and prepared the ground for vigorous ḥadīth-based reform movements in the nineteenth and twentieth centuries.

Shāh Walī Allāh and al-Shawkānī represent the early stages in the emergence of the modern spectrum of approaches to religious authority. The pressures that led them to reemphasize ḥadīth scholarship were a small foreshadowing of the social and political turmoil that would, in the following two centuries, repeatedly drive Muslim thinkers back to scrutinize and to rethink their tradition. In principle, Shāh Walī Allāh and al-Shawkānī followed much the same pattern as would later reformers of the nineteenth and twentieth centuries. In the face of crisis and change, they searched the tradition in which they were grounded for solutions relevant to the dilemmas of their time. For these thinkers the ḥadīth literature itself seemed to offer the flexibility they were looking for. They appealed to the authority of ḥadīth in order to challenge the authority of received legal doctrine. Many of their successors in the nineteenth century adopted and refined the same approach; others, beginning with Sayyid Aḥmad Khān, found it necessary to go one step further, subjecting the ḥadīth literature itself to scrutiny.

Ḥadīth-based reform in the nineteenth century

In India rejection of *taqlīd* and preoccupation with ḥadīth became focused in a single reformist sect, the Ahl-i-Ḥadīth, which drew directly on the tradition of Shāh Walī Allāh and al-Shawkānī.[15] Almost all of the group's early and influential representatives had direct connections with the line of Shāh Walī Allāh and especially with the Indian *mujāhidīn* movement, led by Sayyid Aḥmad Barēlvī, which carried to an extreme the purificationist tendencies within Shāh Walī Allāh's school. The Indian *mujāhidīn* had a close parallel in the Arabian Wahhābī movement, and the two movements were sufficiently similar in general character to encourage the identification of both as Wahhābī. In fact, they grew up quite independently of each other.[16]

The Ahl-i-Ḥadīth may be viewed as a direct outgrowth and quietist manifestation of the *mujāhidīn*. As a basis for their iconoclasm, the *mujāhidīn* had developed Shāh Walī Allāh's rejection of *taqlīd* into a central point of doctrine.[17] Yet, preoccupied as they were with their physical *jihād* against non-Muslims and against syncretism among Muslims, the *mujāhidīn* were little concerned with detailed points of law. This changed after the trauma of 1857, when many of the adherents of this movement opted for a quietistic approach, abandoning the physical *jihād* and confining themselves to the *jihād* of the pen (*jihād bi'l-qalam*).[18] It was out of this core of activist religious leaders that the Ahl-i-Ḥadīth emerged.

There were direct and personal lines of connection between the Ahl-i-Ḥadīth and Shāh Walī Allāh. We see this especially in the case of Naẓīr Ḥusayn Dihlawī (d. 1902), one of the most prominent early leaders of the movement and perhaps the single most influential figure in the spread of the Ahl-i-Ḥadīth.[19] Naẓīr Ḥusayn self-consciously identified himself with Shāh Walī Allāh, claiming to be his true spiritual heir and successor. He studied ḥadīth under Shāh Muḥammad Isḥāq, Shāh Walī Allāh's grandson, and he appropriated the title *miyān ṣāḥib*, a title closely associated with the successors of Shāh Walī Allāh. Another important propagandist for the movement, Ṣiddīq Ḥasan Khān (1832–1890), also identified himself with the line of Shāh Walī Allāh.[20] His father had been a disciple of Shāh ʿAbd al-ʿAzīz and he studied under Ṣadar al-Dīn Khān

(1789–1868) who was himself a student of the sons of Shāh Walī Allāh, Shāh ʿAbd al-ʿAzīz and Shāh ʿAbd al-Qādir.[21] Ṣiddīq Ḥasan Khān was also deeply influenced by the writings of Shawkānī and in this he demonstrates the influence that Yemenī *ʿulamāʾ* in the line of al-Shawkānī were exerting on Indian scholars at this time. Yemenī scholars were especially active at the court in Bhōpāl where Ṣiddīq Ḥasan spent the greater part of his life. Ṣiddīq Ḥasan Khān himself studied ḥadīth with ʿAbd al-Ḥaqq Muḥaddith Banārisī, a scholar who had become a follower of Shawkānī after he was commissioned to travel to Yemen to copy the latter's works.[22] In his own writings Ṣiddīq Ḥasan acknowledged great indebtedness to Shawkānī and he considered the diffusion of the Yemenite scholar's works to be his special mission, claiming to have had frequent contact with him in visions and to have received, in this way, an *ijāza* (permission) to transmit his works.[23]

In their attitude toward legal matters the Ahl-i-Ḥadīth combined rejection of *taqlīd* in the tradition of the later Shāh Walī Allāhī school with an extreme literalism in approach to ḥadīth. In this they departed significantly from Shāh Walī Allāh's moderate doctrine and self-consciously emulated the ideas of the most extreme among the ancient traditionists, those of the Ẓāhirī school.[24] Like the Ẓāhirīs the Ahl-i-Ḥadīth bind themselves to a single, literal meaning of texts of Qurʾān and ḥadīth, denying the efficacy of *qiyās* (the use of logical reasoning to decide a legal question). They refused to acknowledge any authority in the orthodox schools of law, whether in matters of detail or theory (*uṣūl*). Like the Ẓāhirīs, they completely rejected the authority of *ijmāʿ*, except that of the Companions of the Prophet.[25]

For the Ahl-i-Ḥadīth, the whole classical tradition of Islamic learning is suspect. Only in the sunna, represented by authentic ḥadīth, is the legacy of Muḥammad preserved in purity. After the time of the Prophet, history is but a record of decline, a period of darkness punctuated only by brief flashes of illumination when the legacy of the Prophet was given its full importance in the work of a renewer of the faith (*mujaddid*) and the sunna thus revived. In their evaluation of ḥadīth they demonstrated the same pessimistic view, manifested in an unwillingness to question ḥadīth that have been judged authentic by classical traditionists. The science of ḥadīth for these *ʿulamāʾ* is a "repetitive and not a critical one," because the knowledge of those closer to the Prophet is superior to that of later generations.[26] Only the early *muḥaddithūn* had the necessary tools at their disposal to judge ḥadīth adequately. Classical traditionists such as Bukhārī and Muslim were, in the view of the Ahl-i-Ḥadīth, privy to information which is irretrievably lost and their judgments are not liable to challenge by modern scholars.

The apparent contradiction between the Ahl-i-Ḥadīth's "uncritical preoccupation with the traditional corpus of the ḥadīth" and their vehement opposition to *taqlīd* has not been lost on their opponents.[27] Yet the Ahl-i-Ḥadīth themselves would deny such a comparison. *Taqlīd* is, by definition, to deviate from the sunna, to follow innovation; for them adherence to ḥadīth is not *taqlīd* but *ittibāʿ*, following the true practice of the Prophet. The critical question is not whether one is following some precedent, but whether it is the *right* precedent.

The ideal of the Ahl-i-Ḥadīth was to live a holy and ethical life, conforming to the Prophetic example in every detail.[28] Ḥadīth, as the guide to the prophetic sunna, became the central focus of their lives and "the ideal guide to social behavior and individual piety."[29] In politics they were thorough quietists, striving to live lives devoted to scholarship, but in the realm of ideas they relished their intellectual *jihād.* In most matters of law they did not deviate significantly from Ḥanafī views, but on the issues that most set them apart from the Ḥanafī majority, especially in the field of ritual, they invited frequent and sometimes violent conflict. They set themselves apart by highly visible deviations from the majority of Muslims in such features as dress and cut of beard. Their most visible distinction, however, and the most frequent source of controversy with other Muslims was their manner of performing the ritual prayer (*ṣalāt*). The Ahl-i-Ḥadīth considered several aspects of the Ḥanafī form of the *ṣalāt* to be deviations from authentic sunna. Whereas the Ḥanafīs said "*āmīn*" quietly after opening recitations, for example, the Ahl-i-Ḥadīth insisted that it must be said aloud. In a similar fashion they set themselves apart by reciting the *fātiḥa* aloud along with the prayer leader and modifying certain other ritual recitations. It was these differences in ritual practice more than their doctrine that set them apart from the mainstream and brought them into conflict with other Muslims. For the Ahl-i-Ḥadīth themselves such practices were an ever-present reminder of their distinctiveness and the superiority of their faith; to their opponents they were a visible and disruptive challenge. The Ahl-i-Ḥadīth believed that by remaining true to a literal reading of ḥadīth and by rejecting subsequent doctrinal accretions they were emulating the authentic practice of the earliest Muslims and reviving the true sunna of the Prophet.

In the central Islamic lands no ḥadīth-based movement emerged that was comparable with the Indian Ahl-i-Ḥadīth in organization or coherence. The doctrinal tendencies that marked the Ahl-i-Ḥadīth were present, especially in Ḥanbalī circles, but these tendencies were not accompanied by the sectarian trappings of the Indian movement. The movement of Ibn ʿAbd al-Wahhāb had forcefully revived Ḥanbalī traditionism during the eighteenth century. In the nineteenth century the continuing vitality of Ḥanbalī revivalist thought is illustrated in the career of the influential Alūsī family of Baghdad.[30] Three generations of Alūsīs, beginning with Maḥmūd al-Alūsī (d. 1853), were instrumental in preserving and promoting the doctrines of Ibn Taymiyya and of the Wahhābī movement. Nuʿmān al-Alūsī (d. 1899) wrote a celebrated defense of Ibn Taymiyya, his *Jalāʾ al-ʿaynayn,* which gained wide circulation. Maḥmūd Shukrī al-Alūsī (1857–1924), an outspoken advocate of the reform of Islamic law along Ḥanbalite lines as well as a defender and historian of the Wahhābī movement, provided a link to the late nineteenth- and early twentieth-century *salafiyya* movement of which he was a leader. The survival and spread of Ḥanbalī revivalism was also reflected in and further encouraged by the publication and circulation of Ibn Taymiyya's works. These first began to appear at the end of the nineteenth century. Within the first two decades of the twentieth century a significant number of his works was published, in large part because of the efforts of the Indian Ahl-i-Ḥadīth.

These tendencies eventually merged with western-inspired reformist tendencies into what became known as the *salafiyya* movement, an ideological grouping of the late nineteenth and early twentieth centuries which is most closely associated with the work of Rashīd Riḍā.[31] By the mid-nineteenth century the ideas represented by eighteenth-century reformers – rejection of *taqlīd*, promotion of *ijtihād*, and ḥadīth-based reformism – had taken hold among reform-minded men of religion in various parts of the Middle East. Historical circumstances, particularly the spread of secular education and secular legal systems and the resulting disenfranchisement of many *ʿulamāʾ*, gave these ideas new force. Social and economic dislocation seems to have given certain segments of the religious elite reason to reject the religious status quo and the rejection of *taqlīd* proved a popular tool both to oppose more conservative *ʿulamāʾ* entrenched in their positions and to appeal to young men of secular education who sought to understand the reasons for the apparent weakness of Islam in the face of western power.[32] Thus the urgently felt need to catch up with the West was combined with the latent power of the traditionist thesis – the assurance that all could be set right by returning to the unadulterated sunna of the Prophet – to create a powerful reform movement.

This impulse seems to have come to maturity later in the Arabic-speaking lands than it did in India; changes that had taken place a century earlier in India were only beginning to take hold in the Middle East during the nineteenth century. Conservatism weighed heavier on the *ʿulamāʾ* in the Middle East than on their counterparts in the Subcontinent, perhaps because they maintained their social and economic base for a longer time. The *ʿulamāʾ* of India were stripped of their dominant role in education and in the courts by the early nineteenth century. In Egypt and Syria the economic base of the *ʿulamāʾ* – schools, religious endowments (*waqfs*), and the legal system – did not come under serious threat until much later. In Syria, secular schools did not become widespread until the end of the nineteenth century.[33]

As with the Ahl-i-Ḥadīth, the guiding principle of *salafī* reformism was the conviction that Muslims must emulate the first generation of Muslims, the *salaf al-ṣāliḥ*, and recapture the pure Islam of the Prophet. This could be done only by returning to the basic sources of authority, the Qurʾān and the sunna, for only in these sources can the true essence of Islam be found. To this extent, as Merad points out, the reformers did not deviate markedly from traditional Sunni doctrine.[34] It is in rejecting the way the Qurʾān and sunna have traditionally been interpreted and in cutting through the interpretive accretions that classical scholarship had built up around these basic texts that the *salafiyya* set themselves apart. Thus they vigorously opposed *taqlīd*, but like the Ahl-i-Ḥadīth they differentiated between *taqlīd*, which represents imitation of an invalid authority, and *ittibāʿ*, which denotes emulation of a worthy model.

In their search for an authentic model, the *salafī* reformers insisted on returning to the Qurʾān and the sunna anew. This necessarily faced them with the problem of determining exactly how these sources should be understood and applied. With regard to the Qurʾān the reformers insisted on a straightforward interpretation. They rejected any form of esoteric interpretation (*taʾwīl*), arguing that difficult texts should be accepted as a matter of faith without attempting to interpret them. They held that the Qurʾān was not hard to understand as long as its primary objective – to give moral guidance and direction – was kept in mind.

The sunna posed a more difficult problem. From the start the attitude of *salafī* scholars towards sunna was ambivalent. The reformers laid great stress on the importance of sunna as the second canonical source, but they were less prone to trust the results of classical ḥadīth criticism than were their Indian counterparts. Whereas the Ahl-i-Ḥadīth believed that the judgments of the ancient *muḥaddithūn* must be accepted, the *salafī* reformers were willing to concede the need to evaluate the traditions anew. The reformers did not, however, reject the classical system of ḥadīth criticism as such. Their stress was rather on the need for more rigorous application of the traditional criteria. This approach is illustrated in one of the important *salafī* works on ḥadīth, Jamāl al-Dīn al-Qāsimī's *Qawāʿid al-taḥdīth min funūn muṣṭalaḥ al-ḥadīth*. This manual of ḥadīth criticism, which carries a laudatory introduction by Rashīd Riḍā, does not offer a new approach to ḥadīth criticism so much as it emphasizes the need for a renewed application of the classical system. Without striking out on his own – in the tradition of Islamic scholarship the book is largely a compilation of quotations from various authorities – al-Qāsimī manages to emphasize the depth and latitude within the tradition of ḥadīth scholarship. He thus makes it clear that establishing the authenticity of a tradition is a complicated matter requiring more than simple acceptance of the conclusions of earlier ḥadīth scholars.[35]

In their approach to sunna the Ahl-i-Ḥadīth and the *salafī* reformers reasserted the traditionist emphasis on the centrality of practice of the Prophet as the preeminent standard for belief and practice. For both movements departure from sunna was viewed as the critical illness afflicting Islam and the whole of the classical tradition was taken to represent such a deviation. This is especially evident in the case of the Ahl-i-Ḥadīth, who consciously identified themselves with Ẓāhirī doctrine. Their approach to sunna thus departs quite significantly from classical theory. In the orthodox schools, sunna was represented, in practice, by the established doctrines of the particular schools. For the Ahl-i-Ḥadīth, by contrast, sunna became an independent standard, based purely on ḥadīth, against which the classical tradition was judged and found wanting. The *salafiyya* are akin to the Ahl-i-Ḥadīth in their rejection of classical authority and their claim to be capable of reviving the pure, unadulterated sunna of the Prophet. They differ from the Ahl-i-Ḥadīth, however, in their more critical attitude toward ḥadīth.

The underlying principle shared by both of these movements is radical. By insisting that a qualified person need not rely on authorities, and that texts can be approached without intermediary, they advance a democratization of religious knowledge and seek to wrest control of the interpretive process away from the specialists. Moreover, by their emphasis on a return to the Qur'ān and the sunna both movements offer a radical critique of the whole classical tradition.

The tendency represented by the Ahl-i-Ḥadīth and the *salafiyya* continued to thrive through the twentieth century, representing an important band in the spectrum of modern Muslim approaches to religious authority. But within each of these groups there were some individuals who felt the pressure for reform more urgently, whose ideas were refracted more dramatically. These thinkers took this call for a return to first principles one step further, subjecting not just classical *fiqh* (legal interpretation) but also the ḥadīth literature itself to criticism.

Early modernists: Aḥmad Khān and ʿAbduh

The first major challenge to sunna in the modern period came from the great Indian modernist Sir Sayyid Aḥmad Khān (1817–1898), who eventually came to reject almost all ḥadīth as unreliable.[36] He was severely critical of the classical methods of ḥadīth criticism and eventually came to believe that only traditions dealing with spiritual matters were of relevance to contemporary Muslims, and traditions dealing with worldly (*dunyāwī*) matters were non-binding. Without altogether rejecting the authority of sunna, he severely curtailed its scope, called for new methods of evaluating it, and insisted on its subordinate position *vis-à-vis* the Qur'ān.

Sayyid Aḥmad's critical attitude toward ḥadīth evolved only gradually, however. His early religious writings display a devotion to sunna and an opposition to *taqlīd* characteristic of the reformist ṣūfī tradition within which he grew up. His family was deeply involved with the Mujaddidī branch of the Naqshbandiyya – the reformist ṣūfī line traced back to Shaykh Aḥmad Sirhindī.[37] The Naqshbandīs particularly emphasized devotion to the Prophet and Sayyid Aḥmad Khān's first religious writing, a biography of Muḥammad entitled *Jalā' al-qulūb,* reflects this background: the essence of Islam is love for the Prophet and love for the Prophet will be reflected in following his sunna. Sunna in this context implies an ethical pattern, an *imitatio Muḥammadi*, rather than a principle of legal authority; ṣūfī thinkers emphasized personal spirituality and piety rather than the details of *fiqh*.[38]

Sayyid Aḥmad Khān's concern for following sunna necessarily led to preoccupation with discovering the authentic content of the sunna. This preoccupation ushered in a stage in Sayyid Aḥmad Khān's religious outlook during which he expressed ideas about sunna virtually identical to those being promoted by the Ahl-i-Ḥadīth.[39] He never really abandoned his affinity for the spirit of the Ahl-i-Ḥadīth reformers. As Troll notes: "He regards it as the ultimate motive of his endeavor in religious thought to contribute to the re-establishment of 'true' Islam, the pure and essential Islam of the origins, unencumbered by the accretions of later developments."[40] This was precisely the objective of the Ahl-i-Ḥadīth, and although his vision of this "true" Islam came to differ markedly from that of the Ahl-i-Ḥadīth, he expressed great respect for them, especially Naẓīr Ḥusayn Dihlawī, to the end of his life.[41]

The influence of Shāh Walī Allāh, the *mujāhidīn* movement, and the Ahl-i-Ḥadīth left Sayyid Aḥmad Khān with an aversion to *taqlīd* which shaped his views throughout his career. By the 1870s, however, he had ventured beyond the traditionalism of the Ahl-i-Ḥadīth. The important aspect of this change is the stress he placed on reason as a basis for understanding Islam and especially for exegesis of the Qur'ān. But in the course of the broader evolution in his religious thought he also began to take a critical approach toward the authenticity of ḥadīth and the authority of sunna.

The evolution of Sayyid Aḥmad Khān's ideas about ḥadīth was directly affected by orientalist scholarship and missionary polemics. At the same time, he assimilated these influences into a pattern of basic religious attitudes which had already been established. In other words, the conclusions that Sayyid Aḥmad Khān came to with regard to the nature of sunna and the authenticity of ḥadīth, while hastened and partly shaped by western influences, do not represent the adoption of alien ideas. His ideas are quite consistent with the reformist currents of thought to which he was heir: he conceded to his western opponents only what could be reconciled with his own vision of Islam.

Sayyid Aḥmad had known Europeans from early in his career. His father had served in a high position with the East India Company and in 1837 Sayyid Aḥmad followed his father into the service of the company. From this point his contacts with Europeans increased in frequency and cordiality. His early years with the company were spent in Agra, a major center of missionary activity, and he was there at the time of the "Mohammedan Controversy" touched off by the polemics of Carl Pfander (1803–1865).[42] Sayyid Aḥmad became personally acquainted with several missionaries in Agra, most importantly with the missionary-orientalist William Muir (1819–1905).[43] At the same time, as Troll points out, he was exposed to western scholarly method through the influence of Alois Sprenger who was then principal of Delhi College.[44]

Sayyid Aḥmad Khān's views of ḥadīth and sunna were directly affected by these contacts and by his responses to them. Two works in particular, his *Tabyīn al-kalām* and the rejoinder to Muir in his *Essays on the Life of Muhammad* illustrate this process. The first work, a commentary on the Bible, was an attempt to establish an Islamic framework within which the Bible could be understood and accepted as a product of divine revelation. In the course of this venture, Sayyid Aḥmad Khān was confronted with western methods of biblical criticism and with questions of inspiration and revelation which caused him to examine his attitudes on corresponding Islamic questions. By accepting the Christian scriptures as revealed, he was faced directly with the problem of reconciling the form of the biblical text with Muslim preconceptions about what a revealed book should look like. The Bible, he concluded, is indeed a form of revelation (*waḥy*), but it is not the same kind of *waḥy* as the Qurʾān. Jewish and Christian scriptures differ from Qurʾānic revelation in just the same way as does the sunna. Both contain the meaning and the general sense of the divine message, but they cannot be considered to be the very words of God.[45] He invoked the classical distinction between recited revelation (*waḥy matlū*), found only in the Qurʾān, and unrecited revelation (*waḥy ghayr matlū*), i.e., sunna. He reinforced this analogy between the Christian scriptures and the sunna by an unusual application of the terminology of ḥadīth criticism to the biblical text. Inconsistencies and corruption in the biblical text can be explained and reconciled with the general revealed character of the Bible by distinguishing, within the text, between *matn* and *riwāya* passages. The former constitute revelation itself, while the latter represent merely the explanatory notes of those who transmitted the text.[46] By implication then, both pre-Qurʾānic revelations and the sunna are less trustworthy than the Qurʾān and, unlike the Qurʾān, are liable to corruption. In the course of subtly undermining the authority of the Bible in relation to the Qurʾān, Sayyid Aḥmad Khān also widened the gap between Qurʾān and sunna.

The most far-reaching of his conclusions in *Tabyīn al-kalām* concerns the possibility of distinguishing between revealed and non-revealed materials on the basis of whether the subject matter of the text concerns religious (*dīnī*) or worldly (*dunyāwī*) matters.

> Only such a word is taken to be *waḥy* which he has enounced under the heading of religion, or where he has said something which otherwise would be far from [the reach of] reason or concerning which he made it clear himself that he is saying this by way of *waḥy* or *ilhām* or where it becomes clear from the situational or literary context that something has been said by *waḥy* or *ilhām*. But apart from this, his other speech and what pertains to the everyday behaviour of man and what relates to worldly affairs, that has nothing to do with *waḥy*.[47]

Thus only when the intent is unequivocally religious is a text to be taken for revelation.

A much more direct challenge to Sayyid Aḥmad Khān's thinking about sunna and ḥadīth came from the pen of the missionary and orientalist Sir William Muir. In his *Life of Mohamet* Muir had argued that the Qurʾān alone represents a reliable source for Muḥammad's biography – a true and accurate portrait of Muḥammad's own thought.

> The Coran becomes the ground-work and the test of all inquiries into the origin of Islam and the character of its founder. Here we have a store-house of *Mahomet's own words recorded during his life*, extending over the whole course of his public career, and illustrating his religious views, his public acts, and his domestic character.[48]

The ḥadīth literature, he contended, was plagued with corruptions and of limited value as a source for the earliest history of Islam. Muir completely discounted the value of classical ḥadīth criticism based on an examination of the chain of transmission, the *isnād*. He insisted that the text of the tradition itself, the *matn*, "must stand or fall upon its own merits."[49] He distrusted any tradition that furthers a general bias common to all Muslims (e.g., "the universal desire of Mahomet's glorification"[50]); he rejected all traditions in which the narrator appears to have a "special interest, prejudice or design"; and he expressed suspicion of traditions in proportion to their "particularity of detail."[51] Traditions narrated by individuals who were very young at the time of the events they report, or which relate events prior to the time when Muḥammad became a well-known public figure are, in his view, of doubtful authenticity.

Sayyid Aḥmad Khān, deeply troubled by Muir's work, prepared a rebuttal, in his *Series of Essays on the Life of Mohammed and Subjects Subsidiary Thereto.*[52] In this work, and in all of his subsequent writings on ḥadīth, Sayyid Aḥmad Khān demonstrated a preoccupation with the issues raised by Muir: he defended the value of *isnād* criticism; he argued that Muir was unreasonable in attributing bias to the early narrators of ḥadīth; and he suggested that his opponent had vastly underrated the power of memory. But despite his apologetic tone in the face of Muir's attacks, he also made a critical concession, agreeing that all traditions, even those in the canonical collections, should be subject to criticism.

Sayyid Aḥmad Khān adopted Muir's concern for problems connected with the oral transmission of ḥadīth and particularly with the practice of transmitting traditions according to the sense *(bi'l-maʿnā)* rather than verbatim *(bi'l-lafẓ)*, a practice which opened the way for numerous corruptions in the ḥadīth literature. He agreed with Muir that criticism of the content of traditions is essential and that traditional ḥadīth criticism was flawed by its reliance almost exclusively on external criticism. He pointed out, however, that criticism of the content of traditions was not entirely unknown among classical scholars and that a number of them set out detailed rules for this branch of ḥadīth criticism.

Most significantly, Sayyid Aḥmad Khān was influenced by Muir to emphasize the subordination of sunna to the Qur'ān. Following Muir, Sayyid Aḥmad Khān came to regard the Qur'ān as the supreme standard against which other information about the Prophet should be tested. He came to consider only *mutawātir* traditions – those transmitted by a great enough number of persons to eliminate the possibility of collusion to deceive – to be a reliable basis for belief independent of the Qur'ān; of these he claimed to have found only five. So, in the end, Sayyid Aḥmad Khān's approach to sunna was ambivalent. On the one hand he neither rejected the historicity of ḥadīth in principle, nor did he reject the theoretical authority of sunna. On the other hand, he so severely restricted the application of ḥadīth that he came to be viewed by conservative opponents as a *munkir-i-ḥadīth,* a denier of tradition, and on the theological level, by distinguishing between religious and secular in Muḥammad's words and actions, he greatly restricted the scope of sunna.

The evolution of Sayyid Aḥmad Khān's ideas presents us with a microcosm of the transition through which Indian Muslim thought was passing during his career. His admiration of the West pulled him farther and farther in the direction of adaptation, but he always maintained a deep rootedness in the tradition. Western ideas and western challenges were important in shaping Sayyid Aḥmad Khān's views, yet these external influences were not, on their own, decisive. They were, rather, a challenge and a catalyst leading him back to reexamine and draw inspiration from the sources of his own intellectual tradition.

In Egypt Muḥammad ʿAbduh began to express skepticism about ḥadīth at about the same time as Sayyid Aḥmad Khān, but much more cautiously. Direct evidence for ʿAbduh's attitude toward the authenticity of ḥadīth rests on a very brief statement in his *Risālat al-tawḥīd* which suggests that he considered only *mutawātir* traditions to be definitively binding. As for traditions with only a single narrator (*āḥād*): "He to whom the tradition has come, who has satisfied himself of the truth of what it contains, is obliged to believe it. But he to whom it has not come, or receiving it had misgivings about its validity, he cannot be blamed as an unbeliever if he withholds acceptance of it since it is not verified by sustained narration."[53] ʿAbduh thus opened the door to personal judgment in deciding what traditions to accept or reject. He made it clear, however, that he did not reject the authority of sunna as such, for "He who denies something he knows the Prophet said or affirmed impugns the truth of his message and characterizes it as lies."[54]

ʿAbduh's reluctance to lend credence to *āḥād* traditions simply on the basis of their having been declared sound according to the traditional methods of ḥadīth criticism is confirmed by statements from later writers. Muḥammad Ḥusayn al-Dhahabī reports that ʿAbduh was reluctant to accept any *āḥād* tradition as the basis for *tafsīr*. He was especially critical of the so-called *isrāʾīliyyāt,* but he also rejected other traditions normally considered authentic.[55] Rashīd Riḍā also confirms that ʿAbduh rejected certain categories of traditions outright, especially the *isrāʾīliyyāt* and *fitan* traditions, even when these were found in the *ṣaḥīḥ* collections of ḥadīth.[56]

These snatches of information give us only a vague indication that ʿAbduh was willing to depart from traditional approaches to ḥadīth in certain cases. But nowhere does he offer a systematic approach to the criticism of ḥadīth. ʿAbduh was more at home with questions of theology than of jurisprudence, and more speculative than scripturalist in his method. He found it unnecessary to tackle the difficult question of ḥadīth in detail. In this he differed from what was to become the mainline doctrine of the *salafiyya.* For his scripturalist successors the authenticity of ḥadīth and the status of sunna became central concerns.

Qurʾānic scripturalism

In the generation following Aḥmad Khān and ʿAbduh, another band in the spectrum of modern approaches to Prophetic authority took shape with the emergence of Qurʾānic scripturalism. The first signs of this tendency were in the Punjab in the early twentieth century with the emergence of the self-designated Ahl-i-Qurʾān.[57] The movement began as a dissident faction of the Ahl-i-Ḥadīth. Just as the Ahl-i-Ḥadīth viewed *taqlīd* as the source of corruption and division in Islam, so the Ahl-i-Qurʾān came to view adherence to ḥadīth as the cause of Islam's misfortunes. Just as the Ahl-i-Ḥadīth claimed that the authentic legacy of the Prophet could be regained only by returning to ḥadīth, so the Ahl-i-Qurʾān argued that pure and unadulterated Islam is to be found only in the Qurʾān. The Qurʾān alone, they argued, supplies a reliable basis for religious belief and action.

Ahl-i-Qurʾān activity was concentrated in two important Ahl-i-Ḥadīth centers in western Punjab, Lahore and Amritsar. In Lahore the movement was initiated by a minor religious functionary, ʿAbd Allāh Chakṟālawī (d. 1930).[58] The Amritsar group was established by Khwāja Aḥmad Dīn Amritsarī (1861–1936).[59] Chakṟālawī was apparently the first to make use of the term Ahl-i-Qurʾān some time around 1906, but the Lahore and Amritsar groups vied for recognition as the originators of the doctrine. An Amritsar biographer credits Khwāja Aḥmad Dīn with converting Chakṟālawī, although, as Mājid points out, a comparison of their writings suggests that Khwāja Aḥmad Dīn did not espouse Ahl-i-Qurʾān doctrines until 1917, about ten years after Chakṟālawī's first writings on the subject.[60] After being forced out of his home town, reportedly by opponents of his views, Chakṟālawī fled to Lahore where he established an association, the Jamāʿat-i-Ahl-i-Qurʾān. Under the auspices of this organization, he began to promote his doctrines. He became engaged in bitter debates with the Ahl-i-Ḥadīth, most notably with the newspaper editor Muḥammad Ḥusayn Batālawī, and he so aroused their fury that he had to be rescued on one occasion by the government authorities. In 1921 a disciple of Chakṟālawī established a journal, *Ishāʿat al-Qurʾān*, which continued until 1925.

The Amritsar group appears to have been more influential and had more lasting effect. The founding figure, Khwāja Aḥmad Dīn, first opposed reliance on ḥadīth in favor of the Qurʾān in 1917 with his book *Muʿjizāt al-Qurʾān*, in which he attempted a reinterpretation of the laws of inheritance on the basis of the Qurʾān alone.[61] Khwāja Aḥmad Dīn had been educated at a mission school and as a young man had been active in interreligious debates. Following the pattern typical of the Ahl-i-Ḥadīth, and indeed of most of the reformist Muslim groups of the day, he claimed to have come by his views on his own. The same account may be found in almost any Ahl-i-Qur'ān autobiography: an ardent student of ḥadīth comes across traditions that shock his moral sensibilities. In the course of trying to explain the presence of such traditions, he digs deeper and deeper into the study of ḥadīth only to become more and more disillusioned, concluding in the end that no ḥadīth can be trusted.[62] In 1918, after his conversion and the publication of his book on the subject, he founded the Anjuman-i-Ummat-i-Muslima, an organization which actively promoted Ahl-i-Qur'ān views at least until 1952. The Anjuman began publishing a journal, *al-Balāgh*,[63] which became the leading voice for Ahl-i-Qur'ān views until Ghulām Aḥmad Parwēz established the journal *Ṭulūʿ-i-Islām* in 1938.

The central concerns of the early Ahl-i-Qur'ān fall squarely within the tradition of the Ahl-i-Ḥadīth. They were preoccupied with the same matters of ritual practice that divided Ahl-i-Ḥadīth and Ḥanafīs, especially the precise form of the *ṣalāt*. They did not sound the call to prayer, they recited "God is great" silently, and they knelt on only one knee in the prayer ritual.[64] They established their own mosques, refusing to pray with other Muslims, and they eliminated special prayers for the dead as well as *ʿīd* prayers. But in most matters of doctrine and practice, again like the Ahl-i-Ḥadīth, they did not differ significantly from other Muslims. Indeed, one of their dominant intellectual preoccupations was an effort to prove that all of the essentials of Islam could be derived from the Qur'ān alone. Again, this effort was especially focused on the problem of the prayer ritual. Just as the *ṣalāt* had become a central distinguishing mark of the Ahl-i-Ḥadīth, establishing their difference from the Ḥanafī majority, in much the same way the Ahl-i-Qur'ān made use of the *ṣalāt* to set themselves apart from the Ahl-i-Ḥadīth. These common concerns clearly establish the close relationship between the two groups.

The second generation of deniers of ḥadīth in the Subcontinent repudiated attempts to find every detail of Islamic practice in the Qur'ān in favor of a more speculative and rationalistic approach to Qur'ānic exegesis. But even Muḥammad Aslam Jayrājpūrī (1881–1955), the individual most responsible for advancing the focus of Ahl-i-Qur'ān discourse beyond parochial matters of ritual and moving it out from under the shadow of the Ahl-i-Ḥadīth, had Ahl-i-Ḥadīth roots himself. Jayrājpūrī's father, Salāmat Allāh Jayrājpūrī (d. 1904), had been a leading member of the Ahl-i-Ḥadīth in Aʿẓamgarh, and had studied ḥadīth under Naẕīr Ḥusayn Dihlawī.[65] Jayrājpūrī reports that he began questioning the authenticity of ḥadīth as a young man, after coming across traditions that shocked him. In 1904 he went to meet Chakṟālawī in Lahore, but came away unsatisfied, convinced that Chakṟālawī was wasting his efforts on obscurities. Apparently he was more impressed with the work of Khwāja Aḥmad Dīn and his Anjuman-i-Ummat-i-Muslima in Amritsar; he translated Aḥmad Dīn's *Muʿjizāt al-Qurʾān* into Arabic under the title *al-Wirāthāt fī al-Islām* and became a frequent contributor to *al-Balāgh.*[66]

Whereas Jayrājpūrī and later deniers of ḥadīth moved away from the specific concerns of the Ahl-i-Ḥadīth, it is clear that the original impulse for the development of Ahl-i-Qurʾān ideas was a direct outgrowth of the anti-*taqlīd* doctrines of the Ahl-i-Ḥadīth movement. The Ahl-i-Qurʾān were not rationalists, nor were they deeply affected by western ideas. The movement was, in essence, an extension and a more extreme manifestation of Ahl-i-Ḥadīth scripturalism. Moreover, the transition from the tradition-based scripturalism of the Ahl-i-Ḥadīth to the Qurʾān-based scripturalism of the Ahl-i-Qurʾān did not require any great change in orientation. The basic impulse – returning to Islam in its original and pure form – was the same for both groups. The Ahl-i-Qurʾān simply substituted different criteria by which this "pure" Islam was to be defined. They turned the basic Ahl-i-Ḥadīth argument, that accretions must be bypassed and authentic Islam regained, against the ḥadīth literature itself. As Ikrām notes, the Ahl-i-Ḥadīth had in some respects become more inflexible and dogmatic than the classical tradition against which they had protested.[67] We see in the conversion accounts of those who became deniers of ḥadīth evidence that by focusing attention so sharply on the tradition literature and by insisting so dogmatically on the acceptance of all that was considered reliable by the ancient traditionists, the Ahl-i-Ḥadīth brought crisis on itself. Virtually every denier of ḥadīth, in describing his conversion, insists that at one time he was devoted to the authority of ḥadīth but that extensive study of the tradition literature faced him with allegedly sound traditions which he simply could not accept. Thus the Ahl-i-Qurʾān may be viewed as the product of conflict within the Ahl-i-Ḥadīth between the essentially radical impulse that gave rise to the movement and the conservatism demonstrated in its treatment of ḥadīth.

While these ideas were percolating in Lahore and Amritsar, similar arguments made a surprising, and quite anomalous, appearance in Egypt. In 1906, the year Chakṟālawī published his first major work, Muḥammad Tawfīq Ṣidqī, an associate of Rashīd Riḍā, a regular contributor to *al-Manār* and an active Muslim apologist, published an article in *al-Manār* which introduced ideas remarkably similar to the doctrine being propagated by the Indian Ahl-i-Qurʾān. Ṣidqī's article sparked a debate in *al-Manār* which lasted four years.[68]

Ṣidqī argued that the details of Muḥammad's behavior were never meant to be imitated in every particular. Thus Muslims should rely solely on the Qurʾān. Ṣidqī's own motivations, made explicit in the article itself, were directly related to the central doctrines of the *salafiyya* – rejection of *taqlīd* and a quest for authenticity.[69] He simply extended these principles a step further than they had previously been taken. It is clear, however, that his views do not represent a sharp break with *salafī* ideology. The rejection of ḥadīth as a source of authority was simply a new variation on an old *salafī* theme.

Ṣidqī's article and the controversy it set off is also important for what it reveals of Rashīd Riḍā's attitude to questions of sunna and of the authenticity of ḥadīth. Why did Riḍā, who took a stand against Ṣidqī's views and forced his recantation, allow the article to run in the first place? Riḍā's retrospective review of Ṣidqī's works after the latter's death suggests that Riḍā was motivated primarily by a desire to shake up the Azhar establishment; he wanted to rouse them to the defense of their views on sunna. In other words, Riḍā's motives in allowing a radical challenge to sunna to be published, even though he disagreed with it, were connected with his general opposition to *taqlīd* and his contempt for the passivity of the *ʿulamāʾ*.

Riḍā's own views about sunna were expressed in detail only after the appearance of Ṣidqī's article and his approach may be viewed as a compromise between complete rejection of sunna and adherence to classical ideas about ḥadīth. On the one hand he would not countenance a wholesale rejection of Prophetic authority. On the other hand, he reserved for himself the right to review and reevaluate the sources of sunna (i.e., ḥadīth) on the basis of his own *ijtihād*.[70] The only source of sunna that is beyond dispute for Riḍā is the sunna *ʿamaliyya* which has been practiced and passed on by each generation of Muslims in a *mutawātir* fashion. This includes, for example, the prayer ritual and the details of other central rituals. But traditions that were transmitted verbally by a single line of reporters, the so-called isolated (*āḥād*) traditions, must be subject to reexamination according to new criteria. Such a reexamination must encompass even traditions in the sound collections.

It is clear that Riḍā's and Ṣidqī's motivations in their treatment of the problem of sunna are essentially the same. Both were motivated primarily by the desire to shake off the fetters of *taqlīd* and to assert the right to return to the sources and to rediscover the original and authentic Islam for themselves. We may conclude, then, that the basic background to the emergence of challenges to ḥadīth in Egypt is similar to that of corresponding ideas in the Subcontinent. In both environments anti-ḥadīth ideas grew up within groups that had made the rejection of received authority and the search for authenticity cardinal points in their doctrine.

Despite the similarities in their roots, however, these ideas grew up in very different forms. In the Subcontinent anti-ḥadīth sentiment developed in vigorous sectarian forms and discussions of sunna have taken a speculative turn, focusing on theoretical issues such as the nature of revelation and of prophecy. In Egypt anti-ḥadīth ideas have been the province of a small number of isolated writers, and they have never found fertile ground or developed an institutional base. Moreover, the Egyptian critics of ḥadīth hardly venture into theological speculation, confining their arguments mostly to historical and technical questions.

Anti-ḥadīth views, such as those of the Ahl-i-Qurʾān and Ṣidqī, have never attracted a large following. In the twentieth century, however, there have been a handful of important writers, most notably Ghulām Aḥmad Parwēz in Pakistan and Maḥmūd Abū Rayya in Egypt, who have developed sophisticated arguments to defend anti-ḥadīth views. Although the radically revised views of religious authority proposed by such writers have not gained wide acceptance, they have had a major influence as a catalyst, sparking controversy and setting the agenda for modern discussions of Prophetic authority. The issues raised by these deniers of ḥadīth – the nature of revelation, the scope of Prophetic authority, the reliability of the tradition literature – have been the main concerns in the modern crisis of religious authority, and it is on these issues that the remainder of this work will be focused.

3 Boundaries of revelation

The issue of sunna confronts Muslims with urgent questions about the nature of revelation. Where does revelation end and interpretation begin? What distinguishes the divine voice from the human voices that transmit or interpret it? What part does the humanity of the messenger play in the process of revelation? All prophetic religious traditions share these dilemmas, for these questions arise from the fundamental paradoxes of prophecy: in the prophetic message the transcendant becomes immanent, the universal becomes particular, the perfect is transmitted through imperfect channels. It is not surprising, then, that the nature and purpose of the Qurʾān is a central concern of modern discussions of sunna.

The classical view of the relationship between the Qurʾān and the sunna is concisely stated in the maxim "The Qurʾān has more need of the sunna than the sunna has of the Qurʾān." The Qurʾān, in this view, cannot stand on its own. Without the sunna to guarantee its meaning, to clarify its intentions, and to supplement its commands, it is incomprehensible. This argument was central to al-Shāfiʿī's defense of sunna; the primary function of sunna, he argued, is to clarify the Qurʾān. The Qurʾān provides general commands, the sunna specifies the exact intent. When the Qurʾān lays down the penalty of eighty lashes for adulterers, it uses general and inclusive language, implying that all adulterers are included (24:2). The sunna, however, makes it clear that only a particular category of adulterers is intended by this command.[1] In addition to clarifying the precise intent of the Qurʾānic text, the sunna offers additional information which is absolutely essential to religious practice but which does not appear in the Qurʾān. Where, for example, can one find a detailed explanation of ritual prayer or the fast in the Qurʾān? The Qurʾān refers to these requirements in general terms only; the sunna provides the detailed explanation.[2]

Challenges to this view of the organic relationship between Qurʾān and sunna are not completely unprecedented in the history of Islamic thought. Some of the opponents of al-Shāfiʿī argued that the Qurʾān "explains everything" (16:89) and needs no supplement.[3] Their viewpoint was snuffed out after the triumph of the traditionist view, however, and it was not until the nineteenth and twentieth centuries that the argument was revived. The factors that entered into the emergence, or reemergence, of this doctrine included the challenge of Christian polemics, the influence of Protestant scripturalism, and the effects of western scholarship. These external influences encouraged an emphasis on the Qur'ān to the exclusion of ḥadīth. There were also indigenous factors. Among these were the general impulse toward reform and the accompanying reaction against adherence to tradition (*taqlīd*) which was rooted in eighteenth-century reformist movements. Such factors encouraged, among the Muslims most affected by them, an almost complete rejection of classical interpretations. For early reformers and for groups such as the Ahl-i-Ḥadīth this meant rejecting *ijmā'* in order to interpret the Qur'ān and the sunna for oneself. For later and more radical reformers it came to mean freedom from reliance on ḥadīth as well. Their intention was to get at the Qur'ān directly and to bypass the ḥadīth-bound *tafsīr* literature. The pressure for reform and for revision of traditional viewpoints thus drove a wedge between the Qur'ān and its traditional sunna-based interpretation.

In the Subcontinent this new emphasis on the independence of the Qur'ān is first evident in the work of Sayyid Aḥmad Khān.[4] The principles of interpretation which he lays down free the discipline of *tafsīr* from ḥadīth, substituting instead the principles of reason and "nature." He assumes, throughout his work, that the Qur'ān stands on its own, requiring only the application of a dedicated and enlightened mind for its understanding. The principles of interpretation he outlines make no mention of sunna, focusing instead on the use of philological and rational principles to interpret the text.[5] For Sayyid Aḥmad the great miracle of the Qur'ān is its universality. He was struck by the fact that each generation continues to find the Qur'ān relevant despite the constant increase in human knowledge. Too heavy a reliance on ḥadīth for the interpretation of the Qur'ān puts at risk this eternal and universal quality. Ḥadīth-based *tafsīr* tends to limit the meaning of the Qur'ān to a particular historical situation, thus obscuring its universality.[6]

The Ahl-i-Qur'ān further developed this tendency to emphasize the Qur'ān as the sole source of religious authority to the exclusion of all others into a full-blown Qur'ānic scripturalism. For the Ahl-i-Qur'ān the elevation of the Qur'ān and the explicit rejection of all aids to its interpretation, including sunna, became central tenets of dogma. Their doctrine implied, first of all, that the Qur'ān needed nothing external for its interpretation. Like the early Qur'ānic scripturalists who show up in al-Shāfi'ī's work, the Ahl-i-Qur'ān held that the Qur'ān was intended to be clear, accessible, and readily understandable. This meant, first, that the Qur'ān was self-contained and must be interpreted according to internal logic, a conviction summed up in the proposition that "the Qur'ān ought to be interpreted by its own verses."[7] In other words no external aids were needed for its interpretation except, as Jayrājpūrī says, a sufficient command of Arabic.[8] This conviction that the interpretation of the Qur'ān could and should be freed from the restraints of tradition gained popularity beyond the narrow confines of those directly affiliated with the Ahl-i-Qur'ān. Thus Ināyat Allāh Khān Mashriqī, the founder of the radical khākhsār movement, wrote:

> The correct and the only meaning of the Qur'ān lies, and is preserved, within itself, and a perfect and detailed exegesis of its words is within its own pages. One part of the Qur'ān explains the other; it needs neither philosophy, nor wit, nor lexicography, nor even ḥadīth.[9]

This aspect of the doctrine of the sufficiency of the Qur'ān found its expression in a new genre of Qur'ān commentaries which set out to prove the point that "the Qur'ān is its own best commentary." Among the earliest was a commentary by ʿAbd Allāh Chakṟālawī, *Tarjumat al-Qur'ān bi āyāt al-furqān.*[10] The attempt to interpret the Qur'ān on the basis of internal criteria alone became the hallmark of Ahl-i-Qur'ān *tafsīr* and the basis for the sophisticated exegetical works of Jayrājpūrī and Parwēz.[11]

Besides encouraging new methods of exegesis, the Ahl-i-Qur'ān also argued that the Qur'ān is comprehensive, a book in which all the requirements of the faith are revealed. It is a self-contained and fully sufficient guide for belief and practice and all that is a necessary part of religion can be derived from it. Among the early Ahl-i-Qur'ān, especially ʿAbd Allāh Chakṟālawī and his followers, this assertion found expression in attempts to prove that all of the essential details of ritual practice, i.e., the five pillars, could be distilled from the Qur'ān. By this means the Ahl-i-Qur'ān sought to demonstrate to their erstwhile colleagues in the Ahl-i-Ḥadīth that ḥadīth was, in fact, superfluous; all the details of ritual allegedly supplied only by ḥadīth could be distilled from the Qur'ān.

The greatest preoccupation of Chakṟālawī and his followers was with the details of *ṣalāt*, the ritual prayer. The object of one of his first works, *Burhān al-furqān ʿalā ṣalāt al-Qur'ān,* was to prove that the details of the five daily prayers can all be derived from the Qur'ān. "The Muslims offer, and should offer, five prayers a day," he wrote, "not because they are found in ḥadīth, but because they are enjoined by, and are proven from, the Qur'ān."[12] His conviction that every detail should be demonstrated from the Qur'ān led him to reject a number of practices for which he could find no justification. He considered the call to prayer (*adhān*) an innovation with no basis in the Qur'ān, he modified the ritual recitations, and he would allow no more than the obligatory number of ritual acts of prayer (*raka'āt*).[13] But on the whole his modifications to ritual worship were fairly minor; Chakṟālawī was more concerned with justifying the main elements of the existing ritual than with promoting radical changes.

In the course of making his point, however, Chakṟālawī frequently embarked on exegetical fantasies. In order to defend the practice of grasping the ears during the *takbīr* (repetition of the phrase "God is Great"), for example, he appealed to the following verse: "Say: 'Consider, if God took away your hearing and your sight and sealed up your hearts, who – other than God – could restore them to you?'" (6:46); to which he offers the following highly unusual translation and commentary:

> O Prophet, Say [*to those people who do not humble their ears and hearts in prayer, that is, who do not grasp their ears, do not prevent their eyes from wandering, and who have no fear of God in their hearts*]: "Tell me, after thinking, if God grasps your ears [*enlarges them*] and your eyes [*blots them out*] and binds your hearts, then who do you have but God to return them to you?" [*Since there is no one, you had better grasp your ears in prayer, keep your eyes from wandering and maintain the fear of God in your hearts.*][14]

This example illustrates both the lengths to which Chakṟālawī was willing to go to prove that everything of value could be distilled from the Qur'ān and the fantastic interpretations that were possible when the restraining influence of sunna was removed from the discipline of *tafsīr*.

Proving that the details of prayer were contained in the Qur'ān was a tenuous venture. It was not at all easy to find justification even for the number of prayers, let alone minutiae of ritual. Thus divisions grew within the ranks of the Ahl-i-Qur'ān itself. One of Chakṟālawī's disciples, Mistrī Muḥammad Ramaḍān (1875–1940),[15] broke with him ostensibly over the number of daily prayers, although underlying their differences over matters of detail were more important differences in exegetical technique. Ramaḍān rejected some of the more extreme exegetical extravagances of Chakṟālawī, arguing that they demonstrated a continued adherence to the Islam of the ḥadīth. Thus while Chakṟālawī believed he could justify the details of existing prayer rituals, including the requirement of five daily prayers, from the Qur'ān, Ramaḍān found only three prayers. He also modified other elements of the prayer ritual, reducing each prayer to two *raka'as* and eliminating all recitations.[16] He left Chakṟālawī's group and returned to his home in Gujrānwāla to found a rival organization, the Anjuman-i-Ahl-i-Dhikr wa al-Qur'ān and a rival journal, *Balāgh al-Qur'ān*.[17] Another Ahl-i-Qur'ān figure, Sayyid Rafī' al-Dīn of Multān, is reported to have insisted that only four prayers could be proven from the Qur'ān.[18]

These developments indicate a gradual migration away from the Ahl-i-

Ḥadīth roots of the movement. The preoccupations of Chakṟālawī and his followers are clearly shaped by the concerns of the Ahl-i-Ḥadīth. His close relationship with the Ahl-i-Ḥadīth is also shown by the polemics between the two groups which displayed all the characteristics of a squabble among siblings.[19] Soon, however, the logic of the Ahl-i-Qur'ān position began to take on a force of its own. Ramaḍān's ideas represent the beginnings of an advance in Ahl-i-Qur'ān thought away from mere justification of the doctrine of sufficiency towards a more systematic development of its implications.

The sufficiency of the Qur'ān also became a focus of discussion in Egypt after Ṣidqī inaugurated modern controversies over sunna there. Ṣidqī set out to prove that "what is obligatory for man does not go beyond God's book." Thus the Qur'ān describes itself as "the book which explains all things" (16:89), and God Himself bears witness that He has "omitted nothing from The Book" (6:38). Ṣidqī admits that the Qur'ān commands obedience to the Prophet – on this there is no dispute. Where there is room for dispute, he says, is on the question of whether the Prophet placed any requirements on Muslims which were not already commanded by the Qur'ān. Muḥammad's authority, he implies, is strictly limited to implementing the Qur'ān.[20] These ideas are virtually identical to those that were being spread in India at the same time.

The most striking parallel between Ṣidqī's arguments and those of Chakṟālawī and his followers is their common concern to prove that the essentials of Islam – especially the requirements for *ṣalāt* – can be derived from the Qur'ān alone without any reference to sunna. Ṣidqī based his argument that the prayer ritual can be established without any help from sunna on the instructions for the shortening of prayer in times of danger (*ṣalāt al-khawf*).[21] From the exception, he claimed, the rule becomes clear. Since Muslims are instructed to shorten the prayer to only one *rakaʿa* (a segment of ritual prayer) during times of danger, the normal minimum requirement must be two *rakaʿas*. Beyond this basic requirement Ṣidqī believed that Muslims have a measure of freedom as long as they do not exceed what is reasonable. Any additional *rakaʿas* performed by the Prophet were purely optional.[22] *Zakāt* presents a similar case. Since the Qur'ān did not establish the precise amount of *zakāt* to be levied, it is clear that this is a matter of flexibility. Changes in circumstances will require changes in the required amounts.[23]

Ṣidqī's direct assault on the foundations of sunna is an anomaly in Egyptian religious discourse. Although his article set off a debate on the pages of *al-Manār* which lasted two years, Ṣidqī's ideas left almost no positive trace.[24] In fact Ṣidqī himself recanted, and consequently the debate was resolved more or less amicably.[25] In later treatments of sunna Ṣidqī's arguments are cited only for the purpose of refutation and his approach has never been taken up by any other writer in Egypt. This outcome contrasts sharply with the fate of similar ideas in the Subcontinent where the doctrine of the sufficiency of the Qurʾān quickly gained clear institutional expression and has continued to attract a small but dedicated following up to the present. In Punjab during the 1930s this viewpoint was widespread enough to support three separate journals. The contrast is illustrative of general differences between approaches to the problem of sunna in Egypt and the Subcontinent. Whereas Ṣidqī's arguments, like those of the Ahl-i-Qurʾān, go to the heart of the theory of sunna, the dominant tendency among Egyptian critics of ḥadīth has been to avoid theoretical and theological issues and to focus instead on questions of the historicity of ḥadīth. As a result speculative approaches to the authority of sunna which found fertile ground in the Subcontinent failed to take root in Egypt.

In the Subcontinent the doctrine of the sufficiency of the Qurʾān continued to evolve as it attracted new followers. A second generation of adherents to this doctrine largely abandoned exegetical exercises designed to prove the comprehensiveness of the Qurʾān which had been Chakṟālawī's stock-in-trade. This trend was already evident in the early twentieth century among the followers of Khwāja Aḥmad Dīn in Amritsar whose organization, the Ummat-i-Muslima, refused to endorse any attempts to revise basic ritual practices.[26] Later writers, particularly Jayrājpūrī and Parwēz, did not feel any urgency about proving that every essential detail of Islamic belief and practice can be found in the Qurʾān. They were content to assert that the Qurʾān contains all the necessary *principles* for right belief and action. The job of elaborating these principles they assigned to reason and to divinely sanctioned political authorities. It was enough for Jayrājpūrī that the Qurʾān is sufficient to guide human reason and morality, providing the principles necessary for people to come to their own conclusions about details. For these thinkers, Islam has an unchanging core, but in application it is adaptable and fluid. This implies that texts of revelation do not have a single, fixed meaning. Rather, each new generation can expect to find in the Qurʾān new treasures as their own capacity to understand its teaching grows. The Qurʾān's capacity to provide guidance is infinitely adaptable to new circumstances. By extension, it also becomes the right of each believer to read, interpret, and apply the Qurʾān for her- or himself, bypassing both the classical tradition of *tafsīr* and the keepers of that tradition. Furthermore, no one's understanding of the Qurʾān – not even that of Muḥammad himself – is completely binding on others.[27] Khwāja Aḥmad Dīn Amritsarī took this argument to an extreme, claiming that the Prophet had no more understanding of the Qurʾān than has been given to us. Muḥammad's understanding of revelation, like ours, was based on reason (*ʿaql*) and like us he was quite capable of making mistakes in his interpretation.[28]

Such arguments fuel deep suspicions among more conservative Muslims. To defenders of sunna it seems that the doctrine of the sufficiency of the Qurʾān is simply an excuse to play loose and free with the meaning of the Qurʾān. While Qurʾānic scripturalists view it as a primary concern to establish the independent authority of the Qurʾān, their opponents respond by arguing that the Qurʾān cannot stand on its own apart from the Prophetic witness. The sunna, in this view, far from being superfluous, is absolutely essential to clarify the meaning of the Qurʾān, to guarantee its correct interpretation, to demonstrate its practical application, and, finally, to guarantee the divine origins of the text of the Qurʾān itself.

The argument that sunna performs an indispensable clarifying function is often a simple reiteration of al-Shāfiʿī's argument: without the sunna to clarify its meaning, the Qurʾān becomes "a closed book," devoid of the information necessary for its understanding.[29] While the Qurʾān provides general principles, practical details can be found only in the sunna. Examples are numerous: the form and frequency of the ritual prayer, the rules for the fast, and obscure verses which would remain a complete mystery without the sunna to explain them.[30] Without the sunna Muslims would be left without guidance on essential points of belief and practice.

According to Abū al-ʿAlā Mawdūdī, one of the most vehement opponents of the doctrine of the sufficiency of the Qurʾān, the central function of prophets is to guarantee the interpretation of the revelation they bring. Prophecy is an indispensable guarantee that the Divine message will be correctly understood. Could not God have had angels distribute a book of guidance to each individual? Yet if such a book was sent without a prophet, divisions would arise over its interpretation and there would be no one to offer an authoritative decision on such disputes. Mistakes would be made in implementing God's commands with no one to set them right.[31] The experience of earlier communities makes it clear that having a divinely revealed book is no guarantee against error: were not the Jews and the Christians also blessed with revealed books?

In this view, then, prophets hold a privileged position as authoritative interpreters of revelation. Here we have a manifestation of the idea, ubiquitous in Islamic thought, that the closer an individual is to the source of an event, the more authoritative is their interpretation of that event; because they were closest to the event of revelation, prophets are naturally its most capable interpreters. Therefore no one was better placed than

Muḥammad to understand the full context and meaning of each passage of revelation, according to Mawdūdī. But Muḥammad's interpretation of the Qur'ān involved more than just proximity to the events. The Prophet also had a God-given insight, *khudādād baṣīrat*, by which he was able to rightly understand and act upon the Qur'ān. Hence his words and conduct, the stuff of sunna, represent an authoritative interpretation of the revealed text.[32]

It follows that Muḥammad's sunna is a clear and practical demonstration of the divine will put into action. Since the purpose of revelation is to guide human behavior, it is impossible to separate the Qur'ān from its concrete implementation, that is, from sunna. S. M. Yusuf provides a clear exposition of an argument for the necessity of sunna based on the inseparability of revelation from its active implementation. In the Qur'ān, he says, this relationship between abstract word and concrete implementation is referred to in the collocution "*al-kitāb wa al-ḥikma.*"[33] According to Yusuf, "*ḥikma* signifies propriety of judgment as manifested and embodied in propriety of conduct." The whole purpose of the Qur'ān is to establish *ḥikma*: "The progression from *kitāb* to *ḥikma* is essential; to tear the one from the other is to destroy the common entity of both."[34] The manifestation of this divine *ḥikma* is in the sunna of the Prophet. As a result, the Qur'ān and the sunna "cannot be fundamentally divorced from each other. For Sunnah is, more or less, a concrete implementation of the divine will."[35] Revelation, in other words, cannot be separated from the particulars of its practical application and, in the case of the Qur'ān, these particulars are to be found in the sunna of the Prophet.

Finally, some supporters of sunna argue that the Prophetic witness is not only the clarification and the practical demonstration of the meaning of revelation, but also the chief guarantee that it really is revelation. In other words, Muslims only know the Qur'ān is revelation because of Muḥammad's testimony to this fact. If the Prophetic word is not to be trusted, then the Qur'ān itself is open to suspicion. The sunna thus provides the essential foundation for the authority of the Qur'ān, or put in technical terms, "The word of the Prophet is a *ḥujja* [evidential proof] for the Qur'ān."[36] If the word of the Prophet had not been preserved, or if this word could not be considered completely trustworthy, then we would have no assurance about the reliability of the Qur'ān.[37]

The basic issue between those who support the sufficiency of the Qur'ān and their opponents reduces to a fundamental disagreement over the nature of revelation and its application in Islamic society. In the view of those who uphold its sufficiency, the Qur'ān is a basic set of principles and a general guide for moral behavior. Details of the law, however, must be worked out according to circumstances. Their opponents charge that this simply means molding the Qurʾān according to personal whim. They allege that the Ahl-i-Qurʾān take whatever comes into their minds and project it onto the Qurʾān, and thus claim the interpretive authority that they deny to the Prophet himself. "[The deniers of ḥadīth] completely deny the authority (*ḥujjiyyat*) of ḥadīth in order to dismember the Qurʾān and mold it according to their own desires."[38] Consequently, "they made the Qurʾān a sort of camel which anyone can take by the halter and lead wherever they please."[39] Adherents of the doctrine of the sufficiency of the Qurʾān respond that conservatives, by their attachment to ḥadīth, obscure the inherent flexibility of Islam and make it impossible for society to adapt to changing circumstances. God never intended, they insist, for every detail of life to be eternally established by revelation.

Such differences about the nature of revelation are sharply focused in questions about the manner of Prophetic inspiration and the relationship of Muḥammad's ordinary words and actions – his humanity – to his divine mission as Prophet. In classical doctrine one of the fundamental pillars of the theory of sunna is the argument that Muḥammad was the recipient not only of Qurʾānic revelation, but also of special revelation apart from the Qurʾān.This doctrine was established by the time of al-Shāfiʿī and was a subject of controversy between him and his scripturalist opponents among the *ahl al-kalām* who argued that the Qurʾān alone was revelation from God. After al-Shāfiʿī, the view that sunna could be defined as extra-Qurʾānic *waḥy* achieved general acceptance, and traditions were circulated which stated that Gabriel brought the sunna just as he had the Qurʾān.[40] Thus classical doctrine posited a duality of revelation:

> While the Qurʾān is the basic source for the law, when we examine it we find that it requires obedience to the Prophet of God in everything he commands and we find that God, referring to the Prophet, clearly says, "It is no less than *waḥy* sent down to him." (53:4) This proves to us that God distributed two kinds of *waḥy* to Muḥammad: The first is *waḥy matlū*, recorded verbatim by miraculous arrangement; this is the Qurʾān. The second is the *waḥy* of tradition, which is not verbatim, is not inimitable, and is not ritually recited . . . and we find that God requires obedience to this second type of *waḥy* in the same way that he requires obedience to the Qurʾān. There is no distinction, for God says "Obey God and obey the messenger."[41]

In this doctrine of dual revelation, the formal superiority of the Qurʾān was maintained by distinguishing, as Ibn Ḥazm does here, between recited revelation (*waḥy matlū*), the accuracy of which is attested word for word, and unrecited revelation (*waḥy ghayr matlū*), for which only the meaning and not the exact words can be attested. For the purposes of the jurists, however, the authority of the two sources was equal. In al-Ghazālī's words, "On occasions, God indicates His word by the Qur'ān, on others, by words in another style, not publicly recited, and called sunna."[42] Both the sunna and the Qur'ān therefore originate with God, both are mediated through the agency of prophecy, and no distinction can be drawn between them with regard to their authority.

There was some disagreement in classical scholarship about the precise manner in which God delivered the sunna to Muḥammad. While most scholars held that the sunna was a product of direct revelation (*waḥy mubāshir*), revealed through angelic agency, others believed that the Prophet himself was more intimately involved in the process, and that sunna, at least in part, was a product of his inspired *ijtihād*. The disagreement made little difference, however, to the final outcome. Whether direct revelation or inspiration, the sunna still represents divine authority. Thus the essential identification of sunna with divine guidance came to be unanimously recognized in orthodox circles.

In the Subcontinent the identification of sunna with *waḥy* has been an important point of controversy, and the question of whether the Prophet received extra-Qur'ānic revelation has therefore emerged as a major theme in the controversial literature on sunna. The issue has a certain logical priority for both critics and supporters of sunna. For skeptics, denial of this doctrine is a necessary corollary of the sufficiency of the Qur'ān. For those who defend sunna the doctrine remains a central defense for the importance of ḥadīth. If sunna is a part of revelation then it is an essential and undeniable part of Islam and to deny its authority amounts to heresy. But if, as the skeptics claim, Muḥammad's extra-Qur'ānic words and actions are not revealed, if they are nothing more than the product of human effort, then it can be convincingly argued that such precedents are subject to revision and were never meant to be binding on all Muslims for all time.

The Qur'ānic scripturalists' primary argument against the revealed status of sunna takes the form of a comparison between sunna and the Qur'ān: the sunna is measured against the standard of revelation and found to fall short. This argument has ancient roots. The *ahl al-kalām* as portrayed by al-Shāfiʿī claimed that they accept "nothing which has not been guaranteed by God in the same way that he has guaranteed the Qur'ān, of which no one can doubt even a single letter."[43] Modern Qur'ānic scripturalists elaborate this argument. They hold that revelation which God intends to be universal and eternal is dealt with in a special way. First of all *waḥy* must be revealed and transmitted verbatim – every word must be from God. Second, the process of revelation must be external, entirely independent of the influence of the messenger. Finally, revelation must be recorded and preserved in writing and transmitted faithfully without any possibility of corruption or error.[44] Sunna, in the view of the deniers of ḥadīth, does not meet these conditions.

The first weakness of sunna is that, unlike the Qur'ān, it is not preserved in such a way that it can be trusted to represent the exact words of God. This is for two reasons. First, with the exception of the *ḥadīth qudsī*, *aḥādīth* record only the words of the Prophet, not the words of God. Even if it be granted that Muḥammad was speaking in response to revelation or inspiration, the words are nevertheless his own words in a way that the Qur'ān is not. Second, due to the practice of transmitting reports according to their sense (*bi'l-ma'nā*) rather than verbatim (*bi'l-lafẓ*), the words of the traditions cannot be trusted to represent even the exact words of Muḥammad. These facts were recognized by classical doctrine and it is in part for this reason that sunna is defined as unrecited revelation (*waḥy ghayr matlū*). Nevertheless classical scholars still considered the sunna reliable. For the Ahl-i-Qur'ān, however, the inability to guarantee that every word of sunna is divinely revealed represents a fatal flaw. To be considered revelation it is not enough that the meaning be from God; the words themselves must be of divine origin and free from corruption.

A second criterion by which sunna can be shown to fall short of the standard for *waḥy* is closely related to the first: whereas *waḥy* must be externally and verbally communicated, the sunna bears the marks of Muḥammad's personality. *Waḥy* in this view can refer only to the very words of God. "The unique characteristic of *waḥy*, upon which is based the assertion that it is from God," according to one representative of this view, "is that the mentality (*baṣīrat*) of the individual to whom it is sent has no hand in it. If the '*waḥy*' by which the Prophet established the practical application of the basic laws of the Qur'ān, was really from God, then Muḥammad's *baṣīrat* can have no part in it."[45] Any human influence or involvement precludes the possibility that a command or statement is *waḥy*. Khwāja Aḥmad Dīn of Amritsar argued that divine origin of the Qur'ān is established by the fact that the Prophet did not and could not have full understanding of it. By transcending the mentality of the Prophet the Qur'ān reveals its divine origins.[46]

The third and most important weakness of the sunna in relation to the Qur'ān, however, concerns its late registration in writing and its flawed transmission. If God had wished the sunna to be an indispensable part of Islam, He would surely have had it recorded and preserved in writing in the manner of the Qur'ān. Conversely, because the traditions were not registered in writing until long after the time of the Prophet, we can safely assume that sunna is not an essential part of religion (*dīn*). The tradition literature itself alleges that the Prophet prohibited the writing down of ḥadīth, presumably in order to prevent its confusion with the Qur'ān.[47]

Muḥammad's prohibition against writing sunna down is taken to have both historical and theological implications. First, the late recording of ḥadīth casts doubt on the historicity of the tradition literature. How can traditions be trusted if they were not secured in writing close to the time of the Prophet?[48] Second, the absence of reliable written records brings into question the revealed status of sunna; if sunna was *waḥy* it certainly would have been recorded in writing.

The theological implications of the recording of ḥadīth have been discussed in both Egypt and Pakistan. "If anything other than the Qur'ān had been necessary for religion," writes Ṣidqī, "the Prophet would have commanded its registration in writing and God would have guaranteed its preservation."[49] In actual fact, he says, ḥadīth was put into writing only after numerous corruptions had entered the tradition literature.[50] To Ṣidqī's mind, and the Ahl-i-Qur'ān of the Subcontinent are in complete agreement with him on this point, the failure to preserve the sunna in writing implies that it should not be considered an essential part of religion. It is only writers from the Subcontinent, however, who use this argument to attack systematically the classical theory that sunna is *waḥy*. The absence of divine intervention to preserve the ḥadīth, they argue, is incompatible with the classical theory that sunna is *waḥy*. God does not treat His revelation so casually.

The importance that Ṣidqī and Indian critics of ḥadīth place on the issue of the writing of the traditions reveals the degree to which they have come to identify revelation with "book." It also marks an important departure from the emphasis on oral transmission and human attestation that is prevalent in classical Islamic thought. In Ahl-i-Qur'ān polemics, the rhetorical question repeatedly surfaces "Is the Prophet's sunna preserved in any book which is trusted by Muslims to be authentic?"[51] If ḥadīth represents *waḥy*, argues Parwēz, then why didn't God preserve it in the same way that He preserved the Qur'ān? Why would He treat the two kinds of revelation so differently? In the case of Qur'ānic *waḥy*, Muḥammad went to great lengths to assure its complete and perfect registration in writing. From beginning to end every word was both written and committed to memory. As for the *waḥy* allegedly recorded in ḥadīth, it was neither written down, nor memorized, nor systematically collected or preserved. No steps were taken by the Prophet or by his immediate followers to preserve the integrity of ḥadīth.[52]

If the Prophet failed to have his sunna written down, it is also evident, according to the "deniers," that God did not preserve the integrity of tradition after the time of the Prophet. At best the collections of traditions, even Bukhārī and Muslim, are mixtures of truth and falsehood. At worst they are riddled with blatant blasphemies and absurdities.[53] In such a mixture, how can one distinguish what is revelation from what is forgery? Here again arguments discrediting the historical authenticity of ḥadīth mingle with theological assumptions about the nature of revelation. In Ṣidqī's words, "Is it conceivable that God would have subjected the world to something in which it is impossible for anyone to distinguish truth and falsehood?"[54]

According to Parwēz, support for the notion that sunna is *waḥy* can be found neither in the Qur'ān nor in the earliest traditions. Moreover, since neither the Prophet, nor his Companions, nor the early Caliphs considered anything to be revelation except the Qur'ān, it is evident that the elevation of sunna to this status must have been a creation of later Muslims. Parwēz develops the argument that this doctrine was, in fact, an imitation of the Jewish doctrine of the oral revelation of the Mishna.[55] He also speculates about what motives might have led to the establishment of this doctrine. The problem, he argues, arises from the Qur'ān itself where some commands are explicit while others are vague. For example, a penalty for adultery is clearly defined, while no punishment is laid down for consumption of alcohol: does this mean that drinking is allowed? Clearly not. Details such as the penalty for drinking were left to the Prophet and his successors to establish as sunna. According to Parwēz, God's intent was to allow such details to be changed according to circumstance. But later Muslims were faced with a challenge from non-Muslims and from dissenters in their own community: if commands and prohibitions not found in the Qur'ān are important, why did God not establish these details Himself? And by what authority did the Prophet enforce commands not found in the Qur'ān? In the face of such challenges, and afraid that anarchy would result if the basis for the law was undercut, the *ʿulamāʾ* adopted the idea that sunna is *waḥy*.[56]

Defenders of sunna counter by arguing that the idea that sunna is *waḥy* is implicit in the Qur'ān.[57] Whereas the Ahl-i-Qur'ān claim that the Qur'ān makes no mention of any revelation other than itself, their opponents respond that it contains clear evidence of extra-Qur'ānic *waḥy*. The most oft-cited argument in this regard is the identification of the Qur'ānic term *ḥikma* with the sunna. In the Qur'ān the term *ḥikma* occurs on twenty occasions. On eight of these occasions it appears in the collocution "*al-kitāb wa al-ḥikma*," and in all of its occurrences God is identified as the source of *ḥikma*.[58] The identification of *ḥikma* with sunna seems to have originated with al-Shāfiʿī and this argument remains ubiquitous in modern defenses of sunna.[59] Sibāʿī rightly concludes that "the majority of the *ʿulamāʾ* concur that *al-ḥikma* is something other than the Qur'ān, and that it consists of the hidden things of faith and the commands of *Sharīʿa* which God made known to [the Prophet]." Since the Qur'ān makes it clear that *ḥikma* is obligatory and since Muslims are required to obey only God and the Prophet, *ḥikma* can only refer to the authority of the Prophet.[60] *Ḥikma* is a necessary complement to the revelation of the book, offered by God to His prophets. "God did not promise only to give the Prophets a book, but also *ḥikma* along with the book. Every Prophet was granted *ḥikma* along with the book, and just as the book comes from God, so too *ḥikma* was sent from God."[61] Thus *ḥikma* consists in right understanding and practical guidance into the commands and prohibitions of the book that God gave to His prophets. It was not just private revelation, intended only for the personal guidance of Muḥammad, nor does it consist of Muḥammad's personal judgments. The Qurʾān makes it clear that *ḥikma* is revealed and is meant to be communicated and taught.[62]

Defenders of sunna also find support in the Qurʾānic distinction between different modes of *waḥy*: "It is not for man that God should speak to him except by *waḥy*, or from behind a veil, or by sending a messenger to reveal, by His permission, what He wills" (42:51). According to Mawdūdī, the first two categories of *waḥy* are personal guidance for Muḥammad – the basis for sunna. It was only from the third category of revelation, identified with revelation brought by angelic agency, that the Qurʾān was compiled.[63] Moreover, supporters of sunna claim to find plenty of allusions to extra-scriptural revelation in the Qurʾān, occasions when a command of God is described which never appears in the Qurʾān. The case most frequently cited concerns the change in the direction of prayer, the *qibla*, from Jerusalem to Mecca. No explicit command regarding the original direction of prayer is recorded in the Qurʾān, yet God says that He appointed this original *qibla* (2:143). Other cases include the revelation to Muḥammad in a dream that he would enter Mecca (48:27), the case of Muḥammad's marriage to Zayd's ex-wife (33:37), and the controversy over the division of booty after Badr (8:7). All of these instances offer scriptural validation for actions already undertaken according to extra-scriptural revelation.[64] In Mawdūdī's view, they offer "definitive proof that besides the Qurʾān other commands came to the Prophet by the agency of *waḥy*."[65] Besides these examples, as Salafī points out, the Qurʾān tells us that a number of prophets received *waḥy* who were not the recipients of a revealed book (4:163), proving that God's revelation is not limited to books.[66]

The "deniers" answer with exegetical arguments of their own. Jayrājpūrī, for example, insists that *kitāb* and *ḥikma* must both be identified with the Qurʾān. The proof is in the Qurʾānic command that *ḥikma* be recited. Since only the Qurʾān is recited revelation (*waḥy matlū*), if both *kitāb* and *ḥikma* are recited (*matlū*) then both terms must denote the

Qur'ān. Any attempt to draw a distinction between them is futile.[67] *Ḥikma* must be included with the Qur'ān and cannot be considered something separate. As for the different modes of *waḥy*, there is no proof that any of the three kinds of *waḥy* listed in 42:51 is external to the Qur'ān.[68] Parwēz offers a detailed exegesis of the verse to prove his point. Of the three modes of *waḥy* listed in this verse, inspiration, communication from behind a veil, and messengers, the first two are limited to prophets and are purely external in character. Normal prophetic revelations fall into the first category. Only Moses received *waḥy* of the second mode. The third mode of *waḥy* refers not to a different kind of revelation, but to the manner in which revelation is transmitted from the prophets to ordinary people. When a prophet transmits a command to his followers, this too is labeled *waḥy*, but in a non-technical application of the term. So, when a Muslim reads the Qur'ān, for example, we can say that he is receiving *waḥy*. After the ending of prophecy, only this last category of *waḥy* remains operative, since only the Qur'ān remains as a source of revelation.[69]

One of the challenges to the revealed status of sunna that is taken most seriously by defenders of sunna is the allegation that in terms of accuracy, preservation, and registration in writing sunna does not meet the standard for *waḥy*. The most common response is simple denial, accompanied by attempts to prove that the tradition literature was, in fact, recorded and transmitted accurately. A great deal of effort is spent, for example, attempting to prove that ḥadīth reports were in fact put into writing very early, beginning during the lifetime of the Prophet himself. Furthermore, contrary to the allegations of the deniers of ḥadīth, it is claimed that a core of sound traditions was preserved beyond reasonable doubt by following generations. God Himself bears witness to this fact, argues Sibāʿī, when He promises to preserve His *dhikr*, a word which must be inclusive of sunna.[70] For evidence that God has kept His promise to preserve sunna all we need do is look at the method of the *muḥaddithūn* and appreciate the incomparable care and immense effort they exerted in sorting the true from the false in traditions. "The God who preserved his last book," concludes Mawdūdī, "also arranged for the preservation of the example and guidance of his last Prophet."[71]

Most conservative scholars will admit, however, that denial does not resolve the issue, for the difference between the two sources is undeniable. Only the most conservative polemicists will go so far as to claim that "God protected ḥadīth in the same way as the Qur'ān."[72] The deniers of ḥadīth demand to know why, if it really is *waḥy*, the sunna does not come down to us in precisely the same way as the Qur'ān. What is the value of two different forms of revelation? In answer to this challenge defenders of sunna offer several different responses.

According to one view, faith requires that the sunna should simply be accepted as revelation in spite of the uncertainties surrounding its recording and transmission. A leading representative of the Ahl-i-Ḥadīth, for example, suggests that God deliberately allowed these doubts and uncertainties in order to challenge the faith of believers. The Qur'ān teaches that development of faith comes about by overcoming obstacles. If ḥadīth was preserved just like the Qur'ān, no effort would be required to believe it. Therefore, the uncertainties surrounding ḥadīth should not be considered an indication of weakness but a necessary test of faith.[73] Acceptance of ḥadīth (i.e., adherence to the doctrine of the Ahl-i-Ḥadīth) thus becomes a measure of faith and a means of identifying true believers.

Others argue that the deniers of ḥadīth are simply misguided in the criteria they adopt to determine what can be considered revelation. Mawdūdī claims that the differences between the two kinds of *waḥy* – in form, transmission, and preservation – are inevitable, resulting from the nature of the two sources. It is true enough, he admits, that the sunna was not preserved in the same fashion as the Qur'ān, but this is not sufficient reason to conclude that it is not trustworthy. The suggestion that sunna, if it is *waḥy*, should have been recorded in a single authoritative book is simply wrong-headed. Imagine, says Mawdūdī, a modern leader who, for twenty-three years, works night and day to establish a revolutionary movement. Thousands of followers record and propagate his teachings. An entire country undergoes a revolution in thought, morals, and social norms as a result of his work. Under his guidance a new society is brought into being. And throughout his career, in every situation, people look to him for guidance concerning how they should or should not act. They seek his advice on every conceivable topic. Could we expect the record of such a figure to be contained in a single book? Even if this were possible, would we dismiss out of hand all other accounts of this leader simply because they do not appear in this authoritative book?[74] What Mawdūdī suggests here is that sunna and Qur'ān, although both from God, represent fundamentally different genres of revelation and that the differences between them are inevitable. The Qur'ān was revealed in sporadic, discrete bursts of direct revelation. The sunna, however, was continuous throughout the Prophet's life. It is unrealistic to expect the two sources to be recorded in exactly the same way. In fact, the only way that sunna *could* reach us is in precisely the way it has – through numerous reports and from a variety of sources.

There is also a second part to Mawdūdī's argument specifically directed at those who suggest that *waḥy* must be written down. Preservation has nothing to do with writing, he argues. Just as in a court of law a document carries no weight unless attested, so it is with revelation: the attestation of human witnesses guarantees the authenticity of the text. The Qur'ān is not considered a reliable record of the revelation of God to Muḥammad because it is recorded in writing, but because its accuracy is attested to by reliable witnesses.[75] Thus the manner in which the Qur'ān and the ḥadīth are preserved is not really so different after all, for both come via reliable chains of human transmitters.

These arguments reveal deep differences between sunna's supporters and detractors over the nature of revelation, its purposes, and its scope. Those who consider sunna a form of *waḥy* view all revelation as eternal and unchangeable – a comprehensive code, encompassing every area of individual and communal life. Underlying their argument is a basic assumption about God's purposes in the world: "Islam," as the well-worn phrase has it, "is a complete code of life." The purpose of revelation, according to this view, is to establish a fixed pattern of individual and social norms. Here we have a God who does not merely send His prophets a book of commands, but offers them continuous guidance about exactly how He wants His written word to be understood and implemented. He is intimately concerned about minute details of law and behavior. By contrast, those who deny that sunna is *waḥy* assert that God reveals only general principles of guidance, leaving the details for mankind to work out on the basis of reason. He is like a wise parent who sets his children free once they have reached maturity, allowing them to make their own choices within the bounds of his general guidance. Revelation lays down broad guidelines from which each generation must derive its own conclusions in accordance with the circumstances of the time.

At a deeper level, the controversy is also about human interpreters of the Qur'ān and their authority. If sunna is the essential tool for understanding revelation, then experts on sunna are likewise indispensable. But if ability to contextualize revelation is needed, then those who know the modern world will be the most able interpreters of the Qur'ān and knowledge of the tradition will be counted superfluous. The deep sociological rifts between traditional religious leadership and western-educated intelligentsia, between religious scholar and technocrat, are thus projected onto the spectrum of modern Muslim attitudes toward the Qur'ān and its interpretation.

4 The nature of Prophetic authority

One day when Muḥammad was a boy, looking after sheep with a foster brother, two strangers came up to him. They were dressed entirely in white and one carried a silver pitcher in one hand and, in the other, a gold basin full of snow. While his foster brother fled in terror, the visitors took Muḥammad to the top of a mountain where they split open his breast and purified his heart. Muḥammad himself offered a first-hand account: "He approached me and sank his hand in the cavity of my body and pulled out my heart, split it and took out of it a black speck filled with blood, threw it away and said 'That is Satan's part in you, O beloved of God.' Then he filled it with something that he had with him and put it back in its place, then he sealed it with a seal of light, and I still feel the coolness of the seal in my veins and joints."[1]

The story presents a typical initiatory ritual which invokes shamanic parallels, as Eliade pointed out. But for our purposes the anecdote is important because it offers an early, pre-dogmatic assertion of Prophetic infallibility. Muḥammad, from this time on, was pure, immaculate, free from moral impurity. This belief later found formal theological expression in the doctrine of *ʿiṣma*. All prophets, according to this doctrine, are to some degree *maʿṣūm* – that is, protected by God from making mistakes or falling into sin.

In spite of its early origins and widespread acceptance, the idea of Prophetic infallibility does not sit well with Sunni orthodoxy. Why do Muslims need a sinless, or nearly sinless, Prophet? There is certainly little to suggest this idea in the Qurʾān. In fact evidence from the Qurʾān and traditions seems to suggest just the opposite. But the idea of infallibility does make sense in the context of Shīʿite ideas about charismatic human authority. In Shīʿite theology, God does not guide solely through authoritative texts, but through specially equipped humans, the imāms of the community. The stature and authority ascribed to the imām simply did not make sense if the imām was prone to the same weaknesses as other mortals. Thus it was Shīʿites who first articulated and applied the doctrine of *ʿiṣma* – and they applied it not at first to prophets but to the imāms, the spiritual successors to Muḥammad and proper heirs to his authority. But if the imāms were unblemished, how much more so the prophets. From these beginnings the infallibility of the Prophet found its way into mainstream Sunni doctrine by the ninth century of the Common Era.[2]

While Sunni theologians may not have originated the doctrine of Prophetic infallibility, they found it to be indispensable. First, the doctrine of *ʿiṣma* was an important guarantee of the integrity of the Qur'ān itself. If prophets are liable to err or to sin, then how can we know for sure that they have accurately passed on the revelation that they received from God? Theologians agreed almost unanimously on the most basic form of the doctrine: prophets must be considered immune from error in all matters related to the divine message.[3] More significantly, Prophetic infallibility provided the essential foundation for the authority of Prophetic sunna. To the extent that the words or actions of Muḥammad were protected from error they must accurately reflect God's will. If on the other hand certain of his actions were not protected from error, then they can hardly provide a sure foundation for sunna. Authoritative sunna must be limited to those areas of Prophetic activity that are protected from error by God.

Muslims have had no monopoly on ideas of infallibility. Christians of various persuasions have from time to time talked about the infallibility of scripture, and many still do. For Roman Catholics the infallibility of the teaching office of the Church has been a particular point of tension in recent decades. Such doctrines share certain common theological functions. The general theological problem that the doctrine of infallibility addresses is the problem of the *human-ness* of all sources of religious knowledge. God has no choice, it seems, but to communicate in human idiom, through human agents. But if this must be so, then God can at least be expected to prevent human weakness from marring this process. We have here a recognition, albeit in negative form, of the importance of human involvement in the revelatory process. The function of doctrines of infallibility, then, is to assure the believer that human involvement in the transmission of revelation, or in the interpretation of revelation, will not undermine its authority, and to give the interpreters of revelation a powerful justification for their own authority.

But how are believers to distinguish the infallible from the fallible? Delineating the boundaries between divine word and human word becomes a critical task. In the Islamic tradition, jurists and theologians proposed two quite distinct solutions to the problem of distinguishing between fallible and infallible in the Prophetic example. Jurists treated *ʿiṣma* as a technical problem of jurisprudence. In order to distinguish binding and non-binding precedents, they commonly distinguished the personal habits and preferences of the Prophet from actions related to the Prophetic mission. The former, designated *al-sunna al-ʿādīyah*, were of no legal consequence; the latter, categorized as *sunnat al-hudā*, were legally enforceable. Almost all theologians agreed that Muḥammad was free from error when it came to matters of revelation, but there were disagreements over the nature and extent of *ʿiṣma* in matters outside the sphere of revelation. Only a minority held to a doctrine of complete immunity from error; the majority limited *ʿiṣma* to the period after a prophet received his call and considered only matters directly related to the prophetic mission to be completely guaranteed. In matters that would not affect the prophetic mission, prophets could conceivably commit errors or even minor sins, although they would remain protected against major sins.[4] Thus the prophet's *persona* was divided into "human" and "prophetic" spheres. In his everyday life, in personal affairs and in private judgments, he was potentially fallible and his words and actions are not legally binding. In his capacity as prophet, however, his words and actions were divinely guided and represent God's will.

For classical jurists such categorization of the Prophetic sunna was a useful tool to avoid legal application of inconvenient traditions, and in this way the orthodox schools of law maintained the consistency of their legal doctrines in the face of hostile traditions. It was common to draw distinctions between traditions that could be considered legally binding and others that could not, and the simplest way to do this was to interpret individual traditions as giving rise to no legally applicable rule of law. For this purpose a distinction between the human and prophetic roles of Muḥammad was particularly helpful. Actions that fell into the sphere of the human could be defined as, at best, recommended (*mandūb*). Consequently, some distinction between Muḥammad's human and prophetic capacities was unanimously accepted in the orthodox legal schools and the idea found its way into several traditions. The best known of these is the date-tree tradition, which has Muḥammad offering bad advice to some unfortunate date cultivators. When confronted with the results – no dates – he tells his Companions that, except in matters pertaining to revelation, he is simply human and prone to error.[5] Another tradition has the Prophet refusing to eat lizard meat, but with the assurance, "I myself do not eat it, but I do not prohibit it from you."[6]

This was the juristic approach. But for the pious – particularly the Muslim mystics – such a division between binding and non-binding sunna was meaningless. The demands of law were quite distinct from the demands of piety. The great theologian and mystic al-Ghazālī writes:

> Know that the key to joy is following the sunna and imitating the Prophet in all his comings and goings, words and deeds, extending to his manner of eating, rising, sleeping and speaking. I do not say this only in relation to requirements of religion [*ʿibādāt*], for there is no escaping these; rather, this includes every area of behavior [*ʿādāt*].[7]

Taken from this perspective, the distinction between "human" and "prophetic" actions is unimportant; imitation of the Prophet's behavior in every aspect is the ultimate expression of piety. To follow the *uswa ḥasana*, the "beautiful pattern of conduct" (33:21), of the Prophet is meritorious regardless of whether the sunna was defined as obligatory or non-binding in strict legal terms. As Annemarie Schimmel demonstrates, the mystical vision of Muḥammad became all pervasive in later Muslim treatments of the Prophet. The Prophet's position as human leader and lawgiver was obscured by the glory of his cosmic role as "beloved of God," as intercessor, as channel of divine light. The image of Muḥammad was summed up in his image as the cosmic "perfect man" – *al-insān al-kāmil.* It is hardly surprising that later Muslim piety, pervaded by this mystical vision, could not countenance any suggestion of human weakness or fallibility in the Prophet.[8]

To summarize: there was strong precedent in juristic thought for a recognition of the fallibility of the Prophet in matters unconnected with the Prophetic mission, or at least for a recognition that not all of his actions were legally enforceable. Consequently, in the sphere of law, the division of Prophetic sunna into binding and non-binding spheres was almost universally accepted. Only extreme partisans of ḥadīth were unwilling to recognize any such distinction, and the view that all of the Prophet's words and actions carry the force of legal commands, implying reward for their fulfillment and punishment for their neglect, has been limited to the Ẓāhirīs.[9] But at the same time, the juristic approach to the problem of Prophetic infallibility was submerged under the overwhelming weight of later ṣūfī piety.

Humanizing the Prophet

The problem with infallibility is that it leaves so little room for improvement, or for change of any kind. There is a certain inflexibility built into the idea. This is a problem that has become acute in the nineteenth and twentieth centuries as theologians – not just Muslims, but also Protestant and Roman Catholic Christians – have sought ways of adapting doctrine to rapidly changing circumstances. Not surprisingly, challenges to the infallibility of scripture, the Pope, or the Prophet have been an important part of such efforts.

But challenges to infallibility also raise their own problems. For Muslims the question is quite direct and urgent: is it possible to question the infallibility of the Prophet without thereby completely undermining the authority of sunna? And what will be left of Islam without the sunna? Moreover, challenges to infallibility lend special urgency to questions of human religious authority. If our sources of knowledge are not infallible, then who is to decide what to accept and what to reject? The problem – to adapt George Lindbeck's metaphor for the Roman Catholic debate over infallibility – is how to extract a tumorous growth from a vital organ without killing the patient.[10]

In the Muslim context, the early modernists were the first to reopen the question of Prophetic infallibility in the modern period. Both Sayyid Aḥmad Khān and Muḥammad ʿAbduh adopted the juristic distinction between binding and non-binding sunna, admitting that the Prophet was potentially fallible in certain spheres of activity. But while classical scholarship had encouraged the emulation of the Prophet even in spheres of sunna that it defined as non-obligatory, the modernists began to view these categories as deliberately unregulated and subject to change. In the terminology of Islamic jurisprudence, they lowered the status of such actions from recommended (*mandūb*) to indifferent (*mubāḥ*). In effect they placed whole areas of Prophetic activity altogether outside the boundaries of sunna.

More important, the modernists excluded from the scope of binding sunna not just Muḥammad's personal habits and preferences, but also the bulk of his political and legal activity. Sayyid Aḥmad Khān, for example, divides sunna into four categories: (1) that which is connected with religion (*dīn*); (2) that which is a product of Muḥammad's particular situation and the customs of his era; (3) personal habits and preferences; (4) precedents connected with political and civil affairs. Of these only authentic traditions of the first category, those connected with religion, can be classified as *waḥy* and must be observed. All the others are at best optional and may be freely abandoned without fear of penalty when circumstances change.[11] The Muslim community cannot be bound to detailed precedents in civil and political affairs, for if worldly matters require detailed prophetic guidance, then every age will require a new prophet to accommodate changing circumstances.[12] In another passage he suggests that the only binding traditions, i.e., the only traditions that can be called a part of religion, are those that draw attention to the afterlife.[13] ʿAbduh adopted a similar position: of isolated traditions, he accepted without reservation only those dealing with paradise, hell, and judgment.[14]

These ideas reflect a wider tendency in modern portrayals of Muḥammad to emphasize his humanity, as Schimmel has shown. Where pre-modern Muslim piety envisions Muḥammad as a cosmic figure, larger than life and invested with superhuman qualities, modern treatments of Muḥammad bring the Prophet back down to earth. This process of humanizing began in India in the eighteenth century. Three general trends have contributed to the humanizing tendencies. First, the social and political turmoil faced by Muslims in the eighteenth and nineteenth centuries encouraged Muslims to seek a practical model for the restoration of the Muslim community. The decline of the Mughal empire in India, the accompanying breakdown of Muslim society, and the threat of western colonialism left Muslims with an urgent need for a Prophet who offered not just a spiritual message, but a model for the restoration of Muslim strength. The cosmic Prophet of the mystics and philosophers was no longer enough. Beginning with Shāh Walī Allāh Muslim thinkers, especially in India, began to take a new interest in the sunna of the Prophet as a model for social and political reform. Second, the challenge of missionary polemics and orientalist scholarship of Muḥammad encouraged the tendency to demythologize Muḥammad's life. Beginning with Sayyid Aḥmad Khān in the nineteenth century Muslim scholars responded to western challenges with apologetic biographies of Muḥammad which emphasized his greatness as a human leader and played down miraculous elements in his biography. Finally, the ongoing challenge of reforming or reviving Islamic law perpetuated concern for the life of the Prophet as a normative model for human behavior. The place of Prophetic sunna as a basis for Islamic law has given questions about the details of his life *as a human being* special urgency.

In modern biographies the Prophet is only rarely a cosmic figure. Instead, he is a progressive social reformer, a political leader, and a model of human virtue. For Muslim philosophers and mystics Muḥammad was the cosmic "perfect man"; but as Schimmel points out, by the time we come to Gamāl ʿAbd al-Nāsir, Muḥammad has displaced Marx as "the imam of socialism."[15] Schimmel also notes that it is not Muḥammad's miracles by which modern Muslim biographers establish his authority; rather, it is by his success in establishing a viable social order among the Arabs. Even among those who do not seek to strip Muḥammad of his miracles there has been a strong tendency to deemphasize the miraculous elements. Muḥammad's real miracle, and most contemporary historians would probably agree, was not a split moon or a sighing palm tree, but the transformation of the Arabs from marauding bands of nomads into world conquerors.

Modern challenges to the infallibility of the Prophet are one aspect of this humanization of Muḥammad. Bringing Muḥammad down to earth, and casting him as a fallible human being, offers modern interpreters of his legacy flexibility. An infallible Prophet leaves little room for improvement, but the legacy of a human and fallible Prophet, a Prophet more like us, is much easier to mold. Such a view of Muḥammad also provides a way for modern interpreters to more easily identify themselves with the Prophet and claim his authority.

Consistent with this increasing humanization of Muḥammad, modern critics of ḥadīth have tended to restrict the application of *ʿiṣma* to the transmission of the Qurʾān alone. In other areas of activity, Muḥammad must be considered human like the rest of us and subject to normal human limitations and failings. For Muḥammad ʿAbduh prophets, in spite of their unique position, are "purely human and subject to the same experiences as the rest of men. They eat and drink and sleep: they may be inattentive or forgetful in what is unrelated to their mission." He clearly had doubts about the doctrine of *ʿiṣma*, considering it impossible to verify.[16]

For Sayyid Aḥmad Khān and ʿAbduh the denial or attenuation of Prophetic infallibility becomes the basis for an incipient secularism; or, seen from another angle, we might say that their denial of the authority of prophetic sunna *required* an attenuation of Prophetic infallibility. Neither ʿAbduh nor Sayyid Aḥmad Khān were true secularists, however. This was left to their disciples. Both in Egypt and in India, a second generation of modernists advocated a more complete separation between religious and secular spheres of activity and to support this distinction they revised the orthodox account of the nature and purpose of prophecy.

Secularists defended their exclusion of religion from public affairs by denying that the Prophet had any involvement at all in the realm of government. Sayyid Aḥmad Khān's associate, Chirāgh ʿAlī,[17] for instance, argued that Muḥammad "did not interfere with the civil and political institutions of the country, except those which came in direct collision with his spiritual doctrines and moral reforms." Secularists in Egypt, led by ʿAlī ʿAbd al-Rāziq, argued along the same lines that Muḥammad eschewed political authority. His primacy was purely religious in character and his office ended when he died.[18] What Muḥammad did in the way of governing had no relation to his prophetic mission.[19]

The secularist argument renders the doctrine of Prophetic infallibility irrelevant, except as a guarantee for the text of the Qurʾān. If the Prophet's mission was nothing but a spiritual message then it hardly matters whether his other words and actions provide a perfect model. And, conversely, if his words and actions *are* without error, it is hard to see how they could be so easily dismissed. Denial of Prophetic infallibility, in other words, seems to be part and parcel of secularism. But secularists challenge the *ʿiṣma* of the Prophet not so much to undermine his authority as to claim it for themselves. Even while they deny the authority of the Prophet in specific details, the secularists implicitly recognize the general authority of the Prophetic example. Furthermore, they justify their own position by invoking the example of the Prophet, arguing, in effect, that secularism is a valid model because Muḥammad himself was a good secularist.

The Prophet as postman

The Ahl-i-Qurʾān also differentiated between Muḥammad's human and prophetic activities. But they distinguished not between spiritual and secular in the Prophet's career, but rather between eternal and temporal. The Qurʾān they viewed as God's eternal law, while the Prophet's sunna was only intended for the first generation of Muslims; apart from the Qurʾān, none of the Prophet's decisions and actions are binding on later generations of Muslims. In this way the Ahl-i-Qurʾān account for the Qurʾānic emphasis on obedience to the Prophet without accepting the authority of ḥadīth. The sunna was the authoritative application of divine law for particular circumstances, but when circumstances change the details of the law must also change. The Qurʾān represents basic unchangeable principles and the sunna the practical application of those principles.

Muḥammad Tawfīq Ṣidqī calls the sunna a "temporary and provisional law" (*sharīʿa waqtiyya tamhīdiyya*). It is the word of the Prophet valid only for his generation and because it was meant for the first generation of Muslims, the sunna of the Prophet has no binding force on present-day believers. There can be no question, he says, that practices such as *ṣalāt* and *zakāt* have come to us from the Prophet by *mutawātir* transmission. But simple connection with the Prophet, even *mutawātir* connection, does not prove that a practice is binding in every age and every place.[20] Ṣidqī offers ten proofs that the sunna was intended only for those who lived during the Prophet's era. The majority of these proofs are based on the failure of God, Muḥammad, or the Companions to properly preserve the sunna: it was not written during the time of the Prophet; the Companions made no arrangement for its preservation whether in a book or in their memories; they did not transmit the sunna verbatim; it was not committed to memory as was the Qurʾān and differences therefore developed among different transmitters. If sunna had been meant for all people, it would have been carefully preserved and circulated as widely as possible. Moreover, much of the sunna is clearly only applicable to the Arabs of Muḥammad's time and is based on local customs and circumstances.[21]

Whereas in Egypt such ideas bore little fruit, in the Subcontinent the belief that the sunna was only meant to be absolutely binding during the era of the Prophet has become one of the most important and persistent challenges to the theological foundations of sunna. ʿUbayd Allāh Sindī offers a fairly mild version of these ideas which is often cited by writers in the Subcontinent. According to Sindī's view, which he claims to derive from the teachings of Shāh Walī Allāh, the Qur'ān represents what he calls basic law (*qānūn asāsī*) whereas the sunna is provisional or temporary law (*qānūn tamhīdī*). The relationship of Qur'ān to sunna, he suggests, is like the relationship of a constitution and its bylaws. The Qur'ān, like a constitution, provides basic unchanging principles; the sunna represents detailed laws which are derived from these principles and are subject to change.[22] This theory has two results: First, without completely rejecting the efficacy of sunna or denying the authority of the Prophet in secular spheres, it allows a large degree of latitude in the interpretation of sunna; second, it clearly establishes the superiority of the Qur'ān over the sunna.

The early Ahl-i-Qur'ān developed the same thesis, but more systematically, arguing that all of the Prophet's activity apart from his transmission of the Qur'ān was irrelevant for later Muslims. Chakṛālawī held that the Prophet was no more than a messenger and that obedience to the Prophet means only obedience to the divine message he brought.[23] The Amritsar school was more moderate, holding that the Prophet should be obeyed, but not as an independent authority. In other words, any authority Muḥammad wielded was entirely derivative and could only amount to an enforcement of the Qur'ān.[24] In fact, Muḥammad's understanding of the Qur'ān was in no way superior to that of any other Muslim.[25] He himself was subject to the same commands and had no independent authority or privileged understanding. Adherents of the early Ahl-i-Qur'ān movement did not feel the need to elaborate on the nature or status of Muḥammad's extra-Qur'ānic activity; they simply dismissed it as irrelevant. They lowered Muḥammad, in effect, to the status of a postman whose only duty was to deliver the message.[26]

The Prophet as paradigm

Later adherents of the doctrine of the sufficiency of the Qur'ān, Aslam Jayrājpūrī, Ghulām Aḥmad Parwēz, and Ghulām Jīlānī Barq, elaborated this thesis and developed a sophisticated theory of Prophetic authority. Like the early Ahl-i-Qur'ān, these writers limited Muḥammad's prophetic mission to the transmission of revelation. According to Parwēz, Muḥammad's sole responsibility *as Prophet* was to transmit everything

God revealed to him in the way of revelation, without adding to or subtracting from it. The Qur'ān itself affirms this by stating: "The messenger (*rasūl*) has no duty except to proclaim [the message]."[27] As *rasūl* Muḥammad was no more than a transmitter of divine *waḥy* charged with calling others to render obedience to God's commands.

Jayrājpūrī and Parwēz advanced beyond earlier adherents of the sufficiency of the Qur'ān, however, in the way they interpreted Muḥammad's humanity. All of Muḥammad's activity apart from transmission of the Qur'ān must have been done in his human capacity.[28] But even in his human capacity, he held different roles. Decisions that he made entirely on his own, exercising personal *ijtihād*, were subject to error and carry no authority. But what about his role as leader of the Muslim community? It is clear from the Qur'ān that in this capacity he did wield authority, that this authority was divinely sanctioned, and that Muslims were expected to obey him. What these writers challenged of the classical theory of Prophetic authority is: (1) the assertion that this authority was an inseparable part of Muḥammad's prophetic office; and (2) the conclusion that the Prophet's example is free from error, universally binding, and unchangeable.

According to Jayrājpūrī and Parwēz, Muḥammad's authority over his contemporaries was the authority of a ruler and not of a prophet. In fact, his political authority was unrelated to his prophethood (*risālat*). It was derived from a second office held by Muḥammad – that of *amīr* – which was quite distinct from his prophetic calling. In this capacity, Muḥammad was responsible for establishing a governmental system (*niẓām*) in which God's commands were put into practical effect. The role of this government was not to legislate, but simply to enforce God's law. The Qur'ān alone was the supreme and the sole focus of obedience. But Islam is also an integrated social system which requires a high degree of discipline and conformity; it does not sanction individual obedience. An Islamic system cannot function without discipline.[29] Such a system requires a central authority (*markaziyyat*) with responsibility for overseeing the implementation and enforcement of divine law. The name given to this central authority was the *amīr* or the *imām*. Muḥammad himself was the first *amīr*, of course, for who could be better equipped to put the divine commands into effect than the person through whom they were transmitted? Herein lies the true understanding of the Qur'ānic command to "Obey God and obey the Prophet." This command does not signify individual obedience, nor does it imply obeying detailed precedents as are found in traditions. The call to obey the Prophet is a call to submit to the divine system the Prophet established and to the central authority that administers this system. Obedience to God and obedience to the Prophet cannot be separate things, for the basic teaching of the Qur'ān is that obedience is to be rendered to none but God.

Muḥammad's authority as *amīr* suffered several limitations not envisioned in the classical view of Prophetic authority. First, the authority of the *amīr* is entirely derivative. Borrowing the terminology of constitutional government, we might say that Muḥammad, in his role as the head of the Islamic system of government, had executive functions only and that God reserved all legislative authority to Himself. Thus even during his lifetime Muḥammad was not competent to frame laws. He could only enforce them. This, then, is what the Ahl-i-Qur'ān meant when they said that Muḥammad's extra-Qur'ānic words and actions were never meant to be imitated or obeyed. If he was acting as God's agent in implementing the law, then his actions were based on the authority of the Qur'ān. If he was acting on his own, then his actions were irrelevant to religious concerns, being based only on his own preferences or opinions.

The independence of Prophetic authority is further curtailed by the requirement that decisions be made by mutual consultation.[30] Muḥammad was called upon to consult with his Companions in all matters unrelated to revelation. Moreover, traditions attest to situations in which the Prophet and his Companions disagreed with each other and revelation subsequently confirmed the opinion of the Companion.[31] Returning to our analogy, we might say that just as God retains legislative authority, and the *amīr* acts as executive, the right of judicial interpretation of the law is vested in the judicial council, the *shūrā*, of the *amīr*.

According to Parwēz the Qur'ān itself tells us that when Muḥammad made decisions according to *ijtihād*, his decisions were subject to error. For example, with regard to the decision of the Prophet about the prisoners taken at the battle of Badr, the ruling came: "It is not for a Prophet to take prisoners until he has subdued the land" (8:67). During the battle of Tabūk, after the Prophet approved a request for exemption from military duty, the following guidance was received: "God forgive you! Why did you exempt them before those who were truthful were clearly revealed to you and you knew the liars?" (9:43). On one occasion he vowed not to eat a particular food and the order came: "O Prophet! Why do you call forbidden what God has declared permissible?" (66:1). To Parwēz's way of thinking, the reason that the Qur'ān mentions these incidents is to manifest Muḥammad's humanity clearly.[32] Because he was only human, without any supernatural knowledge, he was bound to make mistakes. When making decisions he had to rely on the knowledge he had, incomplete though it might be.[33]

In his position as *amīr*, the fallibility of the Prophet was mitigated through consultation with his Companions. Indeed, this is the very purpose of *shūrā*. If God had given Muḥammad detailed guidance on every matter, asks Barq, why would He have commanded him to consult with his Companions?[34] Thus Muḥammad's legacy falls into at least three parts: first, the Qurʾān, which is divinely revealed and divinely protected against error; second, his decisions as *amīr*, made in consultation with his Companions and binding on his contemporaries by virtue of the need for a central authority to execute the commands of the Qurʾān – these cease to have binding effect after his death; third, his personal decisions, which were subject to error and were never binding even on his contemporaries. The only eternal legacy of prophecy is the Qurʾān. None of the actions or words of the Prophet – the stuff of sunna – were meant to be obeyed by later generations.

It should be stressed that whereas Parwēz and other Qurʾānic scripturalists seem to dispense with the authority of the Prophet altogether, this is not what they themselves claim to be about. None, in fact, would admit to undermining the position of the Prophet or negating the Qurʾānic command to obey him. All of these writers claim to be, in fact, representing and recapturing the true intentions and the true legacy of Muḥammad. It is not, they would claim, the position of the Prophet they challenge, but the manner in which Prophetic authority is misrepresented by the *ʿulamāʾ*. Thus secularists do not reject the importance of the example of the Prophetic legacy; rather, they insist that the Prophetic example supports the exclusion of religion from public affairs and they co-opt the Prophetic example for their own purposes. Similarly Parwēz and Jayrājpūrī do not altogether reject the example of Muḥammad; rather they reinterpret its content, its significance, and the manner of its representation.

For Jayrājpūrī and Parwēz the Prophetic legacy is twofold. On the one hand Muḥammad delivered a revelation from God which is eternal. The Qurʾān is thus the major product of his prophetic mission and the unchanging part of his legacy. On the other hand, he also served as a model of the way in which an Islamic ruler should apply the Qurʾān. The importance of his example is not in the details of his application of the Qurʾān, but in the general pattern he set. Whereas in the sphere of prophecy Muḥammad had no successors because the message itself was eternal, in his role as *amīr*, the case was just the opposite. The products of his authority as *amīr* were specific to his own era, but the office of *amīr* lived on after him. Because his authority as *amīr* is passed on to successive Islamic rulers, later generations of Muslims are not bound to abide by decisions made by the Prophet in every case. In fact, they have the same freedom to interpret and apply Qurʾānic norms as did Muḥammad himself. Parwēz believes that the pattern of the Prophet was actually implemented during the era of the first four Caliphs. ʿUmar in particular exemplified the *amīr* who followed in the footsteps of the Prophet not by slavishly imitating him in every way but by reinterpreting the Qur'ān to meet changing circumstances. With the Umayyads the pattern was lost.[35]

The original pattern established by the Prophet can, however, be regained. Parwēz holds that in the contemporary world Prophetic authority should be manifested not through ḥadīth but through the central government of an Islamic state. This central government – what Parwēz calls the *markaz-i-millat* – stands in the place of the Prophet. The duty of this institution is to interpret the Qur'ān and enforce God's commands in just the same way that Muḥammad did during his own era.

For these writers, Muḥammad is a paradigm rather than an exemplar. The Prophetic example offers not a set of detailed precedents, but a model of how each generation of Muslims should determine the details of Islam for themselves by exercising reason under the guidance of the Qur'ān. Prior to Muḥammad's prophetic mission people were like children, needing to be led along step by step. This is why numerous prophets were needed. But Islam brought the prophetic dispensation to a close, signaling a coming of age for the human race.[36] For this idea Parwēz is dependent on Iqbāl, who writes:

> The Prophet of Islam seems to stand between the ancient and the modern world. In so far as the source of his revelation is concerned he belongs to the ancient world; in so far as the spirit of his revelation is concerned he belongs to the modern world. In him life discovers other sources of knowledge suitable to its new direction. The birth of Islam . . . is the birth of inductive intellect. *In Islam prophecy reaches its perfection in discovering the need for its own abolition.* This involves the keen perception that life cannot for ever be kept in leading strings; that in order to achieve full self-consciousness man must finally be thrown back on his own resources.[37]

Parwēz concludes that prophecy is no longer necessary because mankind is master of his own choices and no longer needs guidance in every detail. Reason, under the guidance of the Qur'ān, is sufficient for all situations.[38]

Parwēz's denial of Prophetic infallibility reduces Muḥammad to human stature so that a human leader can stand in his place. Muḥammad is no longer a superman but a normal human set apart only by his supreme dedication to understanding, teaching, and applying the message of the Qur'ān. This leaves room, in the contemporary world for the leader of the true Islamic state to become, in effect, the representative of Prophetic authority. Prophetic authority is not manifested through detailed precedents laid down in tradition but through human leaders who follow his general pattern.

The Prophet as paragon

In response to the revisionist approach to prophecy of these "deniers of ḥadīth," conservative writers have maintained a vigorous polemical campaign in defense of the orthodox theory of Prophetic authority. For defenders of orthodoxy the Prophet's example is clearly more than paradigmatic; for them Muḥammad's behavior is exemplary in every respect and in every detail. His every word and action is reliable and worthy of imitation. Thus in answer to the challenge posed by the Qurʾānic scripturalists, supporters of sunna continue to uphold the specificity, the indivisibility, and the universality of Prophetic authority.

For conservatives obedience to the Prophet means, first of all, imitation in every particular. This is assumed rather than argued. Refutations of the Ahl-i-Qurʾān are dominated by proofs that the Qurʾān commands obedience to the Prophet in everything. What else could "obedience" mean but specific commands? The very terms used in the Qurʾān imply obedience to specific precedents. *Ittibāʿ* means to follow directly behind; *iṭāʿat* implies complete obedience.[39] Moreover, the very purpose of prophecy was to provide a practical working out of the Qurʾān commands, an example to be followed.

In response to the tendency among the Ahl-i-Qurʾān to divide Prophetic actions into binding and non-binding categories their conservative opponents insist on the unity of the Prophetic personality and play down evidence of Prophetic fallibility. It is commonly argued that to deny the authoritative nature of any aspect of Prophetic sunna throws doubt on the validity of the whole Prophetic mission, including the Qurʾān itself. Al-Salafī, for example, argues that if the Prophet's word cannot be trusted in worldly matters, then it cannot be trusted on religious matters either, for "trustworthiness is a characteristic of personality" and is not divisible into separate spheres.[40] Muḥammad Ayyūb Dihlawī argues in a similar fashion that either all of Muḥammad's words are authoritative (*ḥujjat*) or none are authoritative. It is absurd to hold that some of the Prophet's words are to be trusted and some are not because there is no independent standard by which to judge between the reliable and the unreliable. The Qurʾān cannot serve as such a standard, for it too depends on the trustworthiness of the Prophetic word. If there is no reliable way to judge between binding and non-binding then to doubt any part of the Prophetic mission is to cast doubt on the whole, including the Qurʾān.[41] According to Muḥammad Karam Shāh the whole notion of distinguishing between two classes of action, one related to religion and the other to worldly matters, is foreign to Islam. It was the British who encouraged such a categorization by taking control of all "secular" affairs while leaving the

Muslims free to conduct their own religious affairs. For the Qurʾān however, all that matters is obedience to God's commands, no matter what category they may fall into.[42] When the jurists distinguished between legal and non-legal matters this was merely a formal distinction, indicating what kinds of commands were enforceable. It was not intended to imply that some commands of the Prophet were not meant to be obeyed. On the contrary, it is still incumbent on Muslims to follow non-legal traditions.[43]

Finally, faced by attempts to confine the sphere of Prophetic authority to the era of Muḥammad, defenders of sunna emphasize the universality of Muḥammad's prophetic message. The universality of Muḥammad's prophethood had been an extremely important element of Muḥammad ʿAbduh's stock of ideas. The Prophetic message was for all people and for all time. This, in fact, was the meaning of the ending of prophecy:

> Muḥammad's prophethood brought prophecy to an end. His message terminated the work of messengers, as the Book affirms and the authentic tradition corroborates. The fact is evidenced by the collapse of all pretensions to prophethood since Muḥammad, as well as by the world's contentment with the truth that has come to it from him. The world knows that there is no acceptability now in claims made by pretenders after mission with laws and revelation from God.[44]

Riḍā takes up this theme in his criticism of Ṣidqī. "It is self-evident to us," he writes, "and none contests it, that our Prophet Muḥammad was sent to all people – those of his own era, both Arabs and others, and those who came after, until the Day of Resurrection."[45] If, as Ṣidqī claims, the sunna was valid only for Muḥammad's own generation, then prophecy is stripped of its relevance for later generations and Muḥammad is reduced to a minor figure. This criticism by Riḍā moved Ṣidqī to withdraw his opinions.

Mawdūdī also defends the universality of prophecy but he offers a somewhat different argument based on his ideas about the organic link between the Qurʾān and the Prophetic witness. If the Qurʾān can stand alone now with no need of the Prophetic witness to corroborate or explain it, then certainly the same was true at the time of its revelation. If the Prophet is superfluous for present-day Muslims, then his witness must also have been unnecessary for early Muslims. The Qurʾān should have been sufficient for them as well. But this is patently not the case. Prophecy was absolutely essential to ensure that the Qurʾān would be received as from God. Without the Prophet the Qurʾān would have been without roots and without attestation.[46]

These differences between the "deniers of ḥadīth" and their orthodox opponents over the meaning and significance of prophecy reflect a deep tension over the manner in which religious authority should be manifested in an Islamic society. It is a tension between principles of stability and of flexibility, between the authority of the past and the exigencies of the present, and between scripture and tradition. Most fundamentally, however, it reflects a struggle over the question of who has the authority to represent the Prophet. What individuals, groups, or institutions are the true mediators of the Prophetic legacy, standing in his place and speaking with his voice? Al-Salafī, in his polemics against Parwēz, makes it clear that one of the central issues is the question of who is qualified to interpret Islamic norms. He objects to Parwēz's proposals to democratize the resolution of religious questions. Democracy is a faulty system to begin with and Parwēz's theories will simply put authority in the hands of the ignorant. Almost all of Parwēz's critics express the suspicion that he is stripping interpretive authority from sunna simply in order to grasp it for himself.[47]

The tensions between conservative approaches to sunna and the radical challenges introduced by Qurʾānic scripturalists are perhaps best illustrated by those who seek a middle ground between these extremes. A number of writers are attracted by the basic premise of the Qurʾānic scripturalists going so far as to dispense with sunna altogether. The Institute for Islamic Culture in Lahore has been one important breeding ground for this sort of thinking. In one of the more comprehensive statements on sunna to come out of that institution, Jaʿfar Shāh Phulwārawī tries to establish a middle ground, accepting many of the ideas pioneered by the Ahl-i-Qurʾān but refusing to dismiss the authority of sunna altogether. He recognizes, first of all, a clear distinction between the prophetic and human functions of Muḥammad. Unlike Parwēz, however, he does not limit the prophetic functions of the Prophet merely to the transmission of revelation. *Ḥadīth qudsī* and traditions expressing special prophetic knowledge for example, are also part of revelation. Thus all that Muḥammad received from God is not, as the Ahl-i-Qurʾān claim, limited to the Qurʾān itself. On the other hand, he thinks that most traditions do not fall into the category of *waḥy*. The majority of what Muḥammad said and did was done by exercising his own *ijtihād* and not in response to direct revelation. These traditions should be respected, but they should not be taken as eternal and unchangeable rules. Thus flexibility is maintained without throwing sunna out altogether. The way is opened to reinterpretation without completely sacrificing sunna on the altar of rationalism.[48]

We see another clear illustration of this tension between the conflicting demands for flexibility on the one hand and stability on the other in the writings of Mawdūdī. On the problem of sunna Mawdūdī occupies a sort of no-man's land between opposing camps, drawing both inspiration and criticism from both sides. On the one hand he defends the necessity of sunna as an indispensable source of stability for Islam. On the other hand he wants to find sources of flexibility which will allow for adaptation. This tension in Mawdūdī's thought is demonstrated in three articles in which he develops his ideas about the human and prophetic capacities of Muḥammad. In the first, entitled "The Islamic Conception of Freedom," he draws a clear distinction between different roles of the Prophet and presents Muḥammad as a paradigm of the enlightened democratic leader who allowed complete freedom of opinion and action in areas not legislated by God. The second article, entitled "Obedience to the Prophet," is a critique of Aslam Jayrājpūrī's ideas and takes a very different approach; here Mawdūdī emphasizes the unity and universality of the Prophetic mission, insisting that he is to be obeyed in every respect. Finally, in a third article, "The Prophet's Human and Prophetic Capacities," he tries to reconcile these apparently contradictory positions.[49]

The first article draws on a number of elements characteristic of the Ahl-i-Qurʾān approach to prophecy – the distinction between human and prophetic capacities of Muḥammad, the derivative nature of his authority, and the non-binding character of his personal behavior. It begins with a specific exegetical question surrounding Zayd's divorce of Zaynab. Why, inquires one of Mawdūdī's readers, did Zayd proceed with the divorce in the face of Muḥammad's instructions recorded in the Qurʾān to keep his wife? And how, if Muḥammad's authority was to be obeyed, could Zayd get away with this? Mawdūdī begins his answer with a reaffirmation of God's absolute authority, a theme which runs throughout his writings. The Qurʾān teaches that God alone possesses absolute authority and that no human can claim such authority.[50] The intent of the Qurʾān is to free mankind from bondage to any authority except God alone. Now if this is the case then Muḥammad's authority, embodied in the Qurʾānic command to obey the Prophet, must be entirely derivative. The Prophet is not to be obeyed by virtue of his human status, but simply as representative of God's authority. The Qurʾān thus makes it clear that Muḥammad occupies two distinct roles. He is, in his personal capacity, a human being like us, and he possesses no special authority. As Prophet, on the other hand, he has been made God's agent. In addition to the prophetic office (*nabuwwat*) by which he conveys God's commands, God has granted him the authority (*ḥukm*) necessary to execute those commands. In his prophetic capacity, obedience to Muḥammad equals obedience to God. If a prophet delivers a command from God then his followers must obey it; they have no right to exercise freedom of opinion (*azādī raʾy*) on the matter. On the other hand, if a prophet does something in his personal capacity he cannot demand obedience and his followers are free to decide for themselves on such matters. In another context Mawdūdī goes so far as to say that imitating the Prophet in such things as dress or personal habits is an "extreme form of innovation (*ēk sakht qism kī bid'at*)."[51]

Mawdūdī admits that a problem arises when it comes to distinguishing human from prophetic actions in practice. The two roles are fused in a single personality and separating the two is like trying to separate milk and water. But he does not try to resolve this problem here. Instead, he focuses on what he believes to be the implications of the two roles. Although Muḥammad had the power and respect to demand personal allegiance, he did not do so. He eschewed personal authority and allowed his followers complete freedom in matters left undecided by God and in so doing he demonstrated the extent of freedom available to Muslims. "In his human capacity," writes Mawdūdī, "the Prophet was also fulfilling the duties of a messenger. When he did things as a human he conveyed to his followers the spirit of free-thought, taught them the true principles of democracy, instructed them on how to exercise freedom of opinion, and told them of their right to oppose any human, even a perfect one."[52]

In his second article, "Obedience to the Prophet," Mawdūdī seems to do an about-face. In this article, which was written as a review of Aslam Jayrājpūrī's *Ta'līmāt al-Qur'ān,* Mawdūdī vigorously reaffirms the unity and universality of prophecy. According to Mawdūdī, Jayrājpūrī's argument that Muḥammad's mission was limited only to bringing the Qur'ān is based on faulty exegesis. His first error is to misapply certain verses of the Qur'ān which state that Muḥammad is no more than a messenger. These verses were directed at unbelievers, says Mawdūdī. For believers Muḥammad is not just messenger but also ruler. Jayrājpūrī's second mistake is to distinguish radically between Muḥammad's job as messenger and his other activities. There is not the smallest trace in the Qur'ān of any distinction between Muḥammad's activities as prophet, as ruler, or as individual. On the contrary, the Qur'ān shows that "the Prophet occupies only one position and this is the capacity of prophet and messenger."[53] Moreover, "whatever the Prophet did, no matter the time or occasion, he did as Prophet."[54] The example of Muḥammad is comprehensive in scope:

> In him is a worthy model for the whole world and from [his example] we can know what is permitted and what is not permitted, what is forbidden and what is allowed, what pleases God and what does not, the matters in which we have freedom to exercise *ra'y* and *ijtihād* and the matters in which we do not, how we should obey the commands of God, how we should establish civil law through consultation and the meaning of democracy in our religion.[55]

It is therefore incumbent on Muslims to obey the sunna in its entirety.

In the third article, "The Prophet's Human and Prophetic Capacities,"

Mawdūdī recognizes the contradiction between his earlier two essays and tries to effect a reconciliation.[56] The conflict arises, he says, because the question can be looked at from two different angles. First, the question can be approached from an abstract (*naẓarī*) viewpoint, looking only at the question of the nature of the Prophetic personality and the nature of Prophetic authority in theory. There is also a second way of approaching the problem, however, and this is from the practical (*ʿamalī*) perspective.[57]

From a theoretical point of view the difference between the human and prophetic capacities and functions of the Prophet is undeniable. Here Mawdūdī rehearses the arguments he made in "The Islamic Conception of Freedom." The Prophet came to call people to obey God, not to make them submit to his own personal authority. What authority he had was based not on his own human qualities but on his role as God's messenger and his duty to call people to obedience to God. Moreover, the Qurʾān and the ḥadīth both offer evidence that when he was acting only on the basis of his own opinion (*raʾy*) his followers were not required to submit to him. From this perspective, the difference is clear cut.

From a practical perspective, however, the problem is more subtle because the prophetic capacity and human capacity were melded in a single personality. Thus we find that the distinction is not nearly so clear cut as it appears and his "human" actions often had a prophetic function. Even when he most clearly emphasized his own humanity and distinguished clearly between matters requiring obedience and areas of freedom, Muḥammad was acting as a prophet by teaching his followers how to distinguish between binding and non-binding matters. And in those matters that appear to be entirely personal – habits of eating, drinking, clothing, marriage, family life, etc. – even in such matters he demonstrated by his behavior the basic limits Muslims should observe. Such precedents cannot therefore be dismissed out of hand as irrelevant to Muslim practice.

Despite the clear theoretical distinction, then, it is neither practical nor permissible to decide for ourselves whether some part of the sunna is simply a human precedent and non-binding. We do not have the tools to make such a decision. Even the Companions of the Prophet themselves had to ask on repeated occasions whether something that Muḥammad said or did was said or done as Prophet or simply as a man. There are only two ways to know with certainty whether a particular sunna can be defined as non-binding because it is part of the "human" legacy of the Prophet. The first is by means of specific information from the Qurʾān or ḥadīth which makes this clear. The second is by applying established principles of interpretation – for example, the principle that in matters of food or clothing the details of the Prophetic practice are not binding, but the general limits implied by that practice are binding.[58]

Mawdūdī concludes that Muslims cannot disregard any part of the sunna. Even precedents that seem to be based simply on the personal preferences or habits of Muḥammad may yet contain principles which Muslims are bound to follow. Mawdūdī thus succeeds in disarming an important Ahl-i-Qur'ān argument. He recognizes the distinction between human and prophetic roles which is so important to them, but he draws very different implications from this distinction. The two kinds of actions are different kinds of sunna, but they are sunna nevertheless. The lesson is not that the "human" sunna can be disregarded, but simply that it was meant for a different purpose and therefore must be interpreted in a different way.

Mawdūdī's attitude toward the question of *'iṣma* also shows a desire to reconcile extreme positions. He admits, along with the deniers of ḥadīth, that Muḥammad did make mistakes; this much is clear from the Qur'ān. But he vehemently rejects the implication drawn by the deniers of ḥadīth that the Prophetic example is not meant to be authoritative. He insists that the Qur'ānic indications that the Prophet sometimes strayed in minor ways were not meant to raise doubts, but, paradoxically, to inspire confidence in the Prophet's authority. The reason that they are recorded is to assure believers that God guided even the smallest details of Muḥammad's life and immediately corrected even his smallest mistakes. God could not require Muslims to follow Muḥammad in everything, as the Qur'ān demands, without guaranteeing that his words and actions were a true reflection of divine will. Even his mistakes are part of his prophetic mission.

If we know that Muḥammad's actions belong to differing categories and have different lessons to teach us, then the problem becomes one of interpretation – of sorting out how we are to understand different aspects of the Prophetic example. How are we to tell the difference between Muḥammad's prophetic actions, which demand specific obedience, and his human actions, which have a general didactic purpose? How do we know when Muḥammad was illustrating human freedom and when he was acting out God's specific will? Clearly we need someone like Mawdūdī to help sort it out for us. We need someone, to use Mawdūdī's own expression, who "breathes the spirit of the Prophet." So here again, the issue can be reduced to a problem of human authority. In Mawdūdī's scheme, the Prophet's fallibility becomes the interpreter's opportunity.

Taken together these various illustrations of challenges to Prophetic infallibility offer some general lessons. At issue is not the validity of Prophetic authority, but how that authority is to be understood. Seldom are challenges to Prophetic infallibility used to undermine the status of the prophet. Parwēz, Mawdūdī, and their opponents among the *ʿulamāʾ* are all competing for the place of authoritative interpreters of Muḥammad's legacy, hence heirs to his authority. Even secularists implicitly recognize Prophetic authority when they appeal to the Prophetic example to justify their secularism. Consequently, modern debates about Prophetic authority should be viewed as contests for the right to represent Muḥammad in contemporary Muslim societies.

5 The authenticity of ḥadīth

It is axiomatic, in classical doctrine, that sunna can only be known by means of ḥadīth.[1] The unchanging, incorruptible norms or sunna are thus encapsulated in the corruptible and imperfect vehicle of ḥadīth. In this way knowledge of sunna becomes subject to the vicissitudes of history, and, we might add, the irreverence of historians. The authenticity of ḥadīth – the assurance that the ḥadīth literature conveys an accurate account of the actual words and deeds of Muḥammad – therefore becomes a crucial pillar to the whole doctrine of sunna as well as a major topic in the modern controversy over sunna.

Such preoccupation with the authenticity and continuity of tradition is shared by all of the Abrahamic faiths. For Jews, Christians, and Muslims, history is the field in which God operates; it is in historical events that the transcendant becomes known. But if history is the ground of revelation, later believers only gain knowledge of these events through the witness of those who have gone before. Therefore, establishing a reliable link between the event of revelation and the later community is a central concern. For Rabbinic Jews, continuity with the events at Mount Sinai was secured by an unbroken chain of teachers, preserving both the written revelation and the oral Torah. For Roman Catholics apostolic tradition, preserved in the teaching office of the Church, ensured the integrity of the Gospel. For Muslims, this need for continuity with the time of revelation was formalized in ḥadīth reports which were attested and transmitted by an unbroken chain (*silsila, isnād*) of reliable and pious Muslims. The system evoked firm confidence among those who maintained it; in the famous statement of Ibn Qutayba, "No community has *isnāds* like this community."[2]

Yet the authenticity of the ḥadīth literature has proved to be the most vulnerable element of the classical theory of sunna and the central focus of most discussions of the problem of sunna, both medieval and modern.[3] For opponents of the classical doctrine of sunna, challenges to the authenticity of ḥadīth provide an opportunity to undermine sunna without appearing to question the authority of the Prophet. If only true knowledge of the Prophet's words and actions was available, critics of ḥadīth claim, they would be the first to recognize the authority of Prophetic sunna.[4] Most writers on both sides of the debate seem to agree, in fact, that sunna and ḥadīth must stand and fall together, that sunna has no foundation apart from ḥadīth. But this assumption of an organic link between ḥadīth and sunna has not gone entirely unchallenged; one of the most interesting aspects of modern discussions of sunna has been the emergence of creative attempts to establish a basis for sunna independent of the authenticity of ḥadīth.

The dependence of sunna on the authenticity of ḥadīth was one of the basic assumptions of the classical understanding of sunna, and an elaborate system was developed to evaluate the authenticity of traditions. This system was based on two premises: (1) the authenticity of a report is best measured by the reliability of the transmitters of that report; and (2) scholars can distinguish authentic from spurious traditions by carefully scrutinizing both their individual transmitters (*rāwī*; pl. *ruwāt*) and the continuity of their chains of transmission (*sanad; isnād; silsila*).[5] The rules for evaluating the trustworthiness of a *rāwī* were borrowed from the procedures and technical vocabulary used to test witnesses in legal cases, and a major branch of scholarship, the science of men (*ʿilm al-rijāl; al-jarḥ wa al-taʿdīl*) emerged. Vast biographical dictionaries were compiled out of the need for evidence by which to establish the reliability or unreliability of transmitters of ḥadīth.[6]

When Muslim ḥadīth critics considered a transmitter they were concerned with both their general capacity (*ḍabṭ; itqān*) and their moral character (*ʿadāla*). Transmitters demonstrating excellent memory, linguistic ability, and accuracy might be considered competent (*ḍābiṭ*); but only adult Muslims, fully in control of their mental faculties, aware of their moral responsibility, free from guilt for major sins, and not prone to minor sins could be considered morally upright (*ʿadl*).[7] A transmitter possessing both qualities was called trustworthy (*thiqa*). A transmitter who possessed sound moral character (*ʿadāla*) but who showed signs of carelessness was called honest (*ṣudūq*), and so on to lower grades.[8] In this way the trustworthiness of each transmitter could be precisely classified.

Such tests of reliability and character were applied to each ḥadīth transmitter in an *isnād* with the important exception of those in the first generation, the Companions of the Prophet (*Ṣaḥāba*). Just as the doctrine of Prophetic infallibility (*ʿiṣma*) guarantees that the Prophet is free from error in matters related to revelation, so too the moral integrity of the Companions is assured by the doctrine of their collective moral uprightness (*taʿdīl*). According to this doctrine the Companions must be considered free from major sins by virtue of their direct association with the Prophet, for "God has declared all of them to be trustworthy. He has revealed their purity and He has chosen [to mention] them in the [very] text of the Qur'ān."[9] The Companions are thus excluded from normal scrutiny on theological grounds.

A second criterion by which the authenticity of a tradition was to be measured was the continuity of its chain of transmission. Not only must the general capacity and moral purity of each transmitter be proven, each *rāwī* must also be shown to have received reports *in an acceptable manner* from the preceding authority in the chain of transmission. Transmitters must have lived during the same period, they must have had the opportunity to meet, and they must have reached sufficient age at the time of transmission to guarantee their capacity to transmit. Imprecision, carelessness, or other defects in citing one's authorities in an *isnād* could bring into question the continuity of transmission in much the same way that imprecise documentation opens a modern scholar to the charge of plagiarism. An elaborate technical vocabulary was developed to aid the discovery and classification of such defects.

Acceptable means of transmission were not unanimously agreed upon in detail, but direct contact with the preceding authority was generally required. As a result, classical theory was indifferent to the existence of written versions of ḥadīth. Regardless of whether reference was made to a written record, a report could only be transmitted by direct contact between master and student. Just as in legal matters documentary evidence carried little weight, so too in ḥadīth transmission, a written account was worthless without oral attestation.

The application of these criteria for judging the authenticity of ḥadīth grew into a mature system with the emergence of the great compilations of ḥadīth in the third century A.H. Compilers of ḥadīth assembled the available data on the character of transmitters and the continuity of transmission and based on this data they gave each tradition a general rating. The most reliable traditions were designated sound (*ṣaḥīḥ*). Reports that fell short of some of the standards for sound traditions were designated fair (*ḥasan*), and those with serious defects were labeled weak (*ḍaʿīf*). Spurious ḥadīth were dismissed as fabricated (*mawḍūʿ*).

The result was a sophisticated and, given the assumptions upon which it was grounded, an eminently coherent system for testing the authenticity of ḥadīth. In the eyes of most Muslim scholars, *ṣaḥīḥ* ḥadīth could, with a high degree of confidence, be considered to represent the actual words and deeds of the Prophet. On the other hand, few scholars would have argued that the system was foolproof. In the epistemological universe of classical Islam, no ḥadīth, even *ṣaḥīḥ* ḥadīth, was considered a source of absolute knowledge (*yaqīn*). At best the knowledge derived from ḥadīth had to be classified as conjecture (*ẓann*). Nor, as we have seen, was ḥadīth without its opponents during the formative period in Islamic thought. Into the third century there were still those, doubtless a small minority, who argued forcefully that ḥadīth was not a reliable basis for religious authority. On the whole, however, the general efficacy of the classical system of ḥadīth criticism as a reliable method of ascertaining the actual words and actions of Muḥammad was not seriously questioned.

In modern discussions of Prophetic authority, many of the basic assumptions of classical ḥadīth scholarship have been questioned both by Muslims and by orientalists. The first serious challenges to the classical system came from European scholars who, beginning with Alois Sprenger, began to express skepticism about the reliability of ḥadīth as a historical source.[10] Sprenger was followed in this regard by Sir William Muir, who also maintained a critical attitude toward the authenticity of ḥadīth in his *Life of Mahomet.* European scholarship of ḥadīth culminated in the work of Ignaz Goldziher, whose *Muhammedanische Studien* remains among the seminal works on the subject, and who was unquestionably the most important nineteenth-century critic of ḥadīth. Goldziher was more skeptical than either Sprenger or Muir about the prospect of positively identifying those few authentic traditions of the Prophet that might have survived. But while he denied that the vast majority of ḥadīth could be considered authentic, he came to this conclusion by way of an insight into the value of ḥadīth as a source for the study of Islamic history. In other words, the tradition literature is unreliable as a source for the rise of Islam, but it provides an invaluable source for the beliefs, concerns, and conflicts of the generations of Muslims who came after and who put the traditions into circulation. As he himself put it: "The ḥadīth will not serve as a document for the history of the infancy of Islam, but rather as a reflection of the tendencies which appeared in the community during the more mature stages of its development."[11] Goldziher thus became the first scholar to subject the ḥadīth to a systematic historical and critical method.

Goldziher's *Muhammedanische Studien*, published in 1896, was neither revised nor supplemented in a significant way until the publication of Joseph Schacht's *Origins of Muhammadan Jurisprudence* in 1950. In the course of studying legal ḥadīth Schacht concluded, like Goldziher, that few if any traditions originated with the Prophet. He believed that it was possible, however, by careful study, to arrive at a rough estimate of when a particular tradition was, in fact, put into circulation. In order to arrive at a chronology of legal traditions he made heavy use of the argument from silence, but he also thought that the *isnād* of a tradition could give clues to its origin. The method he proposed was based on the hypothesis that *isnāds* tend to grow backwards. The earlier a tradition, the less likely it will be to have a complete *isnād*; the more complete the *isnād*, the later the tradition. Schacht developed these insights into his *common link theory*, a method which has more recently been revived, in circumscribed form, by Juynboll. Schacht's theories have given rise to almost a half-century of controversy. While certain of his theories have been widely accepted, particularly the conclusion that *isnāds* grow backwards, there has been less enthusiasm for the final results of his study: the conclusion that the ḥadīth literature offers us almost no information about the Prophet himself. Moreover, Schacht's work has been subjected to a good deal of justified criticism.[12]

While Muslims share many of the specific concerns dealt with in these western discussions of the authenticity of ḥadīth, western treatments of ḥadīth have only occasionally had a direct impact on modern Muslim discussions of the problem. The most important discussions of ḥadīth by Muslim authors, with a few important exceptions, show a marked indifference to western scholarship.[13] From Sayyid Aḥmad Khān onward three topics dominate Muslim discussions of the authenticity of ḥadīth: the *ʿadāla* of the Companions; the manner in which ḥadīth were preserved and transmitted; and the efficacy of *isnād* criticism to distinguish authentic and spurious traditions.

The *ʿadāla* of the Companions

The *ʿadāla* of the Companions is a cornerstone of traditional ḥadīth criticism, for the *ʿadāla* of every generation of transmitters must be proven with the exception of the Companions, "whose character is testified to by Allah and his Prophet."[14] The Companions provide an indispensable link in the epistemological chain between the Prophet and the rest of humanity. They are the only agency by which reliable knowledge of Muḥammad and the Qurʾān could be transmitted. Consequently, the question of the collective *ʿadāla* of the Companions is second only to the problem of the *ʿiṣma* of the Prophet in its sensitivity: "Whosoever slanders the Prophet's Companions only wants to demolish the fortress of Islam."[15]

In their attempts to bring into question the doctrine of the *ʿadāla*, critics of ḥadīth have generally pointed to three kinds of evidence. First, the Prophetic traditions themselves show that Muḥammad did not completely trust all those who could be called Companions. According to a well-known tradition, the Prophet said: "Let whoever tells lies about me deliberately take his place in hell." This can be taken to mean that Muḥammad knew that there were those among his Companions who were spreading lies about him.[16]

A second body of evidence brought to bear on this debate by opponents of ḥadīth consists of reports of conflicts and mutual accusations among the Companions themselves. According to Jayrājpūrī, because the Companions so often disagreed with one another Abū Bakr forbade the collection of ḥadīth.[17] Aḥmad Amīn argues that such reports show that the Companions themselves did not trust each other.[18] Examples are not hard to find: ʿĀʾisha and Ibn ʿAbbās were reported to have criticized Abū Hurayra; a number of Companions demanded evidence for the truth of reports passed on to them; ʿUmar allegedly questioned a report from Fāṭima bint Qays; ʿUmar is also reported to have confined three Companions to Medina to keep them from spreading traditions.[19]

One of the more common accusations in early reports is that a particular Companion simply exceeds the bounds of propriety in the number of traditions he transmits, a practice referred to as *ikthār al-ḥadīth*. The problem of *ikthār al-ḥadīth* has attracted the attention of critics of ḥadīth to particular Companions who seem vulnerable on circumstantial grounds to charges of dishonesty or carelessness in transmission of ḥadīth. The major focus of such criticism has been the Companion Abū Hurayra, who, although he was with the Prophet for only three years, is alleged to have been the most prolific in transmitting ḥadīth.[20] It is impossible, according to critics, to believe that he transmitted so much.[21] Moreover, biographical literature provides ample material for criticism of Abū Hurayra's character which has been used to advantage by opponents of ḥadīth.[22]

Such arguments to discredit the *ʿadāla* of the Companions are to be expected from outright deniers of ḥadīth, but challenges to the *ʿadāla* have also come from less likely sources. Mawdūdī, by most accounts a champion of ḥadīth, offers perhaps the most startling example. After discussing the problem of mutual vilification among ḥadīth scholars, Mawdūdī discloses, in a somewhat scandalized tone, that "even the noble Companions were overcome by human weakness, one attacking another."[23] He proceeds to cite examples similar to those offered by deniers of ḥadīth: Ibn ʿUmar called Abū Hurayra a liar; ʿĀʾisha criticized Anas for transmitting traditions although he was only a child during the life of the Prophet, and Ḥasan b. ʿAlī called both Ibn ʿUmar and Ibn al-Zubayr liars.[24] It is clear that Mawdūdī's point is not to discredit the ḥadīth literature as a whole; he simply wants to make a case for his own reexamination of it. By appearing to deny the *ʿadāla* of the Companions, however, he has sided with more extreme critics of ḥadīth and earned the ire of conservative opponents.

The conservative response to such attacks has been fierce and sustained. Challenges to the moral integrity of the Companions are viewed as malicious slander.[25] Mawdūdī's fairly mild statements turned the *ʿulamāʾ* against him and elicited numerous articles and monographs criticizing his alleged slander of the Companions.[26] The response in the Middle East to Abū Rayya's writings has been similar.[27] The detailed arguments of those who defend the *ʿadāla* need not be rehearsed; thousands of pages have been written, but the general form and approach of these refutations can be summarized briefly. Defenses of the *ʿadāla* of the Companions often include a cataloging of their praiseworthy characteristics and piety.[28] The point is that to attribute falsehood to these people is incompatible with everything known about them. How could individuals who cared so much for the Prophet that they counted his gray hairs be accused of deliberately spreading falsehoods about him? In a similar vein, Sibāʿī suggests that to attribute falsehoods to the Companions is illogical, for fabrications would immediately have been recognized and checked by other Companions.[29] Apart from general praise of the Companions and reaffirmation of God's protection of them, the usual method used to refute the arguments of the deniers rests on detailed analysis of the particular traditions or historical reports; traditions that seem to indicate dishonesty or carelessness on the part of Companions must be discredited or reinterpreted to lessen their sting.[30]

The debate over the moral character of the Companions has thus been fought primarily by means of detailed arguments about the authenticity and interpretation of particular ḥadīth reports and biographical reports which seem to bear on the question. Consequently, critics of ḥadīth have found themselves in the awkward position of attacking ḥadīth by means of ḥadīth, a field in which they are at a decisive disadvantage *vis-à-vis* their conservative opponents. More importantly, these discussions illustrate that critics of ḥadīth are willing to use any evidence at their disposal, even if that is from the ḥadīth literature itself, to defend their rejection of ḥadīth. In other words, their rejection of ḥadīth is more a dogma to be defended than a historical thesis to be systematically applied.

Preservation and transmission of ḥadīth

The Companions are but the first and most critical link in the chain that connects the ḥadīth with the Prophet. No less a concern than the reliability of the Companions is the manner in which the tradition literature was preserved and transmitted after them. The central issue is simple: was the process of transmission reliable enough to give assurance that at least a core of authentic traditions about the Prophet was preserved uncorrupted? This question leads, however, to numerous sub-topics. When were ḥadīth first recorded in writing? Was transmission entirely oral or were written records used? Can oral transmission, especially the practice of transmitting the sense (*bi'l-maʿnā*) rather than verbatim (*bi'l-lafẓ*) be considered a reliable means of preserving sunna?

Classical scholarship portrays the process of ḥadīth transmission as primarily oral, at least through the first century. Even after written collections of ḥadīth were compiled, oral transmission remained the ideal. Orality, in this system, was a virtue rather than a vice. Just as Islamic jurists belittled documentary evidence, preferring direct oral testimony, so the scholars of ḥadīth insisted on the superiority of direct, personal, and oral transmission of ḥadīth.[31] Writing is of value only as an aid to memory; it is neither essential, nor, on its own, trustworthy. In theory, then, written collections of ḥadīth are of value only when directly attested to by living transmitters of the tradition who can vouch for their accuracy.

The nineteenth century threatened a reversal of this preference for oral over written evidence, at least among the Muslims most directly affected by the West. Western historians demanded documentary evidence, tending to impugn the trustworthiness of oral transmission. Thus early European critics of ḥadīth stressed the late registration in writing and the flawed process of transmission as the sources of the corruptions with which they alleged the ḥadīth literature was beset.

The substance of the orientalist critique of early ḥadīth transmission was absorbed into Muslim discussions of ḥadīth beginning with Sayyid Aḥmad Khān. Aḥmad Khān, in his response to Muir, accepts the contention that significant writing of ḥadīth did not occur within the first century A.H. He is also cognizant of the problems posed by oral transmission, but he refuses to admit Muir's more extreme allegations with regard to the self-serving and corrupt motives of ḥadīth transmitters. Aḥmad Khān prefers to view transmitters of ḥadīth as essentially well meaning. Corruption in ḥadīth literature is therefore not primarily premeditated but the result of a flawed process of transmission. He locates the problem primarily in the custom of *riwāya bi'l-maʿnā*, transmitting according to the sense rather than the exact words.[32] In his essay on *jinn* he offers an illustration of the devastating results of this widespread practice by comparing textual variations among traditions about *jinn* – differences which go well beyond the wording and affect the essential meaning.[33] As a result, he contends, one can be sure in very few instances that traditions accurately portray the Prophet's words and actions, even if they can be shown to have originated during his lifetime.

A similar emphasis on the essentially flawed character of early ḥadīth transmission became a central theme in the controversial writings of both the Indian Ahl-i-Qur'ān and the Egyptian deniers of ḥadīth. Ṣidqī held that nothing at all of the ḥadīth was recorded until after enough time had elapsed to allow the infiltration of numerous absurd or corrupt traditions.[34] "It is evident," he writes, "in every era and in every nation that people find it hard to preserve traditions, when they are lengthy or numerous and especially if they are reported only once, without corruption of the words and the meaning and without changes, additions or mistakes."[35] On the other hand, there is incentive for transmitters to claim their report is verbatim. This sort of transmission at best approximates the meaning of the original and the result is numerous different readings, contradictions, and outright falsehoods.[36] Aḥmad Amīn comes to the same conclusion, arguing that because the traditions were not written down, fabrication and corruption began very early, perhaps during the lifetime of the Prophet himself.[37]

Jayrājpūrī also lays stress on *riwāya bi'l-ma'nā* as a source of corruption in ḥadīth. Since the Companions had not written ḥadīth down when they were with the Prophet, nor had they consciously memorized his words, the best that they could do was to transmit what they remembered. As a result the *muḥaddithūn* had no choice but to accept such transmissions. But it is inevitable, if words are changed, that some change will take place in meaning as well. The Companions themselves seem to have been aware of this problem and therefore criticized one another's reports from time to time.[38]

Maḥmūd Abū Rayya has promoted similar arguments. Like earlier critics of ḥadīth, Abū Rayya argues that the late date when traditions began to be registered in written form, more than one hundred years after the Prophet's death, became a major obstacle to the fidelity of the ḥadīth.[39] Like Aḥmad Khān, he blames the practice of transmitting the meaning rather than the exact words, a practice which he claims began with the Companions of the Prophet. If the Companions themselves could do no better than to transmit the approximate meaning, one can well imagine how the traditions were transformed in subsequent generations.[40] What began as less than perfect thus continued to be corrupted until it emerged in final form only in the third and fourth centuries A.H.[41] To illustrate his argument Abū Rayya points out that eight different traditions offer eight distinct readings of parts of the Muslim statement of faith.[42] Consequently, even if a tradition is thought to originate with the Prophet, there can be no assurance that its meaning has been preserved intact.

Such arguments from historical reports are sometimes bolstered by an appeal to common experience. Consider, suggests Barq, an event witnessed by fifty different people. If you go to them one by one and ask for details of what happened you will find considerable discrepancies in their accounts. Wait a month or a year, and the differences will be even more considerable.[43] This common tendency is easily illustrated by comparing conflicting news reports of the same event.[44]

It is apparent from these accounts that the deniers of ḥadīth share two common assumptions: first, in line with classical ḥadīth scholarship, they hold that traditions were transmitted in oral form until at least the second century A.H.; second, they hold that oral transmission, and especially the practice of *riwāya bi'l-maʿnā*, opened the door to corruption and forgery in the ḥadīth literature. Thus, by the time the traditions were gathered into the canonical collections during the third century A.H., the corpus of ḥadīth was damaged beyond any reasonable hope of restoration. Parwēz draws parallels between this situation and the alleged corruption of the gospels; if Muslims distrust the gospels, which were recorded within a hundred years of Jesus' death, how much more should they distrust ḥadīth.[45]

The dominant response of conservatives to such challenges has been to defend the traditional account of how ḥadīth was transmitted, i.e., the reliability of oral transmission. Oral transmission, according to the general argument, is not only reliable but superior to isolated written documents. Written records, unless attested by living witnesses, are of little value.[46] Furthermore, the reliability of the oral transmission of ḥadīth is assured by the remarkable memories of the Arabs. Remarkable powers of memory are common among illiterate peoples, and the ability to memorize large amounts of information with precision was especially well developed among the Arabs.[47]

A second response, both more interesting and more fruitful, has been to accept the modern preference for written evidence and to argue that traditions were, in fact, recorded in writing from the earliest times.[48] This project has involved both Muslim scholars and orientalists and has given rise to a large body of scholarly writing, including the works of Nabia Abbott, Fuat Sezgin, and Muḥammad Muṣṭafā al-Aʿẓamī.[49] Abbott and Sezgin play, at best, a peripheral role in Muslim debates about the authenticity of ḥadīth since their works are primarily written for and accessible to the western scholarly community. Aʿẓamī, whose work parallels Abbott's and Sezgin's both in method and conclusions, participates more directly in Muslim discussions; his work has been published in Arabic and he responds to the arguments of Rashīd Riḍā and Maḥmūd Abū Rayya. Like Abbott and Sezgin, however, Aʿẓamī's main preoccupation is with orientalist ḥadīth scholarship. What makes the work of these writers relevant to wider Muslim discussions of ḥadīth is the similarity of their method and argument to numerous lesser-known works in Arabic and Urdu. Their work is, in fact, a scholarly incarnation of arguments that have appeared frequently in less sophisticated forms in both Pakistan and

Egypt. One of the earliest examples is a 1907 article in *al-Manār* which grew out of the controversy touched off by Ṣidqī.[50] Since that time numerous monographs specifically dedicated to demonstrating the early recording of ḥadīth have been published in both Arabic and Urdu.[51]

Proponents of the early recording of ḥadīth must first answer the argument that Muḥammad himself prohibited the writing of ḥadīth. As I have shown in the previous chapter, the alleged Prophetic prohibition on writing ḥadīth has served as an important theological argument for deniers of ḥadīth; if Muḥammad prohibited the writing of ḥadīth, he must never have intended his words to be taken as binding. Similar arguments can be applied to challenge the historicity of ḥadīth reports; if care had been taken to record traditions in writing, surely some of the earliest collections would be in our hands.[52] Conversely, as Parwēz argues, without a fixed text of ḥadīth everyone could shape a revelation to their own liking, and the likelihood of preserving the ḥadīth literature uncorrupted was severely diminished.[53]

Those who argue that Muḥammad's Companions began to record ḥadīth in writing during his lifetime must explain (or explain away) the Prophetic prohibition. Several solutions are possible. First of all, other traditions can be cited in which Muḥammad gives express approval to write down his words. In one of the most frequently cited traditions ʿAbd Allāh b. ʿAmr reports that he was in the habit of writing down everything the Prophet said until he was warned against it. He thereupon approached the Prophet and asked whether he should continue to write down his sayings, and the Prophet replied: "Write . . . I say nothing but the truth."[54] Other similar incidents can also be cited.[55]

On the basis of such reports recourse can be had to the theory of abrogation: one set of traditions can be judged to have originated later in the Prophet's life, thus abrogating the earlier traditions. The argument for abrogation can go either way, of course; Rashīd Riḍā, for example, thought that the traditions prohibiting writing came later, abrogating earlier traditions which permitted writing of ḥadīth.[56] A larger number of scholars argue, however, that the prohibition on recording ḥadīth was made early in the Prophet's career and lifted at a later time. According to this account, Muḥammad at first forbade writing of traditions because he feared that Muslims would confuse them with revelation, compromising the text of the Qurʾān. Later, after the Qurʾān was well established, there was no longer any reason for the prohibition and it was lifted.[57] Other scholars have sought to reconcile the traditions by arguing that the prohibition applied only to combining ḥadīth with the Qurʾān on the same sheet and not to the writing of ḥadīth generally,[58] or by arguing that the prohibition had only to do with making official collections of traditions.[59]

Another focus of debate is the historical tradition that states that the first individual to record the ḥadīth, under orders from the Caliph Hishām, was the traditionist Ibn Shihāb al-Zuhrī (d. 742 A.H.). There is fairly wide agreement among Muslim scholars on the authenticity of this tradition, but disagreement over what it signifies.[60] The tradition has commonly been taken to mean that al-Zuhrī, under duress, became the first traditionist to violate the Prophet's prohibition on recording ḥadīth in writing. Al-Zuhrī is reported to have said: "We disapproved of recording knowledge until these rulers forced us to do so. After that we saw no reason to forbid the Muslims to do so."[61] In other words, before al-Zuhrī writing was the rare exception; after al-Zuhrī writing of traditions became commonplace.[62] This argument is bolstered by numerous accounts that early generations of pious Muslims, including not only al-Zuhrī and traditionists like him but also the first four Caliphs, strongly disapproved of writing ḥadīth.[63]

The revisionist reading of this tradition takes it to mean that rather than being the first to write ḥadīth, al-Zuhrī was simply the first to put together an officially sponsored collection of ḥadīth. In other words, private collections of written ḥadīth may have been common enough but, unlike the Qur'ān, the ḥadīth had not, until the time of al-Zuhrī, become the focus of any official attempts at regulation or systematization. Consequently, the apparent aversion of pious Muslims to the recording of ḥadīth should be interpreted as reluctance to record an official, public collection of ḥadīth.[64]

The most powerful argument for the early recording of ḥadīth, however, is based on overwhelming evidence that, regardless of whether it was officially sanctioned or not, early generations of Muslims wrote down traditions with zeal. There are several components to this argument. First, evidence is mustered to show that, contrary to the common belief, writing was commonly practiced among the Arabs, and knowledge of writing was actively encouraged among the early Muslims. Second, Muḥammad himself is said to have commissioned the preparation of written documents on a number of occasions. Finally, historical sources and the ḥadīth literature provide hundreds of examples of individuals who are alleged to have written down traditions or to have possessed collections of written traditions.[65] Aʿẓamī, the most able champion of this argument, lists fifty Companions who reportedly passed on traditions in written form.[66]

According to these arguments the general belief that traditions were transmitted orally until they were finally put down in writing in the second century A.H. is a historical myth perpetuated by the prejudice of the medieval *ʿulamāʾ* in favor of oral sources. The evidence strongly suggests that early generations of Muslims did record traditions in writing. But can such evidence of the early recording of ḥadīth be convincingly translated into a general argument for the authenticity of the ḥadīth literature as a whole? Having reports about written records is rather different from having the records themselves. A leap of faith of significant proportions is required to go from the general assertion that some traditions were written down at an early date to the specific assertion that those traditions can be identified, uncorrupted, in extant collections.

The justification for such a leap of faith rests on two assumptions: first, that a core of authentic traditions remains extant; second, that the *isnād* system and the classical method of ḥadīth criticism allows us to identify these authentic traditions amidst an ocean of forgeries. The logic goes something like this: suppose we have a report about X, which we judge authentic, alleging that X passed along a certain number of traditions in written form to one or more of his students. Suppose we also have a tradition, with an apparently unimpeachable *isnād*, going back to X. If the *isnād* system is trustworthy, then we can reasonably conclude that we have this tradition in roughly the same form in which X transmitted it. On the other hand, if the *isnād* system is itself subject to corruption, then, even if we are quite certain that X did transmit written traditions, we have no assurance that the tradition we have in our hands actually originated with X. According to Muslim scholarship, however, proper scrutiny of the *isnād* offers an essentially reliable way of rescuing authentic traditions from the mass of forged or questionable reports. The *ṣaḥīḥ* collections of ḥadīth represent the successful outcome of this method. But this assertion has become a central issue in modern discussions of ḥadīth. The issue for Muslim scholars therefore shifts to the reliability of the *isnād* system and the efficacy of classical ḥadīth criticism.

The efficacy of *isnād* criticism

Scholars agree that forgery of ḥadīth took place on a massive scale. The science of ḥadīth (*ʿilm al-ḥadīth*), according to the traditional account, developed gradually as a response to this problem. A formal system of ḥadīth criticism became necessary only when the integrity of ḥadīth was threatened by theological and political schism, by the widespread fabrication of traditions, and by the deaths of the only authorities able to attest personally to the words and deeds of the Prophet, the generation of the Companions. Pious Muslims responded to this crisis first by collecting and writing down traditions in systematic fashion and second by formalizing the use of the *isnād* as a means of documenting traditions.

As we have seen, some traditions were almost certainly put into writing at an early stage, but this was done informally and not in any systematic way. The early written compilations, called *ṣuḥuf,* were little more than random transcriptions or personal collections of what remained an essentially oral body of tradition. Muslim sources identify the first systematic collection and recording of ḥadīth with the Umayyad Caliph ʿUmar b. ʿAbd al-ʿAzīz and with the scholars Abū Bakr b. Muḥammad b. ʿAmr b. Ḥazm and Muḥammad b. Muslim b. Shihāb al-Zuhrī. No such collection has survived, however, although other early collections are extant, most notable the *Ṣaḥīfah* of Hammām b. Munnabih.

The earliest systematic collection is the *Muwaṭṭaʾ* of Mālik b. Anas (d. 179 A.H.). The *Muwaṭṭaʾ* and collections like it, which are labeled *muṣannaf* because they classify traditions according to subject, represent organized attempts to collect traditions of legal importance and to arrange them in systematic fashion. Mālik did not, however, apply a formal standard of criticism to his selection of ḥadīth other than the general standard of legal relevance and his work belongs as much to the category of *fiqh* as to the genre of ḥadīth.

As scholars such as Mālik compiled more sophisticated written collections of traditions, they also began to develop critical methods of documenting and criticizing the authenticity of traditions with reference to their *isnāds*. The approximate date at which the *isnād* came into use in a formalized way has been a subject of scholarly debate.[67] It is fairly clear that the *isnād* was widely used by the second century A.H., although scholars could still get away with applying it only casually, especially in the biographical literature about Muḥammad.[68] The elevation of the *isnād* to a place of preeminence as a measure of the authenticity of ḥadīth probably occurred around the time of the career of al-Shāfiʿī. *Isnāds* were certainly in use before his time, but al-Shāfiʿī forcefully argued that traditions could be considered authentic only if they had *isnāds* that could be traced, unbroken, to the Prophet himself. The next stage in the development of ḥadīth literature, the compilation of *musnad* collections during the third century A.H., reflects the triumph of this emphasis on complete *isnāds*.[69] The *musnad* collections, by including only traditions that have an *isnād* going back to Muḥammad himself, represent the rudimentary beginnings of formal *isnād* criticism. These collections made no clear distinction, however, between strong or weak chains of transmission; they included any tradition with an *isnād* originating with a Companion of the Prophet.

The *musnads* were followed by the great *ṣaḥīḥ* collections, marking the final stage in the development of the science of ḥadīth.[70] The compilers of the *ṣaḥīḥ* collections established formal rules by which the authenticity of a tradition could be judged on the basis of its *isnād*. They sifted through all of the traditions they could find and they selected only those whose *isnāds* met their rigorous standards. Their method of scrutiny was based on several assumptions: they assumed that defects or corruption in ḥadīth could be directly attributed to weakness of character in its transmitters; they believed that such faulty transmitters could be identified; and they had an unquestioning faith in the essential reliability of the *isnād* as an account of the actual transmission history of a tradition. The *isnād* becomes the only possible bridge between what we have before us and that which existed at an earlier date. Therefore faith in the reliability of *isnāds* becomes the main guarantor of the authenticity of ḥadīth.[71] The extraordinary value placed on the *isnād* has been enshrined in tradition: "The *isnād* is [the] matter of religion"; and "But for the isnād anyone could say whatever they wanted."[72]

Challenges to classical ḥadīth criticism often begin by pointing out anomalies in the collections of ḥadīth thought to be the most reliable. Deniers of ḥadīth have especially delighted in exposing traditions in the *ṣaḥīḥ* collections, especially Bukhārī and Muslim, which they take to be vulgar, absurd, theologically objectionable, or morally repugnant. In fact, it is not uncommon for deniers of ḥadīth to claim that they too were firmly devoted to ḥadīth until they came across a *ṣaḥīḥ* tradition that they simply could not accept. For Khwāja Aḥmad Dīn Amritsarī, one of the originators of the Ahl-i-Qurʾān, the decisive moment came when he discovered a report about Moses knocking out the eye of the angel of death.[73] Ghulām Jīlānī Barq's faith in ḥadīth was "finally shattered" by traditions describing sexual details of Muḥammad's life.[74] Similarly, Maḥmūd Abū Rayya began to question ḥadīth when he came across what he took to be vulgarities among the ḥadīth, such as the tradition that "when the devil hears the call to prayer, he flees, farting."[75] Starting with traditions such as these, a number of writers have cataloged similarly objectionable material in the *ṣaḥīḥ* collections.[76] For their part, defenders of the *ṣaḥīḥ* collections of ḥadīth can only respond to such challenges by arguing that the traditions in question, when rightly understood, are not in actual fact vulgar, absurd, or objectionable. In response to criticism of traditions reporting intimacies of Muḥammad's relations with his wives, for example, al-Salafī argues that there should be nothing offensive in this. The Sharīʿa encompasses every area of life; how, then, are men to know how to treat their wives without an example to follow?[77]

The broader question at issue for both the detractors and defenders of ḥadīth is not the authenticity of particular traditions, but the reliability of the method of the *muḥaddithūn*. Even some staunch defenders of ḥadīth are willing to challenge particular traditions in the canonical collections while still maintaining the general reliability of the system of ḥadīth criticism. But the deniers of ḥadīth view such traditions as evidence of deeper problems; if Bukhārī or Muslim, the most scrupulous collectors of ḥadīth, were unable to recognize obvious fabrications, then surely there must be something wrong with their approach.

What is at issue is not the sincerity of the great ḥadīth scholars, but the efficacy of their method.[78] According to the deniers of ḥadīth the *muḥaddithūn*, no matter how dedicated, were simply too distant from the time of the Prophet, and forgery had become too rampant, for authentic ḥadīth to be recovered. The extent of forgery was dramatic. Forgers became active even during the lifetime of Muḥammad, in spite of his dire warning that whoever spread lies about him would burn in hell.[79] In the caliphate of ʿUmar, the problem became so serious that he prohibited transmission of ḥadīth altogether. Forgery only increased under the Umayyads, who considered ḥadīth a means of propping up their rule and actively circulated traditions against ʿAlī and in favor of Muʿāwiya.[80] The ʿAbbāsids followed the same pattern, circulating Prophetic ḥadīth which predicted the reign of each successive ruler. Moreover, religious and ethnic conflicts further contributed to the forgery of ḥadīth. The *zanādiqa* (those who professed Islam but secretly held Manichean ideas), for example, are reported to have circulated over 12,000 fabricated traditions.[81] The degree of the problem that resulted can be seen from the testimony of the *muḥaddithūn* themselves. Bukhārī selected 9,000 traditions out of 700,000.[82]

Even the most well-meaning traditionists were simply unable to stem the tide, a fact amply demonstrated by anecdotes of *muḥaddithūn* who could not prevent forgeries from being transmitted in their own names.[83] There were even well-meaning traditionists who thought there was nothing wrong with circulating fabricated ḥadīth if the cause was good, (e.g., Nūḥ b. Maryam, who passed on false traditions in praise of the Qurʾān).[84] Forged and authentic ḥadīth were therefore thoroughly mixed, and the extent of forgery was such that even the best critics can recognize authentic traditions only with great difficulty. There is no branch of literature and no collection of traditions in which forged and authentic ḥadīth are not found mixed together.[85]

From pointing out the *prima facie* difficulty of identifying a limited number of authentic traditions among so many fabrications, deniers of ḥadīth go on to argue that the method of the ḥadīth scholars was simply inadequate to the massive task. At the very least, they were liable to error; there was no way that they could know everything.[86] More seriously, although what they accomplished may have been admirable, it was at best incomplete. They largely neglected the tools that would have offered the best chance of rescuing authentic ḥadīth, for in their concern for *isnād* criticism they ignored criticism of the content of traditions, the *matn*.

The argument that the major failing of the *muḥaddithūn* was to neglect criticism of the *matn* was pioneered by Sayyid Aḥmad Khān in the Subcontinent and by Rashīd Riḍā and Muḥammad Tawfīq Ṣidqī in Egypt. Subsequently the argument has been adopted by numerous critics of ḥadīth. The *muḥaddithūn* had two tasks according to Sayyid Aḥmad Khān: to examine the trustworthiness of the narrators (i.e., *isnād* criticism) and to examine the content of traditions. Because of the difficulty of the first task, they never got around to the second. Later scholars failed to recognize this deficiency in their work and, impressed by their achievement, treated the work of the *muḥaddithūn* as though it was infallible.[87]

Many critics follow Sayyid Aḥmad Khān in arguing that the *muḥaddithūn* were so concerned only with the continuity of transmission and the character of the transmitters that they completely ignored the subject matter of the traditions and failed to look at either internal or historical evidence.[88] Others, notably Jayrājpūrī, argue that the *muḥaddithūn* did not so much ignore such criticism as evade it by means of creative exegesis *(taʾwīl)*. They paid lip service to the principle that traditions should not conflict with either the Qurʾān or with reason, but instead of rejecting such traditions, they made every effort to interpret difficult traditions in such a way as to remove the apparent conflict. This fact explains why there are numerous unacceptable traditions even in the canonical collections.[89]

The deniers thus agree that the results of classical ḥadīth criticism are entirely inadequate; but they disagree about whether anything of value can still be retrieved. According to the most optimistic assessments, authentic ḥadīth can be rediscovered by righting the deficiencies of classical ḥadīth criticism; that is, by criticizing the content of traditions on the basis of reason or historical considerations.[90] The more extreme critics of ḥadīth argue, however, that the damage is irreparable and that authentic ḥadīth can never be recovered.

In addition to criticizing the *muḥaddithūn* for neglecting scrutiny of the *matn*, modern ḥadīth critics also argue that the assumptions behind *ʿilm al-rijāl* are essentially flawed. This argument is made on a number of grounds. First, as Sayyid Aḥmad Khān points out, it is difficult enough to judge the character of living people, let alone those long dead. The *muḥaddithūn* did the best they could, but their task was almost impossible.[91] Information is scanty, conflicting reports abound, and there can be no assurance that all the relevant information has been gathered.[92] Furthermore, ḥadīth scholars could easily have been deceived by clever hypocrites (*munāfiqūn*) who made every appearance of being upright and careful but who were in actual fact seeking to undermine Islam.[93] Honesty and dishonesty are internal qualities which cannot be known with any certainty by observers. As a result, *ʿilm al-rijāl* is only an approximate (*qiyāsī*) science, and one can never be absolutely certain that one's judgment about a transmitter is correct.[94]

Furthermore, what renders trustworthy the historical reports about the transmitters themselves, upon which *ʿilm al-rijāl* is founded? Did those who recorded this information do so accurately, or could it have been doctored or fabricated? It is necessary to judge biographical reports with just as much rigor as we judge other traditions. When this is done the reasoning behind *isnād* criticism is exposed as circular: the only way of judging the character of transmitters was by means of biographical traditions, but biographical traditions are subject to all of the same weaknesses and corruptions as any other branch of tradition.[95]

Even a prophet, according to Jayrājpūrī, would need divine inspiration to sort out the forgers from among 100 to 150 years' worth of ḥadīth transmitters, many of whom were well-known and honored people. *Rijāl* traditions were transmitted orally until into the third century and there is evidence that they were often the product of conflict.[96] This explains the serious contradictions within the biographical literature over the reliability of individual transmitters. Most of the Islamic biographical literature is therefore suspect and the wealth of detail it offers, far from representing a great achievement of Muslim historiography, has simply contributed to virtual idolatry of the *riwāyat* (*riwāyat parastī*) at the expense of balanced historical criticism.

Perhaps the most serious challenge of all to the classical system of ḥadīth criticism is the assertion that *isnāds* were forged on just as large a scale as the content of traditions but that the *muḥaddithūn* completely discounted this possibility. There was clearly great incentive to attribute one's information to the most reliable authorities. Even prominent ḥadīth transmitters falsely claimed to have heard traditions from prominent teachers, a practice called *tadlīs,* for if a transmitter was of low station there was great incentive to attribute his traditions to the most trustworthy authorities. How can we judge a tradition reliable on the basis of its chain of transmission when we know that forgers commonly fabricated *sanads* in order to hide their forgery?[97]

Defenders of ḥadīth by no means deny that fabrication of ḥadīth took place. Indeed, they painstakingly document the circumstances and reasons for such fabrication.[98] They argue, however, that the extent of forgery is exaggerated by critics, that the signs of forgery are clear, and that right from the start the great scholars of ḥadīth, the *muḥaddithūn,* took adequate measures to combat the spread of forged ḥadīth. The extent of forgery is greatly exaggerated, according to al-Salafī, because of misunderstanding of essential facts about the ḥadīth literature. When

Bukhārī reports that he selected from over 700,000 traditions, for instance, he is counting every different *isnād*, even when the substance of the traditions are the same. Furthermore, it is clear that the collectors of *ṣaḥīḥ* ḥadīth passed over numerous traditions that are, in fact, authentic when judged by the same criteria as those that are included in their collections.[99] Not every tradition outside the *ṣaḥīḥ* collections can be regarded as a forgery. Furthermore, right from the start, the *ʿulamāʾ* took measures to counteract forgery of ḥadīth. These efforts began informally, by consulting the Companions themselves, for example, to check on a doubtful report, but gradually informal means of checking ḥadīth gave way to formal methods of ḥadīth criticism. The point is that ḥadīth criticism did not begin during the third century, but was practiced continually from the time of the Companions onwards.[100] The gap that critics of ḥadīth claim exists between the time of the Prophet and the beginnings of serious ḥadīth criticism does not, in fact, exist.

Defenders of ḥadīth also turn on its head the argument that the *muḥaddithūn* were simply too distant in time from the Prophet to be able to rescue authentic ḥadīth. Who are we to judge, when we are so much farther removed from the events than they themselves were? The early experts in ḥadīth certainly knew much more than we do. All the research in the world will not turn up anything new that the *muḥaddithūn* did not take into account; any reassessment will therefore amount to nothing but personal opinion. New research cannot change past events.[101] Earlier scholars, because they were closer in time, were far better equipped to make judgments about transmitters because they were privy to sources that have long since been lost.

According to supporters of ḥadīth the assertion that the *muḥaddithūn* paid no attention to the content of traditions is an inaccurate representation of classical ḥadīth criticism. The *ʿulamāʾ* did, in fact, examine the *matn* of ḥadīth according to rigorous criteria.[102] The scrutiny of ḥadīth and the rules for authenticating ḥadīth reached such a level of perfection that no further research is necessary or fruitful. The *muḥaddithūn* went far beyond what was necessary in order to be absolutely certain that no forgeries slipped through. In fact, the trend was for the rules of ḥadīth criticism to become more and more stringent as time went on.[103] The science of ḥadīth is therefore unrivaled, the ultimate in historical criticism.[104] The deniers of ḥadīth act out of ignorance of what the ḥadīth literature is all about. They have enough knowledge to make them dangerous, but they are like intruders breaking into a house that does not belong to them and parading the loot that they find even though they have no idea of what is valuable and what is not.[105]

Al-Salafī's depiction of the deniers of ḥadīth as bumbling thieves is an apt portrayal, for while there may be much to commend their conclusions, the methods by which they achieve them are lifted from *ʿilm al-ḥadīth* itself. This flaw in the method of many anti-ḥadīth activists can be illustrated in the work of Aslam Jayrājpūrī. Jayrājpūrī argues that the connection of ḥadīth reports with Muḥammad is uncertain (*ghayr yaqīnī*) and ḥadīth can therefore give knowledge of history, but not of religion (*dīn*). He does not appear to deny that there may be some traditions that originated with the Prophet himself; he holds, rather, that these are very few, that neither the Prophet nor his Companions intended that these traditions be treated as a source of religious knowledge, and that they are submerged in an ocean of forged traditions. His thesis seems to rest on two arguments: that genuine traditions are very few, and that forgery of traditions, beginning in earnest under the Umayyads, was on such a scale that it is virtually impossible to distinguish genuine traditions from forged.

Each of these assertions is defensible and they clearly parallel the arguments of Goldziher. But Jayrājpūrī seriously compromises his case by the manner in which he documents his assertions – that is, by relying uncritically on ḥadīth to discredit ḥadīth. Jayrājpūrī makes full use of a body of anti-ḥadīth traditions, some of which, ironically, have found their way even into the canonical collections, without any hint of suspicion that they are almost certainly products of controversies of the second and third centuries A.H. He thus falls unwittingly into the same trap as the early opponents of ḥadīth who opposed the proliferation of ḥadīth in principle, but contributed to it in practice by tacitly accepting its authority as a legitimate basis for argument and by circulating their own anti-traditionist ḥadīth. He argues, for instance, that few if any traditions were transmitted during the time of either the Prophet or the first four Caliphs on the basis of reports that Muḥammad, Abū Bakr, ʿUmar, ʿUthmān, and ʿAlī each discouraged the circulation of ḥadīth. Similarly, he cites the Prophet's prohibition on setting ḥadīth down in writing in support of his argument that the first written collections of ḥadīth did not appear until the time of the Umayyads. His method mirrors that of his conservative opponents and thus plays into their hands.[106]

Sunna without ḥadīth?

The majority of Muslim discussions of ḥadīth, as we have seen, are grounded on the assumption that an organic relationship subsists between ḥadīth and sunna; they stand or fall together. But the assumption that ḥadīth and sunna are inextricably linked has not gone unchallenged. One of the more interesting outcomes of discussions about the authenticity of ḥadīth has been the emergence of attempts to separate the question of the authority of sunna from the problem of the historical authenticity of ḥadīth – to accept the results of modern ḥadīth criticism, at least in part, while in principle preserving the authority of sunna.

The most accessible expression of such an argument is an essay by S. M. Yusuf which reflects the general approach to sunna promoted by the Lahore-based Institute of Islamic Culture.[107] Yusuf begins by clearly differentiating sunna from ḥadīth; sunna refers to "practice as distinct from any documentation of it [ḥadīth]." It is the action that is normative, forming the basis of recorded ḥadīth, and not vice versa.[108] In other words, according to the traditional way of seeing it a ḥadīth says X, and from that ḥadīth we therefore derive a certain normative practice, Y. But for Yusuf, the normative practice, Y, is prior to and independent of any ḥadīth report, X, which merely provides its documentation. In fact, the validity of sunna does not depend on its documentation in ḥadīth because "practice is best transmitted through practice," and "so long as the practice is unbroken and untainted it constitutes a proof of itself by itself." All that is needed is assurance of the continuity and purity of the practice and ḥadīth can be dispensed with.[109]

This, in fact, says Yusuf, is what actually occurred among the early generations of Muslims. The Companions became "living models" and "purveyors of a living tradition."[110] This explains why the early schools of law did not differentiate between Prophetic sunna and caliphal sunna or between reports about the Companions and ḥadīth. The practice of the Companions was the best possible guide to sunna, for they were transmitting the Prophetic sunna in practice. Thus in the early ḥadīth literature it was enough to name someone well versed in sunna as your authority; it was unnecessary to trace every practice back to the Prophet himself.[111]

Yusuf's emphasis on the practice of the community as the most reliable vehicle for sunna has ancient roots. Some of al-Shāfiʿī's opponents, for example, contended that the sunna could be much more reliably established by examining the practice of the community than through ḥadīth. The Companions had acted in the spirit of the Prophet, the Successors had followed the example of the Companions, and by the third generation the Prophetic sunna was so well established in practice that there could be no need for ḥadīth to support it. Indeed, there was great danger in ḥadīth because of the difficulties in establishing its authenticity.[112]

By following this line of argument, emphasizing the transmission of sunna through practice rather than by means of ḥadīth reports, Yusuf aims to give a basis for sunna independent of the historicity of ḥadīth. If sunna is represented by the continuous practice of the Muslims and if ḥadīth is simply a record of that practice, then it matters little whether a tradition can be shown to be strictly historical – the practice is proof enough. But if authentic sunna is proven by continuous practice, what is the proof of continuous practice? Does ḥadīth play any role in validating correct practice? Yusuf fails to address these problems and in the end he falls short of offering a coherent or persuasive argument for how the "living sunna" is to be rediscovered by contemporary Muslims either within the ḥadīth or apart from it.

A similar but much more sophisticated attempt to separate the authority of sunna from the strict authenticity of ḥadīth is found in the work of the Pakistani modernist Fazlur Rahman. Rahman articulated his views on ḥadīth, sunna, and their relationship during the 1960s when he served as director of Pakistan's Central Institute for Islamic Research, an institution established by the regime of General Ayyūb Khān to aid in promoting modernist interpretations of Islam compatible with the needs of the regime. His work on sunna must be understood against the background of religious politics in Pakistan during the 1960s and, in particular, against the background of the controversy between Ghulām Aḥmad Parwēz and his opponents among the Pakistani *ʿulamāʾ*. Parwēz's radical rejection of sunna and his particular vision of the Islamic state as true heir to Prophetic authority was associated in the minds of his opponents with the efforts of the Ayyūb government to bypass the *ʿulamāʾ* in order to promote modernist Islam. A number of controversial government actions seemed to suggest that Ayyūb was sympathetic to Parwēz's ideas.

Opponents of the government suspected, quite correctly, that Ayyūb was intent on bypassing traditional sources of religious authority in his formulation of policy. They concluded, probably incorrectly, that Parwēz's ideas were exercising an undue effect on government policy. Thus the debate over the relationship between religion and state and the relative role of the *ʿulamāʾ* and the government in formulating policy on religious questions became focused on Parwēz's ideas, and particularly on the issue of sunna. Attention was also focused on the regime's major voice in religious matters, the Central Institute for Islamic Research and its director. Against this background of heated controversy, Fazlur Rahman entered the fray with the publication of a series of articles on the authority of sunna and the authenticity of ḥadīth.[113]

Rahman's argument begins with a redefinition of sunna, or as he would have it, a return to its original definition. He does not abandon the standard definition of sunna as the normative example of the Prophet, but he insists that sunna should also be understood in another sense – as the Muslim community's collective interpretation of the Prophetic example. Sunna in the first sense is logically prior to sunna in the second sense, since the example of the Prophet is the formal source of all sunna for the

Muslim community. The actual content of the Prophetic example is general rather than specific, however. Muḥammad was not a pan-legist, but a moral reformer; he did not so much set down specific precedents as point the Muslims in a general direction. Thus the Prophetic sunna was "a general umbrella concept rather than filled with absolutely specific content."[114] It was never meant to remain static, but to evolve and develop. Consequently, sunna in the second sense represents the community's interpretation, elaboration, and application of Prophetic sunna in specific situations; it is inspired by the Prophetic example and absorbs it, but its specific formulation is the work of the Muslims themselves.[115] The Muslim community is itself responsible for creating sunna, based on the spirit of the Prophetic example, and guaranteed by the principle of *ijmāʿ*. Sunna is therefore "co-extensive with the *ijmāʿ* of the community" and sunna and *ijmāʿ* are "materially identical."[116]

The relationship between the evolving sunna of the early community and the example of the Prophet was dynamic. The Prophet's sunna was not a set of rigid guidelines, but "an ideal which the early generations of Muslims sought to approximate."[117] They were engaged in a "ceaseless search for what the Prophet intended to achieve."[118] Rahman cites several examples to illustrate this understanding of sunna. Ḥasan al-Baṣrī, for instance, in his letter to ʿAbd al-Malik, contends that although there is no specific ḥadīth defending his position on human freedom, he is nevertheless following sunna.[119] In other words, says Rahman, it is the general spirit of the Prophetic mission, passed along to his followers, that establishes sunna, rather than a specific statement of dogma. Similarly, the *Muwaṭṭaʾ* illustrates that in Mālik's time sunna was understood as the agreed-upon practice of the community (*al-amr al-mujtamaʿ ʿalayh*).[120] Shāfiʿī's opponents assumed, likewise, that it is the practice of the community that establishes sunna. Rahman claimed to be resurrecting the methodology of the pre-Shāfiʿī legists and thus reestablishing the ancient understanding of sunna over and against the classical, ḥadīth-based theory of sunna.

For Rahman, as for Yusuf, ḥadīth is consequent to sunna and not prior to it; ḥadīth is simply the reflection and documentation of the "living sunna" of the community. Thus ḥadīth grew up parallel to the sunna. Most early traditions were traced not to the Prophet but to later Muslims who were busy in the formulation of this "living sunna."[121] As the ḥadīth movement progressed, however, there was inexorable pressure "to project *Ḥadīth* backwards to its most natural anchoring point, the person of the Prophet."[122] In this regard Rahman accepts the findings of Schacht as "irrefutable in their basic outlines." He thinks that it is extremely doubtful "whether the literal Prophetic Sunnah, in its entirety, can be disentangled from the 'living Sunnah' reflected in the *Ḥadīth*."[123] A small number of traditions, at best, can be traced with any certainty to the Prophet himself.

But even if the majority of Prophetic traditions are not authentic in a strictly historical sense, contends Rahman, this in no way reduces their importance as a source of sunna. He resists labeling traditions forgeries, for "although *Ḥadīth* verbally speaking does not go back to the Prophet, its spirit certainly does, and *Ḥadīth* is largely the situational interpretation and formulation of the Prophetic model or spirit."[124] Back-projection was neither unnatural, nor insidious, as opponents of ḥadīth contended. The traditionists recognized this fact, for they established the principle that any edifying statement can be attributed to the Prophet irrespective of whether this attribution is strictly historical or not.[125] In other words, says Rahman, the traditionists themselves did not view their work as strictly historical. Attribution of a statement to the Prophet did not necessarily mean that the Prophet had, in reality, said what was attributed to him; it could just as well signify that given the right circumstances, *he surely would have made such a statement*. Hence the tradition, "Whatever of good saying there be, I can be taken to have said it."[126]

The ḥadīth literature thus represents the record of the Muslim community's understanding and application of the Prophet's example – what the Prophet *would have done*. It is for this reason that ḥadīth must be accepted as a guide to the sunna for "the ḥadīth is nothing but a reflection in a verbal mode of this living sunna."[127] Ḥadīth represents "the interpreted spirit of the Prophetic teaching" and although not strictly historical, it "must nevertheless be considered as normative in a basic sense."[128] But the sense in which ḥadīth is normative, for Rahman, is not the same sense in which it is normative for the *muḥaddithūn*. The problem is this: although ḥadīth records the growth of the "living sunna," and therefore provides a guide to it, it differs from the living sunna by encouraging rigidity. While the living sunna was a "living and on-going process," the ḥadīth movement sought to "confer absolute permanence" and the result was the "fixation" of the sunna in static, rigid form.[129] The sunna cannot, therefore, be rediscovered by simply applying ḥadīth formalistically.

Now the question arises, if ḥadīth simply promotes rigidity, and if the true sunna is, in fact, to be found in the *ijmāʿ* of the community, then why not dispense with ḥadīth altogether? In addressing this question Rahman makes it clear that he has Parwēz in mind. "There are strong trends in society," he writes, "which in the name of what they call 'progressivism' wish to brush aside the *Ḥadīth* and the Prophetic Sunnah." But such an approach, he contends, is akin to Nero's method of rebuilding Rome. To do away with ḥadīth, as Parwēz does, is to do away with the only link that Muslims have with their early history; if ḥadīth is thrown out then nothing will remain between modern Muslims and the Prophet but "a yawning chasm of 14 centuries."[130] The results of such an approach are alarming, for even a principle as basic to Islam as *ijmāʿ* would be devoid of foundation.[131]

The example of *ijmāʿ* provides an illustration of the method by which Rahman seeks to establish Prophetic authority for a tradition or practice that arose after the time of the Prophet:

When we test the *Ijmāʿ-Ḥadīth* on what is historically known about the Prophet, we find that the former develops out of the Prophetic Sunnah; for the Prophet not only made every effort to keep the community together, he both encouraged and elicited a unity of thought and purpose. The Qurʾānic term "*Shūrā*" refers to this activity.[132]

This passage implicitly demonstrates what Rahman subsequently makes explicit: that the general outlines of the life of the Prophet provide his main standard for judging whether a tradition breathes the spirit of the Prophet. He gives more credence to historical reports and to the *sīra* literature than to ḥadīth in a technical sense, and he is willing to judge the ḥadīth in the light of the former. He thinks that the main outlines of the Prophet's biography are absolutely clear, and "it is against this background of what is surely known of the Prophet and the early community . . . that we can interpret ḥadīth." As Rahman points out, this preference for history over ḥadīth proper reverses the bias of the traditionists, who held technical ḥadīth superior to historical reports.[133] If a practice or tradition seems, in its general tenor and overall effect, to advance the spirit of the Prophet's mission as recorded in the biographical records, then it may be said to derive, in some sense, from the Prophetic sunna.

All of this still begs the question of how ḥadīth is to be used by contemporary Muslims to recover the "living sunna." Clearly Rahman opposes any sort of formalistic or literalistic application of ḥadīth. What is needed instead is "to study ḥadīth in situational context – to understand their true functional significance to extract the real moral value."[134] The ḥadīth must be treated as a "gigantic and monumental commentary on the Prophet by the early community."[135] Muslims should study this commentary not in order to apply it directly, but for clues to the spirit behind it. Viewed in this way, the whole of the ḥadīth literature proves its value, for even where the specific content of a ḥadīth must be rejected (e.g., that a Muslim will enter paradise even if he commits adultery and theft), the spirit behind such a tradition (i.e., opposition to schism and the need for catholicity in the community) can be appreciated.

Because no particular tradition is tied to the Prophet with any degree of certainty – at best ḥadīth embody the "spirit" of the Prophet – Rahman is free to accept, reject, or reinterpret traditions without appearing to flout the example of the Prophet. A particular practice or law might well be considered to be a true outworking of the sunna in one era or one circumstance, but the same law might be interpreted as dispensable or incompatible with sunna in another era. Sunna is not fixed, but dynamic; not static, but evolving. Rahman's primary example is the case of *ribā* (usury). The spirit behind the prohibition on *ribā* clearly does extend back to the Qur'ān and to the Prophet. But the particular definition given to *ribā* formalized by early generations of Muslims and enshrined in the ḥadīth (i.e., that it represented any amount of interest on certain categories of loans) need not be applied. So long as they abide by the spirit behind the prohibition, Muslims are free to work out the detail of its application for themselves.[136]

Rahman succeeds brilliantly in defining sunna in such a way as to uphold the authority of Prophetic sunna without insisting that its every detail must be directly traced to the Prophet. His approach to Prophetic authority might be fruitfully compared to some theological responses to the problem of the historical Jesus. Just as some Christian theologians have attempted to separate the Christ of faith from the Jesus of history, Rahman sought a theology of sunna that will not be vulnerable in the face of critical historical research, separating, so to speak, the sunna of faith from the ḥadīth of history. On the other hand, Rahman's approach to sunna was grounded on a firm assurance that early biographical and historical sources on Muḥammad are reliable and the basic outlines of Muḥammad's career are thus established.

Rahman also succeeds in preserving a dynamic relationship between sunna and ḥadīth. He offers a coherent method of deriving sunna from ḥadīth while taking full cognizance, and indeed making use of, the historical problems with the latter. But in the end Rahman's method seems to make of ḥadīth not so much a detailed guide as a source of inspiration. In this sense he is not, after all, so distant from Parwēz. For all their differences, and they are many, the two are similar in their focus on the Qur'ān, in their emphasis on the Prophet as a dynamic rather than a static model, and not least in the inevitable arbitrariness that infects their approach to ḥadīth. While Rahman's sense of history was far more acute than Parwēz's, it is clear that, like Parwēz, his judgments about which ḥadīth to accept and which to reject were based as much on his theological and legal preferences as on historical considerations.[137]

This assessment of Rahman's work demonstrates, paradoxically, how much preoccupation with the tradition has united Muslims even as it has become a focus of conflict. The tradition literature serves as a sort of vast museum of Muslim ideas to which modern Muslim thinkers go for evidence to support their arguments. They argue over the authenticity and provenance of certain items; they dispute the accuracy of the labels attached to them. Yet the nature of their arguments shows that they continue to occupy the same intellectual space. However much they may dispute over method, they share a common body of evidence, and they are engaged in a common venture, fighting to interpret and to represent a shared tradition.

6 Sunna and Islamic revivalism

In 1989 Shaykh Muḥammad al-Ghazālī, a prominent spokesman for moderate Islamic revivalism in Egypt, published a book on sunna entitled *The Sunna of the Prophet: Between the Legists and the Traditionists.*[1] The book became an immediate focus of attention and controversy. A commentator in *al-Ahrām* compared Ghazālī's program with the restructuring of the Soviet Union, exclaiming "This is Islamic Perestroika! . . . This is a true revolution!"[2] Ghazālī's work became a best seller, running to five impressions in its first five months and a second enlarged edition within a year. Within two years at least seven monographs were published in response to the book.[3]

In his book Ghazālī takes up many of the central themes in modern Muslim discussions of religious authority – the relationship between Qur'ān and sunna, the place of Prophetic authority as a source of Islamic law, and methods of ḥadīth criticism. But the book is not primarily a work of theory; Ghazālī's main concern is with the sort of practical questions that have dominated the political and religious discourse of Islamic revivalists: the veiling of women, the place of women in society and economy, Islamic criminal laws, questions of economics and taxation. In fact there is not much that is substantially new in this book. The themes are familiar ones in the works of Ghazālī, who has been a prolific author and is no newcomer to the world of contemporary Muslim religious discourse, and his positions are substantially the same as those he has advocated throughout his career. Neither are his views about sunna extreme. He proposes to "purify sunna of adulterations" by redressing imbalances in the way that ḥadīth criticism is understood by contemporary scholars, but he insists that imitation of the Prophet is the only way to please God and that the classical approach to ḥadīth criticism, when rightly applied, is eminently trustworthy and a fully sufficient guarantee of the soundness of ḥadīth. He does not challenge either the authority of Prophetic sunna or the authenticity of ḥadīth.[4]

Yet Ghazālī's book and the vigorous response to it illustrate important trends in modern Muslim discourse on questions of religious authority. It illustrates, first, the growing centrality of Islamic revivalists in the continuing debate over questions of religious authority in contemporary Muslim societies. Increasingly since the middle of the twentieth century revivalist ideas have been at the storm center of Muslim discourse on issues such as the authority of sunna, the authenticity of ḥadīth, and the relationship of these sources to the Qurʾān. Ghazālī's work represents a continuation of this trend.

Islamic revivalists have moved to the center of the modern debate over religious authority by virtue of the simple fact that they are *revivalist*, committed to a revitalized, reinvigorated, and self-assertive Islam. Emphasis on the ongoing struggle to reinvigorate and restore Islam to ascendancy in a world that has turned away from God is the single most important defining characteristic of revivalism. Consequently, most Islamic revivalist leaders have been activists first, and scholars only secondarily, preoccupied with practical issues of Islamic law and impatient with theory. Ghazālī's work illustrates this revivalist preoccupation. For Ghazālī questions about Prophetic authority, the relationship of Qurʾān and sunna, or the authenticity of ḥadīth are supremely practical questions, which are important not as points of theology but because they have direct relevance for the implementation of Islamic law. In fact for the vast majority of Muslim scholars in Egypt and Pakistan the study of religious texts is a practical exercise rather than a theoretical discipline, and the principal questions facing Muslim scholars are issues that have immediate relevance for particular problems of Islamic law: the appropriate penalty for adultery or the allowability of a particular kind of economic activity. Such legal questions raise numerous problems of method: what is an acceptable method for judging, or justifying one's judgment about, whether a tradition is genuine or forged, reliable or unreliable, applicable or not applicable? How trustworthy are the judgments of the ancient ḥadīth scholars who compiled the great collections of *ṣaḥīḥ* ḥadīth? What attitude should be taken toward ḥadīth that seem to conflict with reason, with accepted dogma, with superior traditions or with the Qurʾān? If such contradictions are identified, how can they be resolved? In the nitty gritty of working out solutions to myriad problems of Islamic law, these questions are of utmost importance to the scholar. Moreover, such problems are peculiar to those who take the tradition seriously; it is precisely the scholars who view the Prophetic example as guidance from God who must struggle to justify to each other the acceptance of one tradition or rejection of another. The dilemma faced by such Muslims is how to achieve knowledge of God's will from an admittedly imperfect corpus of tradition.

It is in their solutions to this dilemma that Islamic revivalists have both aroused controversy and made their own peculiar contribution to modern Muslim discussions of religious authority. Two broad features define the revivalist approach: first, a deep distrust of the classical tradition of Islamic scholarship, reflected in a vehement rejection of *taqlīd*; second, a commitment to the authority of the canonical sources, the Qur'ān, and the sunna. Yet, in line with their rejection of *taqlīd*, this commitment to the authority of the Qur'ān and the sunna has not excluded a willingness to rethink how these sources should be understood. With regard to the Qur'ān this has meant a rejection of esoteric interpretations and a revival of straightforward *tafsīr*. But the real crux of revivalist treatments of religious authority has been the problem of sunna. The revivalist problem has been to maintain a commitment to Prophetic authority without accepting a rigid attachment to the classical corpus of ḥadīth; to ensure authenticity without sacrificing flexibility.

Revivalist treatments of sunna must be understood against the background of the classical approach to ḥadīth to which they respond. According to the classical science of ḥadīth criticism, the genuineness (*ṣiḥḥa*) of a tradition rests primarily upon three criteria: the degree to which a report can be corroborated from other identical reports from other transmitters; the reliability, in character and capacity, of each individual transmitter; and the continuity of the chain of transmission. The highest degree of reliability is assigned to a tradition that is corroborated through numerous different chains of transmission. Such a tradition is described as *mutawātir*. For traditions that stand alone, uncorroborated by other reports, the latter two criteria are essential to the establishment of *ṣiḥḥa*. Untrustworthy transmitters or discontinuity in the chain of transmission constitute fatal flaws. To be considered *ṣaḥīḥ*, an isolated tradition must pass five tests:[5]

- continuity of transmission (*ittiṣāl*);
- *ʿadāla* of narrators, i.e., they must be upright, upholders of religion, and not guilty of major sins;
- accuracy (*ḍabṭ*) of the process of transmission, i.e., narrators must not be prone to carelessness or known to have poor memories;
- absence of irregularities (*shadhūdh*), i.e., contradictions with a more reliable source;
- absence of corrupting defects (*ʿilla qādiḥa*), i.e., inaccuracies in reporting the actual chain of transmission.[6]

These rules represent in summary form the method applied by the *muḥaddithūn* to distinguish authentic traditions. The systematic application of this method is thus embodied in the great collections of *ṣaḥīḥ* ḥadīth which represent the pinnacle of classical ḥadīth scholarship. But the compilation of collections of *ṣaḥīḥ* ḥadīth did not end criticism or debate. For one thing, even classical traditionists were by no means united on the degree or nature of the soundness of the canonical collections of ḥadīth. There was a great deal of latitude both in the evaluation of the collective authenticity of the canonical collections and on the authenticity of particular traditions within them.[7] Moreover, even in classical ḥadīth scholarship proving the *ṣiḥḥa* of a tradition did not immediately ensure its applicability as sunna. Jurists applied a variety of methods which had the effect of subordinating sound ḥadīth to other overriding principles of jurisprudence.[8] When it came to practical concerns, establishing the authenticity of a tradition was only the beginning of the process of evaluating its actual *Sharīʿa* value.[9] Consequently, although there was periodic pressure to apply ḥadīth more systematically, especially from Ḥanbalī scholars, the *madhhabs* maintained their established doctrine even in the face of contradictory traditions. In such an environment, the study of ḥadīth tended to become a theoretical discipline somewhat removed from the practical concerns of jurisprudence. It was useful to cite ḥadīth as a basis for one's position, but ḥadīth was not necessarily decisive in forming that position.

All of this changed in the modern period when pressure to reform, reformulate, and reintroduce Islamic law rendered the study of ḥadīth dramatically relevant once again. After the middle of the nineteenth century the classical *madhhabs* were replaced in practice by secular, western-inspired law codes and challenged in principle by movements such as the Ahl-i-Ḥadīth and the *salafiyya* in most Muslim societies. As a consequence of the collapse of the dominance of the classical schools of law, the field was left clear for reexamination of the sources of Islamic law and the place of sunna among them. Furthermore, since the emergence of Muslim societies from colonial domination after the 1940s, movements to reintroduce Islamic law in some form have given practical urgency to questions about the sources of *Sharīʿa* and the methods by which it might be revived. Among those who have advocated a return to *Sharīʿa*-based law in some form there is widespread and implicit agreement that it is impossible simply to step back in time and to return to Islamic law in its classical form; some reformulation of *Sharīʿa* is necessary. Reformulation requires returning to the sources, and returning to the sources requires some agreement on how they are to be interpreted and understood. Central to this process, most scholars agree, is the reassessment of ḥadīth.[10]

What place, then, is ḥadīth to take in the modern reformulation of Islamic law? The Ahl-i-Qurʾān would dispense with ḥadīth altogether; the Ahl-i-Ḥadīth accept uncritically the work of the medieval traditionists. Revivalists, by contrast with both of these extremes, are unwilling to accept at face value all of the traditions passed on to them as *ṣaḥīḥ*, the results of the classical sciences of ḥadīth criticism, but they are also unwilling completely to reject the value of ḥadīth.

The revivalist approach to sunna is characterized, first of all, by unwavering support for the authority of sunna and for the authenticity of ḥadīth literature in general. Several of the staunchest defenders of sunna met with in previous chapters, especially Mawdūdī in Pakistan and al-Sibāʿī in Egypt, have been prominent leaders in revivalist movements. These thinkers have been at the forefront of the battle against the deniers of ḥadīth and their works are among the most frequently cited writings in defense of sunna. They consider sunna fundamental to their program for the revival of Islam and will countenance nothing that seems to undermine its basic authority. There is another side to the revivalist approach to sunna, however, which is of more direct concern to us here. While they staunchly defend the theoretical authority of sunna, the revivalists' commitment to the reintroduction of Islamic law in *relevant* forms makes them pragmatists in practice. The revivalist attitude toward sunna seeks a *modus vivendi* between two extremes, an alternative approach to ḥadīth which will supplement the classical system and lend it new flexibility without undermining it.[11]

Traditionists vs. legists

Wherein lies the flexibility sought by Islamic revivalists? What are the grounds for reassessing the position of ḥadīth as a basis for a modern revival of *Sharīʿa*? The first method of reassessment is simply to reexamine the authenticity of traditions according the same criteria and method as those applied by the *muḥaddithūn*. In accord with their rejection of *taqlīd*, revivalist thinkers have insisted that, at minimum, the work of the *muḥaddithūn* in criticizing *isnāds* must be open to reassessment.[12] Modern scholars must not rely on the work of the great traditionists of the past; they must do the work themselves.

But for many the classical system of ḥadīth criticism is insufficient to the task. Such thinkers seek a method that transcends the limitations of the classical ḥadīth scholar. They find inspiration for such a method in the legacy of the classical schools of law, especially the Ḥanafī school, before the ascendancy of the great traditionists. Whereas a previous generation of reformers, the Ahl-i-Ḥadīth in particular, appealed to ḥadīth to break the monopoly of the *fuqahāʾ* over the interpretation of *Sharīʿa*, some revivalists now seek to reverse the process, appealing to the method of the great *fuqahāʾ* as a corrective to a literalistic and doctrinaire attachment to ḥadīth.

Such an approach to ḥadīth is represented by the juxtaposition of two ideal types of scholar: the *muḥaddith*, or traditionist, and the legal scholar, the *faqīh*. This opposition of traditionist and legist is portrayed as an opposition of theoretician and pragmatist which works itself out in fundamentally different attitudes toward ḥadīth. The *muḥaddith* will be concerned almost exclusively with the *sanad* of a tradition, basing judgments of authenticity entirely on formal grounds; the *faqīh* will be concerned with the content, the spirit, and the relevance of a tradition within the context of the *Sharīʿa* as a whole.

The central feature of the method of the legal scholar, according to those who appeal to them for inspiration, is the willingness to go beyond external criticism of traditions to examine their content, or *matn*. The contention is essentially this: the ultimate measure of a tradition's authenticity is located in its content rather than its chain of transmission. The effective application of ḥadīth in the reformulation of Islamic law requires not just that the *sanad* be examined, but also that the *matn* be scrutinized by scholars knowledgeable in Islamic law. Consequently, the ultimate arbiters of the authenticity of ḥadīth are not the *muḥaddithūn* but the *fuqahāʾ*.

Scrutiny of the *matn* of ḥadīth is not entirely foreign to the classical science of ḥadīth criticism, but its emphasis among modern writers has gone far beyond what classical traditionists seem to have envisioned.[13] We have already encountered discussions of *matn* criticism in the writings of some deniers of ḥadīth. Unlike the deniers of ḥadīth, who appeal to *matn* criticism as a means of discrediting ḥadīth, revivalists take *matn* criticism seriously as a means of inserting a greater degree of flexibility into the method by which traditions are scrutinized. In the Subcontinent one of the first proponents of an approach to ḥadīth based on the revival of *matn* criticism was the theologian, historian, litterateur, and one-time disciple of Sayyid Aḥmad Khān, Shiblī Nuʿmānī.[14] Shiblī became a prominent voice in a neo-Ḥanafī reaction to the polemics of the Ahl-i-ḥadīth.[15] The study of ḥadīth, he contended, cannot be left to traditionists alone, but must also include the *fuqahāʾ*, because a reliable *sanad* does not by itself guarantee the authenticity of a tradition.[16] He agrees with Sayyid Aḥmad Khān that ḥadīth criticism requires the scrutiny of both the line of transmission (*sanad*) and the content (*matn*) of traditions and that the latter task had been largely neglected by the traditionists. Although an essential part of ḥadīth criticism, *matn* criticism is hardly mentioned in many of the standard texts.[17] Corruption crept into the ḥadīth literature through the procedure of transmitting according to the sense (*biʾl-maʿnā*) rather than verbatim (*biʾl-lafẓ*) and through the effects of political conflicts and sectarian prejudices. Even trustworthy transmitters erred in their understanding of what Muḥammad said and unwittingly transmitted misleading reports so that not even the most trustworthy collections of ḥadīth, those of Bukhārī and Muslim, are free from corruption.[18] Such corruption can only be excised by careful criticism of the content of ḥadīth.

In the course of defending Abū Ḥanīfa against the allegations of deficiency in ḥadīth brought by the Ahl-i-Ḥadīth, Shiblī advances his argument that the study of ḥadīth requires the participation of legal scholars, the *fuqahā᾽*. The science of ḥadīth has suffered, he contends, because of domination by traditionists. The offices and attitudes of the *muḥaddith* and the *faqīh* are distinct, and the two groups advance different approaches to ḥadīth. The *muḥaddith* will pick up any tradition that he stumbles upon to add to his collection; he is concerned with quantity and spends his energies traveling in search of new sources of ḥadīth, wherever they may be found. But the *faqīh* is concerned only with traditions that have legal value; he spends his efforts on *fiqh* and cannot devote his life simply to gathering ḥadīth.[19] The *muḥaddith* collects; the *mujtahid* applies. And because of the *faqīh*'s concern for the legal application of ḥadīth, he is naturally more cautious and stringent in his approach to ḥadīth than the traditionist who simply collects whatever he can find.[20]

There are two respects in which the *fuqahā᾽*, represented by Abū Ḥanīfa, are more stringent in their criticism of ḥadīth than the ordinary traditionist. First, they were more stringent in their rules for ḥadīth transmission. Prior to Abū Ḥanīfa there had been no systematic application of ḥadīth criticism, and huge numbers of forged traditions had been put into circulation. In reaction to a situation that was virtually out of control, Abū Ḥanīfa approached ḥadīth with the assumption that very few could be proved *ṣaḥīḥ*.[21] He was not alone in this attitude. His intellectual forebears were known for their caution in ḥadīth and both Mālik and al-Shāfiʿī agreed with Abū Ḥanīfa's assessment of ḥadīth. Both are identified by Ibn al-Ṣalāḥ as severe critics of ḥadīth.[22] Abū Ḥanīfa was particularly severe – and this is what sets him apart from the *muḥaddithūn* – in insisting that only traditions that had been physically heard and accurately remembered verbatim by the transmitter could be accepted. He took a highly critical attitude toward *riwāya bi᾽l-maʿnā*, accepting it only in cases where the transmitter could be expected to understand fully the meaning and significance of the statements made by the Prophet. He insisted, in other words, that the transmitter be a *faqīh*.[23]

In addition to their stringent rules for transmission, the *fuqahā᾽* applied a system of internal criticism, called *ʿilm al-dirāya*, which Shiblī claims the *muḥaddithūn* have largely neglected.[24] *ʿIlm al-dirāya*, or criticism of the *matn* of a tradition, involves judging whether a report is consistent with reason, with human nature, and with historical conditions.[25] By applying such external tests, the *fuqahā'* were able to weed out corruptions that passed the scrutiny of even the most careful *muḥaddithūn*.

Shiblī's viewpoint is echoed in the work of his disciples, most notably Sulaymān Nadvī. But the most influential figure to adopt and develop Shiblī's line of argument was the leading figure of twentieth-century revivalism in the Subcontinent, Mawdūdī. Like Shiblī, Mawdūdī is dissatisfied with the method of the *muḥaddithūn*, but his criticism is more pointed.[26] The traditionists, he contends, take a one-dimensional view of ḥadīth, paying attention almost exclusively to the character of the transmitters and the continuity of the chain of transmission.[27] Thus they are completely *"akhbārī"* in viewpoint and neglect what Mawdūdī calls "the viewpoint of *fiqh*," which requires that, in addition to the *sanad*, the content of a tradition be scrutinized for defects. By neglecting this branch of ḥadīth criticism the *muḥaddithūn* naively accepted traditions that ring false and rejected other traditions that ring true.[28] What is needed, then, is for modern scholars to turn their attention once again to ḥadīth criticism, but this time by emulating the *fuqahā'* and focusing their attention primarily on the *matn* in order to judge whether a tradition is worthy of acceptance.[29]

In Egypt similar attitudes toward the reassessment of ḥadīth can be traced to Rashīd Riḍā, who contended that many traditions of sound *isnād* should still be submitted to criticism of their content.[30] Consequently, Riḍā rejected traditions if they appeared to him to be rationally or theologically objectionable, or if they conflicted with broad principles of *Sharī'a*. Shaykh Muḥammad al-Ghazālī's writings on sunna offer an elaboration of this viewpoint. Like his predecessors, he is at pains to point out that the method by which he proposes to scrutinize ḥadīth is not a new one. Rather, it is inherent in the classical system of ḥadīth criticism. This system, when rightly understood, requires not just that the chain of transmission of a tradition be examined, but also that its *matn* be scrutinized for defects, for what good, he asks, is a tradition with a sound *isnād*, if its *matn* is defective?[31]

To stress his continuity with classical ḥadīth criticism Ghazālī cites the five principles of ḥadīth criticism listed above, but he argues that two of them are intended to be applied not to the *sanad* but to the *matn*; the tradition must be free of *shadhūdh*, i.e., errors or irregularities. This is to be interpreted as contradictions with more reliable sources. Traditions must also be devoid of *'illa qādiḥa* (defect, weakness). Ghazālī interprets this to mean defects in the *matn*. Such defects are primarily of two kinds: contradictions with sources that are superior in weight and internal imperfections in the text. Thus the classical approach to authenticating ḥadīth, when rightly applied, is eminently trustworthy and a fully sufficient guarantee of the soundness of ḥadīth; nothing matches the rigor of this system.[32]

But ḥadīth criticism, properly understood, also involves a division of labor. Traditionists have quite rightly concerned themselves with collecting ḥadīth and examining their chains of transmission for defects. The task remains incomplete, however, until the *fuqahā'* have scrutinized the tradition for defects in its *matn*.[33] In this way, Ghazālī seeks to correct a prevalent tendency among contemporary Muslim scholars, who are prone to attack the great scholars of *fiqh* under the pretense of defending sunna. The *fuqahā'*, he insists, neither deviated from sunna nor belittled sound ḥadīth.[34] The traditionists are laborers whose job is to pass on materials to the engineers, i.e., the *fuqahā'*, who are responsible for the actual shape of the building.[35] A stone that appears adequate to the ordinary laborer may be rejected by the builder as unsuitable. In the same way, traditions shown to be authentic by their *sanad* may be proven weak by defects in their *matn*.[36] The neglect of the second part of the task has resulted in a breakdown of the system.

Sunna within the boundaries of the Qur'ān

The common thread connecting the arguments of Shiblī, Riḍā, Mawdūdī, Ghazālī, and others is an insistence on going beyond the traditionist preoccupation with the *isnād*; to examine the *matn* according to the method of the *fuqahā'*. But what is the method of the *fuqahā'*? Foremost it involves, for all of these writers, allowing general legal principles to overrule specific *aḥādīth*. The fundamental source for such legal principles is, of course, the Qur'ān. Therefore the Qur'ān must be returned to its rightful place as the supreme arbiter of the authenticity of ḥadīth. The tendency in classical scholarship had been just the reverse: the sunna was viewed as a commentary on the revelation, infallible in its own right, and not subject to abrogation by the Qur'ān. Shāfi'ī pioneered the argument that the sunna could not be abrogated by the Qur'ān because the sunna makes specific the general injunctions of the Qur'ān and it is absurd for the more general source to judge the more specific source. In the case of apparent contradiction, recourse must be had to *ta'wīl*. There were, on occasion, voices raised which seemed to challenge this position, most notably that of al-Shāṭibī, but on the whole the sunna was judged to be an independent source not amenable to abrogation by the Qur'ān.

The revivalist tendency to reverse this preference for sunna over Qur'ān is clearly represented in Ghazālī's work. Ghazālī claims that his central aim is merely to bring the ḥadīth back under the aegis of Qurʾānic principles. In contrast to the traditionist, according to Ghazālī, the method of the jurist is to subordinate isolated ḥadīth to higher principles of authority. Among these he counts *mutawātir* traditions, the practice of the community, and, most important, the Qurʾān. When a *faqīh* approaches a problem of law, argues Ghazālī, he gathers all the sources relevant to it from both the Qurʾān and sunna, he sorts the sources according to reliability and rates all of the evidence before coming to an opinion.[37] By contrast, Ghazālī complains, the method of many contemporary *ʿulamāʾ* is to "grab a ruling from any passing ḥadīth." Two concerns should top the agenda of the Muslim community: a concern for greater reliance on the Qurʾān and a strengthening of the ties between Qurʾān and ḥadīth.[38] His desire is not to weaken ḥadīth that may prove genuine, but simply to bring ḥadīth within the boundaries of the Qurʾān.[39] He complains of being fed up with *fiqh* which is heavy on ḥadīth but ignores the Qurʾān, for "there can be no *fiqh* apart from an understanding of the Qurʾān and of modern circumstances."[40]

To justify his method, Ghazālī appeals to the example of the Companions and early *fuqahāʾ* who, he contends, relied first and foremost on the Qurʾān. ʿĀʾisha, for example, when she heard it reported that the dead suffer because of the mourning of their relations, a tradition which is found in numerous versions in the classical collections, retorted by citing from the Qurʾān: "No one will bear the burdens of another."[41] Her objections did not prevent the tradition from being included in *ṣaḥīḥ* collections, however.[42] Similarly, when asked about a tradition that describes God as descending to give revelation to Muḥammad, ʿĀʾisha exclaimed: "Whoever reported this has lied," and she recited: "It is not for man that God should speak to him except by *waḥy* or from behind a veil" (6:103; 42:51). In the same way Abū Ḥanīfa rejected ḥadīth forbidding retribution (*qiṣāṣ*) for the murder of an unbeliever on the basis of the inconsistency of these rules with the text of the Qurʾān which calls for "a life for a life" (5:45, 48, 50). Mālik made a similar ruling in the case of ḥadīth that forbid *qiṣāṣ* in the case of a father who murders his son.[43] Such examples, contends Ghazālī, demonstrate that even the best transmitters made mistakes and that the means of correcting such mistakes, following the method of the Companions and early *fuqahāʾ*, is to compare the *matn* with Qurʾānic teaching. If a contradiction is recognized, the tradition thereby loses its *ṣiḥḥa*, regardless of the strength of its *sanad*.

By ignoring this principle, contemporary scholars are led astray. Thus a leading Syrian *muḥaddith*, Shaykh al-Albānī, declares beef a forbidden meat on the basis of tradition, despite explicit permission in the Qurʾān.[44] More seriously, when an American engineer was killed in Saudi Arabia, the *qāḍī* ruled that *qiṣāṣ* could not be applied on the basis of the ḥadīth "*la yuqtalu muslimun fī kāfirin.*" In Ghazālī's opinion, such a ruling does violence to the very principles of human dignity that are the foundation of the Qur'ānic insistence on a life for a life.[45] The government was forced into bypassing *Sharī'a* and appealing to the principle of *siyāsa shar'iyya* – the discretionary power of the state – in order to invoke the death penalty.[46] Similarly some scholars argue that there is no *zakāt* on commerce, and limit it to a handful of agricultural products although the Qur'ān conceives of no such limitations. Thus obsession with ḥadīth, without reference to wider concerns, distracts from issues of real importance. Muslim youth, for instance, are more concerned with whether a kiss invalidates ritual ablutions than whether elections are free or rigged.[47]

Ghazālī's arguments have drawn both praise and criticism. Critics contend that his use of the Qur'ān to invalidate *ṣaḥīḥ* ḥadīth has no solid basis in the intellectual tradition of Islam; it is merely a smoke screen to disguise unbridled personal opinion. Traditions must be authenticated independently and once declared *ṣaḥīḥ* it is impossible for a tradition to contradict the Qur'ān.[48] Ghazālī's appeal to the example of 'Ā'isha is fruitless; in the cases where 'Ā'isha called sound traditions into question it was she who was in error, not the transmitters she criticized.[49] Moreover, the opinion of a single transmitter or scholar (in this case 'Ā'isha) is hardly sufficient basis to reject an otherwise well-attested ḥadīth. The approach that Ghazālī (and 'Ā'isha!) should have adopted was to seek out ways of reconciling difficult traditions with the Qur'ān rather than rejecting them out of hand. Classical ḥadīth scholarship is full of examples of ways that traditions such as the one concerning weeping over the dead can be reconciled with the Qur'ān.[50]

The basic mistake made by al-Ghazālī is to confuse difficult traditions (*aḥādīth mushkila*) with forged traditions (*aḥādīth mawḍū'a*). His position on the tradition "*lā yuqtalu muslimun fī kāfirin*" presents a case in point. Ghazālī rejects the tradition on the basis of the Qur'ānic insistence on a life for a life, and he appeals to the opinion of Abū Ḥanīfa for support. But in fact there is no real contradiction here. The Qur'ānic verse in question contains within it an indication that unbelievers are excepted from the general rule. More importantly, the tradition has been proven to be genuine, i.e., from the Prophet, beyond any reasonable doubt. Finally, the agreement of the *'ulamā'* confirms its authenticity and its compatibility with the Qur'ān.[51] In summary, Ghazālī's use of the Qur'ān to invalidate sunna runs counter to the *ijmā'* of Muslim scholars; his defense of this method is based on fringe traditions which are easily refuted; and the result of his approach is the undermining of sunna and the free reign of *ra'y*.

On the other hand, Ghazālī's views have been supported, albeit cautiously, in the writings of another Islamic revivalist, Yūsuf al-Qaraḍāwī. Like Ghazālī, Qaraḍāwī claims to advocate a balanced and pragmatic approach to sunna. His approach contains many of the same elements as Ghazālī's, but he frames his method in more moderate terms.[52] Qaraḍāwī eschews theoretical questions related to the authenticity or authority of sunna. He takes for granted the position of the sunna as living commentary on the Qur'ān and practical guide to Islam. The sunna is, in fact, the Qur'ān made manifest and Islam embodied.[53] Whoever desires a practical guide to Islam will find it in the sunna of the Prophet. Coming to a correct understanding of sunna and knowing how to work with it within the context of Islamic law is critical. Muslims face an intellectual crisis and at the heart of this crisis is the problem of sunna. Qaraḍāwī aims to contribute to the resolution of this problem by offering a practical guide to understanding sunna.[54]

Qaraḍāwī, like Ghazālī, aims to define the role of sunna not merely in isolation, but in the broader context of Islamic law. He begins by outlining three general characteristics of the Islamic program as it is reflected in the sunna: universality, balance, and simplicity. The sunna is universal because it is applicable in all times and places, rules every aspect of life, and encompasses every kind of relationship.[55] It is characterized by balance because it eschews extremes, taking into account spirit and body, mind and heart, this world and the hereafter, ideal and reality, freedom and responsibility, the needs of the individual and the needs of society.[56] The simplicity of sunna lies in its tolerance, convenience, and ease; it imposes no undue burdens.[57] By beginning in this way, describing the general character of sunna, Qaraḍāwī offers a clue to his method. Clearly, if the sunna represents all of these things, then any ḥadīth that contradicts them does not represent true sunna. In other words, sunna can only really be known within a broader framework of legal principles.

Qaraḍāwī is cautious, however, in his application of this method. This caution, which distinguishes Qaraḍāwī from Ghazālī, is especially evident on the question of the relationship between Qur'ān and sunna. He affirms the classical maxim "The sunna rules on the Qur'ān" as an indication of the explanatory and specifying function of the sunna *vis-à-vis* the Qur'ān. The sunna distinguishes what the Qur'ān combines, it disentangles what the Qur'ān intertwines, and it specifies what the Qur'ān deals with in general terms.[58] Consequently the Qur'ān can be fully understood and applied only with the help of the sunna. It is also true, however, that the sunna must be viewed in the context of the Qur'ān. Understanding sunna in the light of the Qur'ān is, in fact, the first of Qaraḍāwī's eight rules for working with sunna. It is impossible, he contends, for *ṣaḥīḥ* ḥadīth to contradict the Qurʾān. If there seems to be a contradiction, then one of two conditions obtains: either the tradition is not in fact *ṣaḥīḥ*, or it is misunderstood.[59]

How is the scholar to decide whether a tradition should be rejected or subjected to *taʾwīl*? He must exercise extreme caution in making such a judgment. There must be a firm basis for evaluating apparent contradictions between Qurʾān and sunna. Unrestrained *matn* criticism will lead only to the denial of sound ḥadīth in the manner of the Muʿtazila.[60] So, for example, the Muʿtazila rejected *ṣaḥīḥ* ḥadīth concerning the intercession (*shafāʿa*) of Muḥammad on the basis of theological considerations. In doing so they ignored evidence that the Qurʾān does not entirely preclude intercession – it only rejects the sort of intercession found in Christian theology.[61] The manner of Qaraḍāwī's treatment of the relationship between the Qurʾān and the sunna illustrates that contradictions are in the eye of the beholder. While he follows Ghazālī in admitting to the need for criticism of the sunna on the basis of Qurʾānic principles, his tone of caution makes it clear that he does not expect dramatic results from such an exercise.

The argument of Yūsuf al-Qaraḍāwī and Muḥammad al-Ghazālī that the sunna should be reevaluated in the light of the Qurʾān is by no means unprecedented in Egypt or in modern Islamic thought generally. Their work merely represents the most recent sign of the vitality of this line of argument. The origins of their approach can be traced at least to Rashīd Riḍā. Riḍā argued repeatedly that all traditions at variance with the Qurʾān should be discarded, irrespective of their chain of transmission.[62] He also held that isolated traditions could be overruled by *mutawātir* sunna – that is, sunna transmitted through the continuous practice of the community, e.g., *ṣalāt* and the pilgrimage ceremonies. Such was the practice of the founders of the *madhhabs*, who used their individual judgment to reject even sound traditions.[63] After Riḍā numerous Egyptian intellectuals, most notably Ṭāḥā Ḥusayn and Muḥammad Ḥusayn Haykal, argued that the Qurʾān must overrule ḥadīth. Indeed, Ṭāḥā Ḥusayn uses many of the same arguments and examples that later show up in Ghazālī's work.[64] That Haykal and Ḥusayn take such a position is no surprise, however, since these intellectuals were known to take a critical approach to ḥadīth generally.

This argument survived not only among liberals, but also among Islamic radicals, notably the Ikhwān al-Muslimīn (the Muslim Brotherhood). The Ikhwān inherited, in a general way, the *salafī* rejection of the classical *madhhabs* in favor of direct reference to the sources. As activists who laid out their program for the revival of Islamic law in general terms, the ideologists of the Ikhwān were for the most part content to leave the details to be worked out later. The activist emphasis of the Ikhwān and their hostility to what they viewed as the passivity of the *ʿulamāʾ* tended to discourage systematic expression of their position on such questions as the roots of *Sharīʿa*. For them the demand that *Sharīʿa* be implemented was straightforward. Thus it is difficult to trace their positions with any clarity, especially in their early years. Despite these uncertainties, however, it is clear that many of the Ikhwān tended to favor the Qurʾān above ḥadīth. In other words, they extended the *salafī* skepticism about the classical *madhhabs* to the ḥadīth literature itself, insisting that "there must be serious re-examination of the traditions to determine the true from the false."[65] According to Mitchell, who based his conclusions on oral sources, "a common belief among the brothers was that no more than a handful of traditions would survive such study; an extreme form of this view held that only one tradition would survive, and that this would have the Prophet say 'Take from me only the Qurʾān.'"[66] One member described the sunna as "a kind of supplement to the legal injunctions of the Qurʾān."[67]

On the basis of these accounts the roots of more recent revivalist writings on sunna by figures such as Ghazālī and Qaraḍāwī come into sharper focus. Their work represents a systematization and moderation of a trend in thought which began with ʿAbduh and Riḍā and was adopted in a general way, but not developed systematically, by the Ikhwān. In a sense it represents an apologetic for the vision of Islamic radicals, directed at the scholarly community. Ghazālī wants to demonstrate that he has not abandoned the sunna and that the positions he takes on critical issues of Islamic law are not innovations, but are solidly grounded in the Islamic intellectual tradition. Consequently, he spends the majority of his book returning to practical issues which have been major themes of revivalist thought – the status of women, the economic system, *jihād*, and *shūrā*.

Ghazālī's consideration of the theoretical basis for sunna represents an attempt to lay a solid foundation for his positions on such practical issues. Not surprisingly, he devotes a lengthy section of his discussion to issues concerning women. Three problems occupy his attention: the problem of the veiling and seclusion of women; the problem of women working outside the home; and the question of women's evidence in court. On each of these issues Ghazālī defends well-established positions. Women should wear modest dress, but there is no basis for requiring a face veil or for complete seclusion. Women are permitted to work outside the home – indeed, this is necessary for the health and prosperity of the *umma* (Muslim community) – but they must not sacrifice the integrity of home and family, which remains their primary responsibility. Finally, a woman's evidence is to be calculated at half the value of a man's, in accordance with Qur'ānic teaching, but there is no basis for excluding women from giving evidence altogether in cases involving *ḥudūd* (crimes for which Islamic law requires a fixed penalty) or *qiṣāṣ*.[68]

There are no big surprises here. Ghazālī has argued all of these positions in the past, and although they remain controversial, they have become well established among revivalists. Neither is Ghazālī's reasoning in defense of these positions substantially new. His arguments rest primarily on his own exegesis of the Qur'ān mixed with a heavy dose of *maṣlaḥa* – his own analysis of the needs of the *umma*. Ghazālī's use of ḥadīth is light; he quotes traditions more often to refute them than to support his own arguments. His intentions seem to be focused on undermining and dismantling what he takes to be unnecessarily restrictive rules which are defended on the basis of ḥadīth. A requirement or prohibition of *Sharīʿa*, he concludes, cannot be established except by a definitive proof.

Ghazālī's examples illustrate his subordination of ḥadīth to other principles, primarily to the Qur'ān, but also simple expediency. So, for instance, in his discussion of *jihād* he dismisses the majority of traditions related to the topic not because they are not authentic but because they are irrelevant; times have changed, therefore the rules concerning *jihād* must also change. The obligation to perform *jihād* remains operative, but the means must be adapted.[69] He makes a similar argument with regard to *shūrā*.[70] Thus he aims not so much at establishing a method for understanding and applying ḥadīth as at justifying the subordination of ḥadīth that conflict with his program. Taken in the context of these examples, Ghazālī's position on ḥadīth can be recognized as providing a basis to refute conservative opposition to revivalist ideology. Revivalists have argued all along that the Qur'ān is the primary basis for their program. Ghazālī now offers more sophisticated weapons to combat the attacks of conservatives who charge that the revivalist positions run counter to sunna.

The method of the *faqīh*

As our discussion of Ghazālī illustrates, the revivalist call for a reassessment of the ḥadīth literature based on *matn* criticism begins with reestablishing the preeminence of the Qur'ān, but it does not end there. The method of the *faqīh* involves the deft juggling of numerous sources and principles of legislation. In the context of a practical problem of Islamic law, a tradition that is considered *ṣaḥīḥ* by reason of its *sanad* may yet be rejected or subordinated to other principles even if it poses no apparent contradiction with the Qur'ān. Ghazālī holds, for instance, that *mutawātir* sunna, i.e., the *sunna ʿamaliyya*, takes precedence over ḥadīth reports, even if the latter are sound. Thus the Mālikīs consider the practice of Medina a more solid proof of the sunna of the Prophet than isolated transmissions.[71] For this reason both Ḥanafīs and Mālikīs disapprove of exchanging greetings in the mosque during the *khuṭba* (sermon), despite traditions encouraging this practice. The *sunna ʿamaliyya*, encouraging silence and meditation, takes precedence.[72] He also holds to the principle that traditions can be overridden when conditions change. We have already seen this illustrated in the case of *jihād* and *shūrā*, but there are other examples as well. So, for example, ʿUthmān equalized the amount of *diya* (blood money) for *dhimmīs* (protected minorities) in order to assure their security, although *diya* for a *dhimmī* had stood at half that of a Muslim. On the basis of the precedent set by ʿUthmān, according to Ghazālī, the modern Pakistani law equalized *diya* for men and women, despite traditions that set the *diya* for women at half. On the basis of the equal value of all life, *diya* for everyone is equal under Ḥanafī law.

This point – that understanding of the broad principles of Prophetic legislation and the specific context of a tradition are essential for critical understanding of ḥadīth – has received a good deal of attention in modern discussions of sunna. Shiblī offers two examples, both frequently cited in modern discussions of sunna, to demonstrate what happens when basic principles of ḥadīth criticism are neglected. His first example is the tradition "The dead will be punished as a result of mourning over them." Rather than appealing to the Qurʾān's emphasis on individual responsibility to refute this tradition, as Ghazālī does, Shiblī emphasizes instead the failure of those who narrated the tradition to understand its full context. He relies on a report about ʿĀʾisha, who, when she heard this tradition, allegedly claimed that Ibn ʿUmar had been mistaken in his understanding of what the Prophet had meant. What had actually occurred was that a Jewish woman had died and her relatives were mourning for her. The Prophet had made two comments: her relatives are mourning and she is suffering punishment. Ibn ʿUmar unwittingly conflated these two statements, concluding that the woman was suffering punishment as a consequence of the weeping of her relatives.[73] Shiblī's second example concerns another occasion when the Prophet stood on a grave and spoke, appearing to address himself to the dead. Observers took him to be saying that the dead could hear him. In actual fact, again according to ʿĀʾisha, Muḥammad was simply saying that these people now knew that his message was true.[74]

The point is that reliable transmission of ḥadīth requires full understanding of the legal significance of the tradition by a narrator. Because of the uncertainty created by the practice of transmitting *biʾl-maʿnā*, one can only trust a tradition if there is clear assurance that the narrator fully understood its context and significance. Shiblī is at pains to point out that he is not impugning the character or general reliability of those narrators who erred in their understanding. In other words, such transmitters were completely honest and reliable in transmitting their own perceptions of an event; their only weakness is in not having the training to be able fully to understand the context or significance of what they were witnessing. In this way Shiblī seeks to evade the charge that he is challenging the *ʿadāla* of the Companions or of other well-known transmitters of ḥadīth. In other words, here is a means of rejecting the principle implied by a given tradition without rejecting the authenticity of the transmission or the reliability of the transmitter.[75]

Shiblī's point is to illustrate how the neglect of broad principles of criticism can lead to misunderstanding and corruption in ḥadīth. Conversely, the weeding out of corruption also requires such understanding. In both of his illustrations, those who related traditions erroneously did so first because they misunderstood the context and second because they neglected to compare what they were relating to general Qurʾānic principles. If even the *Ṣaḥāba* erred in this way, comments Shiblī, what can we expect of later generations? For this reason, he says, Abū Ḥanīfa would accept *riwāya bi'l-maʿnā* only on the condition that the transmitter was a proven *faqīh*, able fully to understand the meaning and legal significance of the material transmitted.[76] Moreover Abū Ḥanīfa insisted that the right to transmit *bi'l-maʿnā* belonged only to the Companions and Successors; subsequent generations could only transmit verbatim.[77]

Reference to Abū Ḥanīfa as the model of a pragmatic and balanced approach to sunna is common to almost all of the revivalist authors we are concerned with here. For Mawdūdī, Abū Ḥanīfa is the archetype of the middle path that he advocates. Just as those who deny ḥadīth are in error, so those who evaluate ḥadīth purely on the basis of the *sanad* are also wrong. The true approach is a balance between these two extremes, and this balance is most evident in the work of the great *fuqahāʾ*, chief among them Abū Ḥanīfa. In Abū Ḥanīfa's *fiqh* we find numerous arguments based on traditions with imperfect chains of transmission. We also find cases where he ignores a sound tradition in favor of a weak tradition. There are even occasions when the ḥadīth says one thing and Abū Ḥanīfa chooses another position altogether. Other great *fuqahāʾ* – Mālik and al-Shāfiʿī – although more *akhbārī* in viewpoint than Abū Ḥanīfa, nevertheless gave numerous decisions that were contrary to traditions considered sound by the *muḥaddithūn*.[78]

According to Mawdūdī, these scholars were not guilty of flouting ḥadīth they knew to be sound; rather, they considered the authenticity of a tradition to rest on more than just the *isnād*. The significance of this viewpoint is in the reordering of priorities that it entails. Mawdūdī and the other revivalists we are considering do not discount the importance of the *isnād*, but they think it must be balanced with other considerations. Rather than examining ḥadīth in isolation, scholars must assess it within the context of the whole of *Sharīʿa* and all of the sources of *Sharīʿa*. How does this reordering of priorities work itself out in practice? Here a difference becomes evident between Pakistani and Egyptian revivalists. While Egyptian writers tend to lay stress on the method of the *fuqahāʾ*, their counterparts in the Subcontinent have tended to emphasize the qualities that mark the individual *faqīh*.

Among contemporary revivalists, Qaraḍāwī offers what is perhaps the most extensive exposition of how these ideas about sunna might be developed into a systematic method for dealing with ḥadīth. Three basic principles of ḥadīth criticism underlie his approach to working with sunna. First, the critic must verify the trustworthiness and authenticity of the materials he is working with. This involves using the tools of classical *isnād* criticism to reassess the authenticity of a tradition on the basis of its transmission. Second, the critic must seek to understand the language and context of the text in order to discover its real meaning and intent: he must examine the circumstances surrounding the event or utterance, the reasons for its occurrence, and its place among other texts; he must place it within the framework of general principles and overall objectives of Islam; he must distinguish what was meant to be law and what was not; and he must separate what was meant to be specific to a particular context from what is of general application. Finally, the critic must ensure that the text is free from contradictions with other, more reliable texts. It will not do to take one or two traditions; the scholar must view a problem in the light of the whole of revelation.[79]

A right understanding of sunna, according to Qaraḍāwī, depends especially on the ability to recognize that different categories of traditions have different functions and purposes. It goes without saying, for example, that not all ḥadīth were meant to serve as a basis for legislation. For this reason the *fuqahāʾ* must be involved in the evaluation of ḥadīth. On the other hand, the *fuqahāʾ* have a tendency to be lazy about scrutinizing the *isnād*. Consequently, books of *fiqh* are filled with weak ḥadīth even though there is agreement that weak traditions cannot provide a firm basis for rules of law. Both the *fuqahāʾ* and the *muḥaddithūn* thus play an indispensable role; each group is in need of the other to bring its work to perfection.[80]

The heart of Qaraḍāwī's treatise is his discussion of eight guidelines for better understanding of sunna. The stress here must be placed on the word *understanding*, for Qaraḍāwī is much less interested in the authentication of ḥadīth than in its interpretation. The first step in the process is to view sunna in the light of the Qurʾān; in other words, in dealing with a particular problem, the scholar must begin by examining what the Qurʾān has to say on the subject. The second step is to gather together all of the traditions relating to the particular subject of concern. The third step is to compare these traditions, reconciling them wherever possible, and rating those that seem irreconcilable according to the degree of their authenticity. Qaraḍāwī resists rejecting a tradition when it appears to contradict others; reconciliation of traditions must be attempted before one tradition is chosen in preference to another.[81]

Qaraḍāwī tends, much more than Ghazālī, to separate the work of the *faqīh* from that of the *muḥaddith*. The *fuqahāʾ*, according to Qaraḍāwī's depiction, are not concerned so much with determining whether a tradition should be accepted or rejected as in deciding what it means and what to do with it. If the job of the *muḥaddith* is to judge the authenticity of traditions, the job of the *faqīh* seems to be to bridge the interpretive gulf that separates authenticated ḥadīth from sunna. Consequently, the approach Qaraḍāwī proposes is really an exegetical method for understanding and applying ḥadīth rather than a system of ḥadīth criticism. All of his five remaining guidelines for understanding sunna have to do with interpretation: ḥadīth must be understood in the light of the background and circumstances of their occurrence; changeable elements must be distinguished from permanent principles; figurative meanings must be recognized; apparent and hidden meanings must be distinguished; and the meaning of the words themselves must be thoroughly understood. Qaraḍāwī's intention is to offer a blueprint which will provide a reliable guide for moving from ḥadīth to sunna to *Sharīʿa*. In implementing this blueprint both the *muḥaddithūn* and the *fuqahāʾ* have a part to play – the *muḥaddithūn* by identifying *ṣaḥīḥ* ḥadīth; the *fuqahāʾ* by interpreting and applying those ḥadīth according to sound principles.

Seeking the spirit of the Prophet

In the Subcontinent, writers such as Shiblī and Mawdūdī, while concerned with subordinating ḥadīth to general principles of *fiqh*, and especially Qurʾānic principles, have tended to lay stress less on a particular method for dealing with ḥadīth than on the special capacity for legal understanding that characterizes the *faqīh*. The ability to judge ḥadīth rightly becomes a quality of character, not simply a skill to be mechanically applied. Like Ghazālī, Mawdūdī insists that the ḥadīth is not at the same level as the Qurʾān in terms of reliability; consequently, the Qurʾān should be the first recourse of scholars in determining the *ṣiḥḥa* of ḥadīth.[82] But specific reference to the Qur'ān receives less emphasis from him than the capacity of the scholar to weigh all the evidence before coming to a judgment.

The emphasis here is on a certain ineffable quality in the true *faqīh* which enables him thoroughly to understand the context, significance, and spirit of Prophetic legislation. With Shiblī this emphasis is subtle; in Mawdūdī's writings it becomes explicit. The *fuqahā'*, according to Mawdūdī, possess special abilities and instincts (*dhauq*) which they apply to each tradition that comes under their scrutiny. A true *faqīh* is especially gifted by God in the understanding of *fiqh*; he has internalized the teachings of the Qur'ān and the example of the Prophet to such an extent that he is able, *instinctively*, to ascertain whether a tradition is true or false.[83] The true *faqīh* is like an old jeweler, able at a glance to appreciate a gem; he takes into account the evidence of the *isnād*, but such evidence is not decisive if contradicted by his own judgment.[84] He understands the whole system of *Sharī'a* and recognizes the nature of the system, so that when one small part comes before him, his instinct tells him immediately whether it is compatible with Islam. This becomes the standard by which the *faqīh* accepts or rejects traditions. Even on questions not dealt with in the Qur'ān and the sunna, the true *faqīh* is able to judge *what the Prophet would have said or done in such circumstances.*[85]

Such an individual possesses a quality that Mawdūdī calls *mizāj shinās-i-rasūl* – a sort of internalization of the temperament (*mizāj*) of the Prophet.[86] The *mizāj* of Islām is embodied in the *mizāj* of the Prophet; whoever understands the *mizāj* of Islam and drinks deeply of the Qur'ān and the sunna becomes identified with the temperament of the Prophet in such a way that when he comes across any tradition his insight (*baṣīrat*) indicates to him what is of the Prophet and what is not. This is so because his spirit is absorbed in the spirit of the Prophet; his viewpoint is united with the vision of the Prophet; his mind is immersed in the truth; and he thinks in just the way that Islam prescribes. Once an individual reaches this point, he has no great need for the *isnād*. Certainly he will refer to the *isnād*, but his decision will not be based upon it. He will freely use traditions with defective chains of transmission, and he will freely reject traditions whose *isnāds* are without defect if his instincts tell him they do not accord with Islam.[87]

The subjective character of the method Mawdūdī advocates is obvious, at least to his opponents. As Adams points out, he gives his critics two causes for concern: first, by the degree of latitude he was apparently willing to concede to the independent use of reason in evaluating ḥadīth, and second because his opponents quite naturally took Mawdūdī to be assigning to himself the qualities of *mizāj shinās-i-rasūl* and to be claiming the ability and the right to reject or accept ḥadīth at whim.[88] To conservative opponents, Mawdūdī's proposed method of reassessing sunna represents nothing more than a thin veil calculated to disguise arbitrary judgment and unrestrained reason.

Mawdūdī's theory does, in fact, illustrate the essentially arbitrary quality of most calls for internal criticism of ḥadīth. It also raises the suspicion that calls for *matn* criticism from revivalists are designed to lead to precisely the same result obtained by deniers of ḥadīth, i.e., freedom from any restraint in interpreting the Qur'ān. Even the claim that ḥadīth should be judged in the light of Qur'ānic principles, which sounds innocuous enough, is only a small step removed from the doctrine of the sufficiency of the Qur'ān espoused by the deniers of ḥadīth. The deniers, in fact, appeal to many of the same arguments made by moderates such as Mawdūdī and Ghazālī. Sayyid Aḥmad Khān, for example, says that the first step toward recognizing authentic ḥadīth must be to compare traditions with what is known to be authentic, i.e., the Qur'ān.[89] The more moderate Amritsar faction of the Ahl-i-Qur'ān had likewise contended that ḥadīth contrary to the Qur'ān must be renounced, but that traditions with positive moral or ethical value could be retained.[90] Ghulām Jīlānī Barq suggests a renewal of *matn* criticism and holds that "only such ḥadīth is acceptable which does not conflict with the Qur'ān," or "which does not repudiate morality or human experience."[91] A true hearted Muslim should accept any ḥadīth that is consistent with the Qur'ān and reject any that is inconsistent, irrespective of the strength or weakness of the *sanad*.[92] Even after he repudiated his skeptical views on the authenticity of ḥadīth, Barq continued to hold that the Qur'ān should be the main judge of authenticity.[93]

Among revivalists themselves there are some who are uncomfortable with the arbitrary quality of *matn* criticism. Sibāʿī, in particular, criticizes some approaches to *matn* criticism because they take it beyond reasonable limits. When you are told something, he argues, the first step in judging the accuracy of the report is to consider the reliability of the reporter. Once you are convinced of the trustworthiness of your source, only then do you go on to consider the report itself. But if a report engenders doubts, not because of the reporter but because of the content of the report itself, you should not be too quick to declare the reporter a liar. To do so may be slander. Instead, the right course is to suspend judgment on the matter, hoping that more light will be shed on it later.[94] In certain other respects, Sibāʿī takes a position similar to other revivalists. He interprets quarrels among the Companions as differences in legal interpretation, for example. Not all of the Companions understood the legal significance or the full context of everything they saw or heard from

Muḥammad. As a result, some had to correct the interpretations of others.[95]

On the whole, however, Sibāʿī's approach to *matn* criticism is cautious. When the *muḥaddithūn* applied *matn* criticism, he says, they did so only with great care, and never without attempting *ta'wīl*. They recognized that there are some principles of criticism that do not apply to the Prophet. As the recipient of revelation, Muḥammad possessed knowledge greater than that of normal humans. The occurrence of ideas that we do not understand cannot be grounds for labeling them false. Our understanding changes and thus our limited comprehension cannot be allowed to rule on revelation.[96] For his opponents revelation must conform to reason; for al-Sibāʿī reason is inadequate and must remain subservient to revelation. This is why *isnād* criticism must take precedence over *matn* criticism and why *ta'wīl* must be attempted whenever apparent contradictions arise. To allow the sort of ḥadīth criticism proposed by scholars such as Aḥmad Amīn would be to open the Pandora's box of unrestrained reason. The result would be certain chaos, for each person's judgment would differ and no standard of truth would remain.[97] Sibāʿī's arguments are echoed by an Egyptian *ʿālim*, Abū Shuhba: a rationalistic approach cannot take into account the metaphorical language of many traditions; traditions may be figurative, not intended to be interpreted literally, they may be allegorical, or they may depict mysteries or hidden things not amenable to rational criticism. Often traditions are so hard to understand that one must admit that God alone fully understands them. To discount such traditions on the basis of rational criteria is unwarranted; a far better course is simply to accept them, leaving their interpretation to the wisdom of God.[98]

Reason and tradition

The problems of *matn* criticism lead naturally to the question of the role of reason and personal judgment in the evaluation of ḥadīth. Should a tradition be discarded when it appears to be in conflict with reason? In theory the answer of many classical traditionists was yes. Traditionists listed among their criteria for *matn* criticism the requirement that a tradition should not be absurd or contrary to reason. In reality, however, those who prescribed such conditions seldom resorted to this option unless there were other grounds for rejecting the tradition as well. There was strong pressure to exercise *ta'wīl* when faced with difficult traditions. It is true that Ibn Khaldūn discounted medical traditions with a comment to the effect that the Prophet had been sent to teach religion (*dīn*), not medicine.[99] But this was less a rational judgment than a statement about the purpose of prophecy, and we can point to only a few exceptional cases where traditions were openly rejected on such grounds.

Conservative critics of revivalist approaches to sunna have been quick to label their opponents rationalists and to point out the affinity of the ideas of writers such as Mawdūdī and Ghazālī to the ideas of the deniers of ḥadīth and orientalists. Salafī claims that Shiblī, Islāḥī, and Mawdūdī, while not denying ḥadīth altogether, have done irreparable damage to the cause of ḥadīth by encouraging unrestrained personal opinion in the criticism of ḥadīth.[100] Similarly, Ghazālī's conservative opponents seek to discredit his views by attributing them to the influence of rationalist schools of thought, to the influence of orientalists such as Goldziher, and to his affinity for Europe and the West.[101]

Proponents of *matn* criticism have been extremely sensitive to such charges. Shiblī, for example, even while he insists that ḥadīth must be considered forgeries if they are contrary to reason, clearly recognizes the difficulty of consistently applying such criteria and, lest he be labeled a rationalist in the mold of Sayyid Aḥmad Khān, he is quick to insist that what he means by reason (*ʿaql*) was not the sort of free-ranging speculation that goes by the name of reason or science in modern times.[102] A tradition should only be rejected on the basis of *matn* criticism if it is not amenable to allegorical interpretation, *taʾwīl*.

Despite his caution, however, he goes too far in the eyes of his critics among the Ahl-i-Ḥadīth. In their eyes, his support for a renewal of *ʿilm al-dirāya* simply cloaks unguarded rationalism in another form. The real meaning of *dirāya* is circumscribed: it signifies study of the text of ḥadīth according to the rules of Arabic grammar, the principles of *Sharīʿa*, and in the light of the biography of the Prophet. By contrast, Shiblī's suggestion that ḥadīth can be judged according to external criteria can only result in intellectual anarchy. Thus while Shiblī should not be accused of heresy, for he does not reject ḥadīth, he has nevertheless done irreparable damage by promoting such views.[103]

In Egyptian discussions of ḥadīth similar tensions are evident. ʿAbduh was willing to reject any ḥadīth that violated sense experience, but we have little indication of exactly what he meant by this.[104] In general he was cautious in his attitude toward reason, arguing that once the Prophetic mission is recognized, "reason is obliged to accept all that he brings."[105] If something known to have originated with the Prophet appears to contradict reason, the only recourse is to believe that some other interpretation is called for. There are two legitimate courses for the believer: to seek out an interpretation that eliminates the contradiction or to fall back on the omniscience of God. In the end, for all his apparent rationalism, ʿAbduh falls short of giving full scope to reason.

It is Rashīd Riḍā, however, who provides the clearest illustration of the confusion surrounding the question of applying rational criteria to ḥadīth. While Riḍā shows no reluctance to pursue *matn* criticism when it suits his purposes, his discussions of controversial ḥadīth show that judgments that appear at first to be based on rational criticism turn out, on examination, to be based on dogma. Take, for example, miracle traditions, which suffer particularly under Riḍā's scrutiny. He rejects the accounts of the *isrāʾ* and *miʿrāj* (Muḥammad's miraculous journey to Jerusalem and ascent to heaven) where they include the removal and purification of Muḥammad's heart when he was a boy.[106] He discards the tradition in which the Prophet describes how the sun, after setting, prostrates itself before God.[107] He also rejects the account of the splitting of the moon, one of the most famous miracles attributed to Muḥammad.[108] Each of these traditions is represented within the canonical collections, and his willingness to attack them sets him apart from conservatives. But for Riḍā these traditions are unacceptable not because they are unscientific, but because they violate a key element of *salafī* dogma – that Muḥammad's only miracle was the Qurʾān.

This predominance of theological over rational criteria is further illustrated in Riḍā's discussion of a medical tradition in which the Prophet describes the fly as having disease on one wing and healing on the other.[109] Riḍā is hesitant to reject this tradition out of hand, because to his thinking it can neither be verified nor discredited by medical science. An argument that is weightier for Riḍā is that this tradition violates a basic principle of *fiqh* because it does not warn against something obnoxious or impure.[110] Similarly, his rejection of traditions concerning the *abdāl*, a class of saints thought to preserve the universe, was based on his rejection of ṣūfī excesses rather than any rational criteria.[111]

As these examples indicate, appeals to *matn* criticism are much less far reaching and much less arbitrary than they might appear. We have seen what effort Ghazālī exerts to assure readers that he is not abandoning the tradition or setting out on his own. Nowhere does either he or Qaraḍāwī suggest that reason is of itself sufficient grounds for rejecting a tradition. Even Mawdūdī, the most extreme of the revivalists on the question of the reevaluation of sunna, does not make the use of reason one of the characteristics of his ideal *faqīh*. Such a person is not qualified by rational ability, but by knowledge of revelation.

All of these writers do lay claim to independence of judgment; consequently, there is a certain appearance of arbitrariness in their method. But in reality they show much less independence than appearances might suggest. Ghazālī provides the clearest instance. Although he claims to be reexamining ḥadīth independently, one would be hard put to find a case where he has contested a tradition for which there is no record of controversy. In other words, he challenges *aḥādīth* only when he can find corroborating evidence within the tradition. He is, in actual fact, just as reliant on earlier authorities as the *muḥaddithūn* he criticizes; he simply chooses different authorities. Rather than stepping out on his own, he amasses an alternative set of data out of the wealth of the Islamic tradition. His rejection of traditions limiting *qiṣāṣ*, for instance, is simply a defense of the Ḥanafī point of view; there is little that is new or radical about it. In fact, Ghazālī's entire argument can be interpreted as an attempt to defend the classical *madhhabs* against the attacks of modern *aṣḥāb al-ḥadīth*.

There is a deep tension in the approach of these writers between independence and tradition, authenticity and flexibility. None of them are willing to dispense with ḥadīth, yet they are also unhappy with the consequences of uncritical acceptance of ḥadīth. They seek flexibility, yet the feature that distinguishes the revivalist quest for flexibility from the similar quest of Parwēz or Abū Rayya is the insistence that the results be explicitly grounded in the Islamic intellectual tradition itself. Out of the repositories of that tradition, they seek alternate voices, more attuned to their own concerns. The conflict here is not between reason and revelation or between traditionalism and rationalism – it is a conflict between alternative visions of the tradition.

Perhaps the comparison with Perestroika with which we began is not inapt. Each of these writers is making a conscious effort to insert a degree of flexibility into a system that is perceived to be ossified – to wrest control of the means to define the content of sunna. They are trying to bring about change from within, an internal restructuring of a tradition thought to be in danger of obsolescence. It is important to recall that the position of religious thought in contemporary Islamic societies makes these issues into very practical concerns. Seen in this context these writings are more than theoretical or theological speculation; they represent one part of an ongoing conflict over the definition of what an Islamic society must be.

7 Conclusion: the spectrum of change

Two recurring questions run under the surface of modern discussions of sunna and define the modern Muslim crisis of religious authority. The first is "How does God speak?" and the second "Who speaks for God?" Most of this study has been concerned with issues related to the first question – questions about revelation, prophecy, and how God's will is to be known. But it is the second question that gives discussions of sunna their special urgency. Moreover, the two questions are intimately connected. Views about the nature of revelation and the nature of prophecy serve to justify particular ideas about who has the right to interpret revelation, i.e., who speaks for God. Those who challenge classical ideas about Prophetic authority as well as those who defend the classical theory of sunna struggle for the right to represent the authority of the Prophet in contemporary society.

Modern controversies over sunna clearly reveal this connection between ideas about the authority of religious texts and rival claims to interpretive authority. For the *ʿulamāʾ* the defense of ḥadīth is part of an effort to preserve their own position as interpreters and guardians of ḥadīth, hence guardians of the whole tradition. In the orthodox structure of religious authority, the Qurʾān is viewed through the interpretive filters of both the sunna and the classical tradition. The *ʿulamāʾ* are the guardians of this interpretive process, and the result is guaranteed by *ijmāʿ*. By virtue of their expertise in the sciences of ḥadīth and their knowledge of classical scholarship, the *ʿulamāʾ* are the mediators of the Prophetic legacy. Through ḥadīth they speak with the voice of the Prophet.

At the other extreme, the deniers of ḥadīth reject orthodox ideas about sunna as a means of wresting control of the interpretive process away from the *ʿulamāʾ*. If ḥadīth is not essential, then the experts in its interpretation are no longer needed. Moreover, if Muḥammad was no more than a human interpreter of the Qurʾān, then modern Muslims can lay claim to the same interpretive authority that he had. Rather than mere imitators of the Prophet, scripturalists such as Parwēz claim to be executors of the

Prophet's legacy. Thus the ideas of the deniers about the sufficiency of the Qur'ān and the nature of Prophetic authority pose a direct threat to the traditional structure of religious and legal authority in Islam, cutting at the heart of the traditional role of the *ʿulamāʾ* as the guardians of tradition. It is not those versed in ḥadīth who have the right to authoritative interpretation of Islam, according to the deniers of ḥadīth. Rather, it is those who can understand the relevance of the Qur'ān to modern life.

Revivalist thinkers do battle on two fronts. On the one hand, they defend sunna against the deniers of ḥadīth, establishing their credentials as protectors of the tradition. On the other hand, they lay claim to the right to interpret the tradition for themselves, independent of the conservative *ʿulamāʾ*. Revivalists find in sunna both their source of authenticity and their chief means of asserting their independence and flexibility *vis-à-vis* a religious establishment which they see as inflexible and out of touch with reality.

All of this explains why modern discussions about sunna, which often seem far removed from real world concerns, are taken so seriously. For the participants in these controversies a great deal is at stake. Parochial as some discussions of sunna might seem, they have a great deal of practical and political relevance. The *ʿulamāʾ* are certainly well aware of the practical importance of the issues surrounding the problem of sunna. Consequently, their reaction against the deniers of ḥadīth has been fierce and sustained and they have spent enormous resources and effort in the defense of sunna.[1]

One reason for the violence of their reaction is that the *ʿulamāʾ* perceive that the ideas of the deniers of ḥadīth have a disproportionate influence on policy. In other words, they connect attacks on ḥadīth with their own alienation from the policy-making process. When Pakistan's President Ayyūb Khān issued a constitution in which the basis of the law was reduced from "the Qur'ān and the sunna" to merely "Islam" it was widely suspected that this was done under the influence of Parwēz's ideas. What other reason could there be to drop sunna from the constitution than to free the interpretation of Islam and the Qur'ān from the restraints of ḥadīth?

The threat of anti-ḥadīth ideas has also been felt in the Pakistani judiciary where the subordination of sunna to the Qur'ān has been used to justify liberalization or reform of Islamic laws. One of Pakistan's more famous high court decisions was based largely on the subordination of Prophetic authority to the authority of the Qur'ān. The case involved a custody dispute, but the details are of little concern. Much more interesting is Justice Muḥammad Shafiʿ's systematic subordination of sunna, not just on the basis of the unreliability of ḥadīth, but on theological grounds.

The words and actions of the Prophet, he argues, are not to be confused with revelation. The Prophet was worthy of great respect but he was nevertheless a mere human being.[2] Although protected from grave sins, he was not perfect and his example was never intended to be obeyed in detail. When the Qur'ān demands obedience to the Prophet, "all it means is that one should be as honest, as steadfast, as earnest and as religious and pious as he was and not that we should act and think exactly as he did because that is unnatural and humanly impossible and if we attempted to do that, life will become absolutely difficult."[3]

Other themes characteristic of the Ahl-i-Qur'ān are also reflected in this decision. Justice Shafiʿ stresses the sufficiency of the Qur'ān, for example, and argues that the Qur'ān is revealed "in very simple language so that it may be understood by all."[4] Every believer, he insists, must have the right to read and interpret the Qur'ān for him- or herself. No interpretation can be considered binding.[5] Where legal matters are concerned, when an agreed-upon standard is necessary, the Qur'ān should be interpreted on democratic principles – its interpretation should be based on the will of the majority.

These examples show the degree to which issues related to sunna have penetrated political and legal discourse in Pakistan. The relevance of sunna in the sphere of law is especially evident in Pakistan's experiment with the revival of Islamic law, and especially in the work of the Federal Shariat Court (FSC). The FSC, established in 1980 by the regime of General Muḥammad Zia al-Ḥaqq, was one of the key institutions of Zia's program of Islamization, an initiative intended *prima facie* to reestablish Islamic norms in Pakistan.[6] The court was established with a twofold jurisdiction. First, it was to serve as a criminal appellate court for cases tried under the newly enacted Hadood (*ḥudūd*) Ordinances.[7] Second, within carefully defined limits, it was empowered to "examine and decide the question whether or not any law or provision of law is repugnant to the Injunctions of Islam as laid down in the Holy Quran and the Sunnah of the Holy Prophet."[8] Thus the primary *raison d'être* of the FSC is to give effect to a collection of clauses that have appeared in each of Pakistan's three constitutions calling upon the government to take steps "to enable Muslims of Pakistan, individually and collectively, to order their lives in accordance with the fundamental principles and basic concepts of Islam," and requiring that all laws be brought "into conformity with the Injunctions of Islam as laid down in the Holy Quran and Sunnah."[9]

The constitutional mandate of the FSC required its justices to judge the compatibility with Islam of any law brought before them on the basis of two standards, the Qur'ān and the sunna. The position of the Qur'ān at least, if not its interpretation, is not open to question. Arguments from

Qur'ānic texts were thus limited to questions of exegesis and hermeneutics. The position of the sunna has been more problematic. The definition of sunna, the problem of authenticating ḥadīth, and the question of the relative authority of sunna *vis-à-vis* the Qur'ān immediately became matters of controversy before the court.

The problem of sunna came most dramatically to the fore when the FSC took up the question of *rajm* (stoning to death) as a penalty for adultery.[10] *Rajm* was introduced as a penalty by the Hadood Ordinances, which were enacted by the Zia regime in 1979. The new law was very soon challenged before the FSC on the grounds that the penalty for stoning violated a clear statement of the Qur'ān: "The woman and the man guilty of adultery or fornication – Flog each of them with a hundred stripes" (24:2). In its first decision on the case, the court departed from Islamic juristic tradition and held, by a four-to-one majority, that the Qur'ān, which appears to prescribe one hundred lashes for adultery, and makes no mention of *rajm*, must be given priority over traditions that support the more severe penalty. Faced with an apparent conflict between the Qur'ān and *aḥādīth* the justices argued that the sunna must be interpreted in the light of the Qur'ān and not vice versa. According to Justice Salahuddin Ahmed:

> That the Holy Qur'ān and the Sunnah constitute the Injunctions of Islam is not in dispute. A Muslim must believe in both and must obey Allah and follow the Prophet. The Ahadith, however, must be considered in the light of the Qur'ān, and they do require careful scrutiny as to their authenticity, contents and context, and whether they are consistent with reason.

If the Qur'ān gives a clear command, it is unthinkable that the Prophet would have deviated from it. For, "to say that the Holy Prophet and his successors continued to award 'rajam' to married persons simply amounts to saying that they defied the Holy Qur'an."[11]

Several different arguments were adopted to justify the decision. Some justices attempted to discredit the *aḥādīth* concerning *rajm* as inauthentic; others sought to prove that all of the occasions on which the Prophet prescribed *rajm* preceded the revelation of the Qur'ānic verse in question, i.e., the sunna was abrogated by the Qur'ān; one argued that *rajm* was prescribed by the Prophet, but only as an enhanced sentence for particularly heinous sexual crimes. The general tenor of the Court's reasoning is illustrated in the following statement of Justice Salahuddin Ahmed:

> Apart from the fact that Hadith cannot override the definite and clear injunctions of the Qur'ān, the Ahadith [particular to the case] themselves suffer from infirmities . . . In this circumstance it is neither safe nor reasonable to found a grave punishment like that of [*rajm*] on such Ahadith and make it an obligatory rule of law.[12]

One option explicitly rejected by all of the justices was the possibility that the sunna of the Prophet might abrogate the Qurʾānic injunction. They agreed that abrogation of Qurʾān by sunna is impossible.

In the light of the foregoing chapters, the echoes in this decision of many of the themes introduced by the Ahl-i-Qurʾān hardly need to be pointed out. The result was both ironic and a major embarrassment – an Islamic court created by the regime had struck down one of the showcase laws of Zia's Islamization program. The government moved swiftly to ensure that the decision was reversed; the court was reorganized, the most liberal justices were replaced, *ʿulamāʾ* were included on the court for the first time, and the FSC was given the power to review and reverse its own decisions.[13] A bench of the revamped court heard the case and reversed the decision on the basis of a technicality: the law, as it turned out, was excluded from the jurisdiction of the court because it fell into the category of Muslim personal law, and the constitution excluded Muslim personal law from the purview of the FSC.

Before this technical loophole was discovered, however, the court had already reconsidered the case on its merits. The majority argued that the previous bench had been misguided in trying to effect a reconciliation between the Qurʾān and sunna. The court had no mandate either to distinguish between Qurʾān and sunna or to attempt their reconciliation. When the constitution gave the court the mandate to judge laws on the basis of "the Qurʾān and the Sunnah," it meant that either the Qurʾān or the sunna would do; if a basis could be found in either source, the law must be allowed to stand. The court found a theoretical foundation for this argument in the classical theory of the relationship of Qurʾān and sunna: the example of the Prophet is the most reliable commentary on the Qurʾān, ḥadīth has a binding character like the Qurʾān, and *ṣaḥīḥ* ḥadīth must therefore be accepted even in the face of apparent conflict.

The centrality of sunna for the FSC, and the record of the court in dealing with the issue, illustrates the significance of disagreements about sunna for any attempt to revive Islamic law. The FSC case also illustrates the important function of sunna as a legitimizing principle. Sunna has become the battleground where conflicts over myriad details of Islamic law are waged. These conflicts, in turn, affect how sunna is viewed. The controversy over *rajm* illustrates this process. Public discourse on the issue shows that those who opposed *rajm* had a variety of reasons for their opposition: they thought the penalty cruel and barbaric, they considered stoning anachronistic in a modern society, they feared such a penalty made Pakistan appear backward. The rules of debate, however, required that the issue be discussed in terms of sunna. Consequently, those who opposed *rajm* had to show that the penalty was not, in fact, sunna. They could do this only by asserting the superiority of the Qur'ān over sunna, by discrediting the particular traditions cited in support of *rajm*, by applying the doctrine of *naskh*, or by substituting an alternative definition of sunna.

Why is sunna such a universal legitimizing principle? The answer is to be found by considering the place of prophecy in the structure of Islamic religious thought. In times of uncertainty and flux, it is natural for Muslims to look for guidance to the one era of certainty and stability, the time of the Prophet. The central event of Islam was the bringing of revelation; guidance from God came at a particular period in human history, during the span of a single lifetime. Hence Muslims are inevitably drawn to that period in history for guidance in how to order their affairs and guidance in how to understand God's revelation. Consequently, sunna gains tremendous stature as a source of religious authority and as the source of continuity with the past, with the whole of Islamic history, but especially with the time of the Prophet. Dealing with sunna, whether by using it selectively, rejecting it, or reinterpreting it, is therefore essential to any effort by Muslims to adjust to changed circumstances.

The centrality of sunna as a symbol of authority, legitimacy, and continuity with an ideal past helps to explain one of the most extraordinary characteristics of modern discussions of sunna – that not even the most radical deniers of ḥadīth seem to reject the essential idea underlying sunna. None of the participants in the debates I have described contend that the Prophet's example is completely irrelevant. The most radical of the deniers of ḥadīth, Parwēz, far from rejecting the example of the Prophet, makes his interpretation of the Prophetic mission the underpinning of an elaborate theory of the Islamic state. Even Muslim secularists defend their secularist ideology by claiming they are in fact following the example of the Prophet. Muḥammad, as it turns out, was an ardent secularist. Secularists, Ahl-i-Qur'ān, and *ʿulamāʾ* all claim to be acting in the spirit of the Prophet, following the true sunna. Thus they all demonstrate that an appeal to the example of the Prophet is the only way to justify the claim that an idea is authentically Islamic.

Just as in pre-Shāfiʿī discussions of sunna, modern Muslims are at odds over *how* to emulate the Prophet but not over *whether* to do so. Modern discussions of sunna are, in fact, a mirror of early discussions of sunna recorded in al-Shāfiʿī's work. The parallels between medieval and modern discussions of sunna are striking; in all discussions of sunna approaches to sunna have tended to fall into certain well-defined patterns. The arguments of Parwēz closely follow the approach of the *ahl al-kalām*, who sought to discredit the historicity of ḥadīth and to subordinate it to the Qur'ān. Mawdūdī and Ghazālī emulate the eclectic approach of the *ahl al-ra'y*, insisting on a high degree of latitude in their approach to ḥadīth. The Ahl-i-Ḥadīth resemble the Ẓahirīs in many respects. The reason that ancient and modern debates about sunna look so similar is quite simply that modern interpreters of sunna have quite consciously reached back into the tradition to justify their viewpoints. Hence we find even ardent deniers of ḥadīth appealing to ḥadīth to support their arguments. The sunna becomes the battleground even for controversies about how to understand the sunna itself.

The fact that all parties to these controversies over sunna root their arguments in the tradition itself underlines a point made at the beginning of this study: that controversies over sunna should not be interpreted heuristically, as part of a struggle between modernity and tradition or reason and revelation. Even the most radical of the deniers of ḥadīth come to their position not by opposing reason to revelation, but by taking an essentially scripturalist position to its logical extreme. The chief concern of all of the parties to the debate, in fact, is to prove themselves true to the tradition. One could certainly argue that there are many more elements of rationalist thought in Parwēz than, for example, in his opponents among the Ahl-i-Ḥadīth, but this would be missing the point. Any clear-minded analysis of Parwēz's thought must conclude that he is not a rationalist but a scripturalist. He does not oppose reason to tradition, but scripture to tradition. Consequently he is, in reality, just as much a traditionist as his opponents; he merely appeals to a different part of the tradition. Discussions about sunna should be understood as battles internal to the tradition over the right to interpret that same tradition.

The direction of change

The universal importance of sunna as a problem for Muslims should not be taken to imply that the contours of debates over sunna have not changed. Debates over the authority of sunna are, in fact, contests for the right to interpret Islamic norms; consequently the debates are region or country specific, arise out of issues of local concern, and reflect the interests of particular political or religious groups. The way the issue was debated in Lahore and Amritsar in the 1920s, where the debate was driven by issues of communal identity, was significantly different from the interchanges between Parwēz and Mawdūdī during the 1950s and 1960s. Similarly, the way controversies over sunna were played out in Egypt has been different from the way the issue has been dealt with in Pakistan, as we have had occasion to note.

What is the direction and nature of change in ideas about sunna? Have modern controversies over sunna shown any promise of leaving behind lasting changes in the way Muslims think about the problem of sunna? One thing should be immediately clear: the problem of sunna has lost none of its importance; in the context of efforts in both Pakistan and Egypt to revive Islamic law, questions related to sunna are more relevant than ever. Curiously, however, the sort of radical rejection of ḥadīth that initiated debates over sunna at the beginning of the twentieth century has borne little fruit. Outright denial of the authority or authenticity of ḥadīth, such as we find among the Ahl-i-Qur'ān, Parwēz, or Abū Rayya has never attracted a significant following. It is true that the ideas of the deniers have made a significant impact on Islamic discourse, particularly in the Subcontinent, but this influence is indirect and should not be exaggerated. A casual acquaintance with current religious thought in Pakistan and Egypt is sufficient to give assurance that the sort of ideas proposed by individuals such as Parwēz or Abū Rayya are not taking the Islamic world by storm. Even in Pakistan, where the movement was strongest, its strength has faded. Anti-ḥadīth tendencies are still represented institutionally, in the Idara-yi Tuluʿ-i-Islām, but with none of the vigor or creativity that characterized the movement during the 1950s and 1960s when Ghulām Aḥmad Parwēz was at the center of religious controversy. The reversal of the FSC's *rajm* decision may be taken as a further sign that in the current political and intellectual environment of Pakistan such ideas wield little influence. In contemporary Egypt anti-ḥadīth ideas are not publicly represented at all. Even by the most generous measure, taking into account even the intangible effects that anti-ḥadīth ideas may have had on attitudes toward sunna in Egypt and Pakistan, the anti-ḥadīth movement can hardly be considered the wave of the future.

But this is not to say that the ideas of the deniers have been without effect. Although their position was defeated, the deniers of ḥadīth set the terms of debate and established the centrality of sunna in modern Muslim discourse. This effect is particularly evident in the subtle effect of anti-ḥadīth views on more moderate thinkers, especially Mawdūdī, who was influenced in significant ways through his polemics with the deniers of ḥadīth. Moreover, the contemporary preoccupation of Muslim thinkers with issues of tradition and its authority is understandable only in the context of the controversy inaugurated by the ideas of writers such as Parwēz and Fazlur Rahman.

The center of controversy in debates about sunna has shifted, however, from the deniers of ḥadīth to the revivalists. Ghazālī's book and the vigorous response to it, both positive and negative, provide ample evidence of the vitality of the approach he represents. Both the enthusiasm and the controversy it has stirred suggest that his ideas are significant. Moreover, revivalist approaches to sunna illustrate an important, but seldom represented, face of Islamic revivalism. Westerners often perceive Muslim revivalist movements as prone to violence, hostile to western geopolitical interests, and committed to a reactionary social agenda – and so they sometimes are. But even if these images are not entirely false, they miss the point. What gives revivalist movements their strength is simply the fact that they promise to bring Islam back to life. They claim to represent a vision of renewed Islam which is not only authentic to the ideal Islamic past but also adapted to the modern situation of Muslims. Reality belies the common stereotype of Islamic revivalism as a defensive and reactionary movement, born of frustration, anger, and fear at the encroachment of western cultural values. The revivalist approach to sunna promises flexibility and relevance combined with authenticity. It is an approach well suited to the increasing demands in both Pakistan and Egypt for a vision of society that is at once authentic to Islam and adapted to the modern situation.

It is in this direction that we should look for clues about the ways in which Muslim ideas about religious authority are evolving. The revivalist approaches to sunna we have examined are forward looking and confident rather than defensive. They are born not of fear for the survival of Islam, but of the assurance that it is growing stronger. It is precisely because Islam is regaining initiative that a blueprint is needed to guide the process.

Notes

INTRODUCTION: THE PRISM OF MODERNITY

1. *Encyclopedia of Religion and Ethics*, ed. James Hastings, s.v. Tradition.
2. This recognition has become a commonplace of contemporary scholarship. E.g., Marilyn Robinson Waldman, "Tradition as a Modality of Change: Islamic Examples," *History of Religions* 25 (1986): 318–340; Jean Camaroff, "Missionaries and Mechanical Clocks," *Journal of Religion* 71 (1991): 1–17.
3. Albert Hourani, *Arabic Thought in the Liberal Age, 1798–1939* (Cambridge, 1983), iv–vii.

1 THE RELEVANCE OF THE PAST

1. al-Jurjānī, *Kitāb al-Taʿrīfāt* (Cairo, 1321 A.H.), s.v. Sunna. This study is concerned with Sunni ideas about Prophetic sunna. While imāmī Shīʿī approaches to ḥadīth and sunna overlap with Sunni concerns in many respects, the structure of religious authority in Shīʿī Islam developed in different directions.
2. This assertion has the following implications: first, it *is possible* to achieve knowledge of sunna through the study of ḥadīth; that is, ḥadīth properly approached represents a trustworthy agency for the transmission of sunna; and second, sunna can *only* be arrived at through the agency of ḥadīth ; apart from ḥadīth there is no way of achieving trustworthy knowledge of sunna. These topics are taken up in detail in chapter 5.
3. There is some discussion in classical sources about whether sunna should be classified as *ilhām* (inspiration) rather than *waḥy*. *Ilhām* represents personal inspiration and is especially associated with the ṣūfī tradition. It differs from *waḥy* in being less direct and offering less certainty of knowledge. See William Graham, *Divine Word and Prophetic Word in Early Islam: A reconsideration of the Sources with Special Reference to the Divine Saying or Hadith Qudsi* (The Hague, 1977), 35; al-Jurjānī, *Kitāb al-Taʿrīfāt,* s.v. *'Ilhām'*; *Encyclopaedia of Islam*, ed. D. B. MacDonald (Leiden, 1913–1938; 1st edn., henceforth EI^1), s. v. *Ilhām.* In classical scholarship the difference seems to have been of little consequence for the authority of sunna; in either case, it was of supernatural origin.
4. Joseph Schacht, *The Origins of Muhammadan Jurisprudence* (Oxford, 1950; repr. 1964), esp. 6–20 and 133–137; Ignaz Goldziher, *The Ẓāhirīs: Their Doctrine and their History*, trans. and ed. Wolfgang Behn (Leiden, 1971), 20

ff.; Noel Coulson, *A History of Islamic Law* (Edinburgh, 1964; 1978), 53–61. For a qualification of the view of al-Shāfiʿī I have presented here, see Wael B. Hallaq, "Was al-Shāfiʿī the Master Architect of Islamic Jurisprudence?" *International Journal of Middle East Studies* 25 (1993): 587–605.

5. G. H. A. Juynboll, "Some New Ideas on the Development of Sunna as a Technical Term in Early Islam," *Jerusalem Studies in Arabic and Islam* 10 (1987): 108.
6. Muḥammad b. Idrīs al-Shāfiʿī, *Kitāb al-Risāla*, ed. Muḥammad Shākir (Cairo, 1940), 84. In arguing this position Shāfiʿī was refuting an unnamed interlocutor who altogether rejected the authority of sunna and proposed reliance upon the Qurʾān as the sole and sufficient locus of divine authority.
7. Schacht, *Origins*, 58–81.
8. M. M. Bravmann, *The Spiritual Background of Early Islam: Studies in Ancient Arab Concepts* (Leiden, 1972), 152.
9. *Ibid.*, 155.
10. *Pace* Margoliouth and Schacht who base their argument on false etymologies. Margoliouth, basing his argument on citations from al-Ṭabarī, contends that sunna means "beaten track" and that it implies, in a social context, well-established norms or practices (i.e., custom). D. S. Margoliouth, *The Early Development of Muhammedanism* (New York, 1914), 69; Muḥammad b. Jarīr al-Ṭabarī, *Annales* [*Taʾrīkh al-rusul waʾl mulūk*], ed. M. J. de Goeje (Leiden, 1879–1901) II, 885; Ibn Manẓūr, *Lisān al-ʿArab* (Cairo, 1300–1308 A.H.), XIII, 224. Joseph Schacht adopted Margoliouth's arguments to support his thesis, and argued in his *Origins of Muhammadan Jurisprudence* that for both the pre-Islamic Arabs and the early Muslims "sunna" meant not the specific example of Muḥammad but rather the "accepted practice," the well-trodden path of the community. In Schacht's view, this meaning was adopted and applied by the early schools of jurisprudence and it was not until the time of al-Shāfiʿī that the identification of sunna with specific precedents of Muḥammad took hold. The root meaning of sunna, according to this view, is the "traditional usage of the community" and sunna is linked primarily to the norms of the group rather than to the specific example of an outstanding individual. See Schacht, *Origins*, 3.
11. Juynboll, "Development of Sunna as a Technical Term," 100.
12. That is, if one accepts the traditional outline of Muḥammad's career. Fazlur Rahman argues that "it would be a great childishness of the twentieth century to suppose that people immediately around the Prophet distinguished so radically between the Qurʾān and its exemplification in the Prophet that they retained the one but ignored the other." Fazlur Rahman, *Islamic Methodology in History* (Karachi, 1965), 9.
13. The root S-N-N occurs on sixteen occasions in the Qurʾān, but curiously it is never linked with Muḥammad. Its use is confined primarily to two contexts: (1) warnings to take heed of the sunna of earlier peoples who incurred judgment (most often *sunnat al-awwalīn*: 3:137, 4:26, 8:38, 15:13, 18:55, 33:38, 33:62, 35:43); and (2) statements about the pattern of God's dealings with man (*sunnat Allāh* – usually in the context of God's judgment: 33:62, 35:43, 40:85, 48:23). These uses seem to be somewhat anomalous to the

general development of the idea of sunna. The intention behind the use of the term in the Qur'ān seems to be to illustrate the breaking down of the old order and the establishment of a new. The Qur'ānic connection between sunna and judgment may be viewed as a condemnation of the intransigence of Muḥammad's opponents, based as it was on their attachment to pagan sunna. Pagan sunna is thus contrasted with the sunna of God, who brings judgment upon those who reject His guidance.

14. Rahman, *Methodology,* 7. See also Zafar Ishaq Ansari, "Islamic Juristic Terminology before Safi'i: A Semantic Analysis with Special Reference to Kufa," *Arabica* 19 (1972): 262–263.
15. But it would be precipitate to suggest that Schacht was entirely wrong. While the notion of Prophetic sunna did originate earlier than he thought, its meaning was quite distinct from later notions of Prophetic sunna.
16. Schacht, *Origins*, 12.
17. Juynboll, "Development of Sunna as a Technical Term," 108.
18. For discussion of caliphal sunna and an argument for its importance see Patricia Crone and Martin Hinds, *God's Caliph: Religious Authority in the First Centuries of Islam* (Cambridge, 1986), 43–57.
19. Muḥammad Ibn Saʿd, *Kitāb al-Ṭabaqāt al-Kabīr,* ed. E. Sachau (Leiden, 1904–1940), III/1, 248: "*In astakhlif fa sunnatun wa'illa astakhlif fa sunnatun.*"
20. "*wa kullun sunnatun.*" The tradition is quoted by Abū Yūsuf, *Kitāb al-Kharāj* (Cairo, 1302 A.H.), 99. See Schacht, *Origins*, 75, and Bravmann, *Spiritual Background*, 132.
21. Abū Yūsuf, *Kitāb al-Kharāj*, 99. Quoted in Bravmann, *Spiritual Background*, 132.
22. Ibn Saʿd, *Ṭabaqāt,* III/1, 243. Cf. G. H. A. Juynboll, *Muslim Tradition: Studies in Chronology, Provenance and Authorship of Early Hadith* (Cambridge, 1983); Juynboll, "Development of Sunna as a Technical Term," 101.
23. For further development of the argument that the sunna of the Prophet did not hold any special place *vis-à-vis* other sunna see Crone and Hinds, *God's Caliph*, 50–55 and throughout; Juynboll, "Development of Sunna as a Technical Term," 96–118.
24. It is presumably this use of the term by al-Ṭabarī that led Margoliouth to conclude that "sunna" in the early period was equivalent to "accepted practice" or "custom." See Margoliouth, *Early Development of Muhammedanism*, 69.
25. Crone and Hinds, *God's Caliph*, 66. That the term sunna, when used in a political context, often symbolized justice or right practice in a general sense can be further demonstrated from its use in the arbitration agreement that followed the battle of Ṣiffīn where it occurs in the phrase "*al-sunna al-ʿādila al-jamiʿa ghayr al mufarriqa.*" For the meaning of sunna in this context see Martin Hinds, "The Siffin Arbitration Agreement," *Journal of Semitic Studies* 17 (1972): 93–129.
26. H. Ritter, "Studien zur Geschichte der islamischen Frömmigkeit," *Der Islam* 21 (1933): 65, lines 7–9. See pp. 62–64 for a discussion of this early theological epistle and its attribution; Julian Obermann, "Political Theology in Early Islam," *Journal of the American Oriental Society* 55 (1925): 138–62; Schacht, *Origins*, 74, 141, 229; Josef van Ess, "ʿUmar II and his Epistle

against the Qadariyya," *Abr Nahrain* 1 (1971–1972): 20 ff; Michael Cook, *Early Muslim Dogma* (Cambridge, 1981), 117–123; John Wansbrough, *Qur'anic Studies* (Oxford, 1977), 160–163. The resolution of the problem of attribution does not influence the present argument. Regardless of the authorship or dating of these documents, they clearly represent pre-technical uses of the term "sunna."

27. Wansbrough, *Qur'anic Studies*, 160–163. Wansbrough argues on this basis that the epistle is a product of third-century *uṣūl* controversies.
28. The *Kitāb al-Irjā'* of al-Ḥasan b. Muḥammad b. al-Ḥanafiyya, ed. van Ess in *Arabica* 21 (1974): 20–52; the first letter of Ibn Ibād to ʿAbd al-Malik discussed by Joseph Schacht, "Sur l'expression 'Sunna du Prophet'," in *Mélanges d'orientalisme offerts à Henri Masse* (Teheran, 1963), 361–365; and the *Risāla* of Abū Ḥanīfa addressed to ʿUthmān al-Battī in *Kitāb al-ʿālim wa'l-mutaʿāllim*, ed. M. Z. al-Kawthari (Cairo, 1368 A.H.), 34–38.
29. Harald Motzki, "The Muṣannaf of ʿAbd al-Razzāq al-Sanʿānī as a Source of Authentic Aḥādīth of the First Century A.H.," *Journal of Near Eastern Studies* 50 (1991): 21.
30. *Ibid.*
31. Ignaz Goldziher, *Muhammedanische Studien* (Leiden, 1896), trans. S. M. Stern as *Muslim Studies* (London, 1967), 24–25.
32. Juynboll, "Development of Sunna as a Technical Term," 113–117.
33. For the essential unity of Qur'ān and Prophetic sunna in the perception of early Muslims see Graham, *Divine Word and Prophetic Word*. For a different approach which nevertheless yields similar conclusions see Wansbrough, *Quranic Studies*, 176. Wansbrough argues that the full canonization of Qur'ānic material whereby it was clearly distinguished from other elements of the tradition was completed much later than had been thought. On the failure of early Muslims to distinguish sharply between prophetic sunna and other sunnas see my discussion above and Juynboll, "Development of Sunna as a Technical Term," 96–118. On the importance of caliphal sunna see Crone and Hinds, *God's Caliph*, 43–57.
34. In rejecting ḥadīth as representative of true sunna the *ahl al-kalām* were preceded by certain of the Khawārij, who adopted the slogan "*la ḥukm illa li Allah*" in their rejection of the authority of the caliphal state. Crone and Hinds, *God's Caliph*, 57 and 63 n. 4; Michael Cook and Patricia Crone, *Hagarism: The Making of the Islamic World* (Cambridge/New York, 1977), 27; Gianroberto Scarcia, "Scambio," *Annali Dell'Istituto Universitario Orientale di Napoli*, NS 14 (1964): 636.
35. Muḥammad b. Idrīs al-Shāfiʿī, *Kitāb al-umm* (Cairo, 1321–1325 A. H.), VII, 250.
36. *Ibid.*
37. John Burton, *The Collection of the Qur'an* (Cambridge/New York, 1977), 19.
38. Ibn Qutayba, *Kitāb ta'wīl mukhtalif al-Ḥadīth*, trans. Gerard Lecomte, as *Le Traité des Divergences du Hadit d'Ibn Qutayba* (Damascus, 1962), 6–8. We find unmistakable echoes of this viewpoint in many modern criticisms of ḥadīth.
39. *Ibid.*, 251.

40. Charles Pellat, *Le Milieu Baṣrien et la formation de Ǧāḥiẓ* (Paris, 1953), 83.
41. Two doctrines in particular, the belief that the Qur'ān is uncreated (*ghayr makhlūq*) and the doctrine of its inimitability (*iʿjāz*), emphasize the unique and unparalleled position of the Qur'ān. The controversy over whether or not the Qur'ān was created was a major issue between the Muʿtazila and their traditionist opponents led by Aḥmad b. Ḥanbal (d. 241/855). The controversy came to a climax in 218/833 with the famous inquisition (*miḥna*) of al-Maʿmūn which required officials to profess the Muʿtazilite doctrine of the createdness of the Qur'ān. The doctrine of *iʿjāz al-Qur'ān* – that the Qur'ān was a miracle (*muʿjiza*) given by God to Muḥammad in proof of the Prophetic office – arose around the same time. At the core of this doctrine was the argument that the Qur'ān was unsurpassed and unsurpassable in beauty, eloquence, and style. The inability of any challenger to match its eloquence serves as proof of its divine and miraculous origin. Both of these doctrines serve to elevate the Qur'ān and to emphasize its unique status and divine origin. A. T. Welch, "The Qur'ān in Muslim Life and Thought," in *Encyclopaedia of Islam,* ed. H. A. R. Gibb (et al.) (Leiden, 1960–; 2nd edn., henceforth *EI*[2]), s. v. "Kur'ān."
42. Dārimī, Muqaddima, 49. Aḥmad b. Ḥanbal, *Musnad* (Cairo, 1312–1313 A.H.), IV, 126. Wensinck, *A Handbook of Early Muhammadan Tradition, Alphabetically Arranged* (Leiden, 1927; repr. 1971), 556.
43. Ibn ʿAbd al-Barr, *Jāmiʿ* (Cairo, 1346 A.H.), II, 191.
44. On the identification of sunna with revelation among early Muslims see Graham, *Divine Word and Prophetic Word. Pace* Burton, *Collection,* who argues that Qur'ānic revelation was canonized early and from the start held a unique position. The elevation of sunna to the status of revelation was, in this view, a late development. Goldziher also held this position. It is my contention that the tendency to identify sunna with revelation came early, as Graham argues, while the formal doctrine, which is what the ḥadīth literature reflects, came much later.
45. Discussions about whether sunna should be considered *waḥy* or *ilhām* should be kept in mind, however. See n. 3 above.
46. al-Shāfiʿī, *Kitāb al-umm,* VII, 271.
47. The fullest treatment of this subject is John Burton, *The Sources of Islamic Law* (Edinburgh, 1990). The argument that certain verses of the Qur'ān were abrogated by others is an exegetical technique traceable to the earliest *tafsīr* literature. The technique was adopted and given technical definition by legal scholars. Its use is evident in the earliest extant work of jurisprudence, Mālik's *Muwaṭṭa'*, and the principle is well developed in Muḥammad b. al-Ḥasan al-Shaybānī, *Kitāb al-Siyār al-Kabīr* (Hyderabad, 1335–1336 A. H.),I, 68.
48. Burton, *Collection,* 55.
49. Ibn Qutayba, *Kitāb ta'wīl mukhtalif al-Ḥadīth,* 217, 232.
50. al-Ghazālī, *Kitāb al-Mustaṣfā* (Cairo, 1322 A.H.), I, 125. The translation is from Burton, *Collection,* 57.
51. Burton, *Collection,* 18.
52. On the many ways that the orthodox schools mitigated the impact of traditions see Goldziher, *The Ẓāhirīs,* 63–80.

53. *Ibid.*, 63.
54. Muslim, Kitāb al-faḍā᾿il, 31.
55. Bukhārī, Janā᾿iz, 32, 33, 44.
56. Burton, *Collection*, 14–15.
57. Marshall Hodgson, *The Venture of Islam* (Chicago, 1974), I, 160.

2 THE EMERGENCE OF MODERN CHALLENGES TO TRADITION

1. The Ḥaramayn, the holy cities of Mecca and Medina, played a special role in the development of eighteenth-century reform. Mecca and Medina provided the atmosphere in which trends in progress in various parts of the Islamic world could coalesce and prosper. The Subcontinent had already felt the effects of the reformist movement of Shaykh Aḥmad Sirhindī (d. 1624) and the reformist branch of the Naqshbandī order which he inaugurated. In the central Islamic lands Ḥanbalī ideas and particularly the purificationist thought of Ibn Taymiyya survived despite Ottoman patronage of the Ḥanafī school, while in West Africa a tradition of ḥadīth scholarship was maintained which was based on the study of Mālik's *Muwaṭṭa᾿*. See John Obert Voll, *Islam: Continuity and Change in the Modern World* (Boulder, 1982), 53–67; John Obert Voll, "Hadith Scholars and Tariqahs: An Ulama Group in the 18th Century Haramayn and their Impact in the Islamic World," *Journal of Asian and African Studies* 15 (1980): 264–73; Rudolph Peters, "Idjtihād and Taqlīd in 18th and 19th Century Islam," *Die Welt Des Islams* 20 (1980): 131–145.
2. For Shāh Walī Allāh's biography see Aziz Ahmad, *Studies in Islamic Culture in the Indian Environment* (London, 1964), 201–209; S. M. Ikrām, *Rūd-i-Kawthar* (Lahore, 1968), 527–568; G. N. Jalbani, *Life of Shah Waliyullah* (Lahore, 1978); S. A. A. Rizvi, *Shāh Walī Allāh and His Times* (Canberra, 1980). For considerations of his religious thought see J. M. S. Baljon, *Religion and Thought of Shāh Walī Allāh Dihlawī, 1703–1762* (Leiden, 1986). Marcia K. Hermansen, "Shāh Walī Allāh's Theory of Religion in *Ḥujjat Allāh al-Bāligha*" (Ph.D. thesis, University of Chicago, 1982); Mohammad Daud Rahbar, "Shah Wali Ullah and Ijtihad," *Muslim World* 45 (1955): 44–48. For discussions of his relationship with the tradition of ḥadīth studies in the Ḥijāz see the works by Voll and Peters cited in n. 2 above.
3. Shāh Walī Allāh, *Izālat al-khafā᾿ ʿan khilāfat al-khulafā᾿* (Bareli, 1869), I, 260. Cited in Baljon, *Religion and Thought*, 122.
4. Ikrām, *Rūd-i-Kawthar*, 543.
5. Shāh Walī Allāh, *Ḥujjat Allāh al-Bāligha*, (Delhi, 1954), I, 2; Baljon, *Religion and Thought*, 152.
6. This position was not a new one in the Subcontinent. The tradition of ḥadīth studies established by ʿAbd al-Ḥaqq Dihlawī had tended to emphasize this point and Shāh Walī Allāh himself claims to have been a "*ghayr muqallid*" before traveling to the Ḥijāz. His experience in the Ḥijāz apparently had a moderating influence on this aspect of his thought; he came away convinced of the value of the law schools and committed to discovering their relative merits.

7. Based on the tradition "I am only a Human being; whenever I give a command in religious matters, you should obey it, but whenever I give you a direction based on my personal opinion, then keep in mind that I am only a human being." Muslim, Faḍā'il, 140. Walī Allāh, *Ḥujjat Allāh,* I, 128. Baljon, *Religion and Thought,* 155.
8. Mohammed Iqbal, *Reconstruction of Religious Thought in Islam* (London: Oxford University Press, 1934), 163.
9. Shawkānī, a Yemenite scholar and the chief *qāḍī* of Yemen from 1795 until his death, came from a Zaydī background but rejected strict adherence to Zaydī views in favor of *ijtihād.* He was a contemporary of Muḥammad b. ʿAbd al-Wahhāb and had contact with the first Saʿūdī state but he came to his views quite independently of this movement. Indeed, both Ibn ʿAbd al-Wahhāb and Shawkānī were later products of the same reformist movement in the Ḥijāz which had influenced Shāh Walī Allāh. The most extensive, though uncritical, account in English of Shawkānī's life is in Husayn b. ʿAbdullah al-ʿAmri, *The Yemen in the 18th and 19th Centuries: A Political and Intellectual History* (London, 1985). On the importance of his ideas see Fazlur Rahman, *Islam* (Chicago, 1979), 196; and Peters, "Idjtihād and Taqlīd," 134.
10. Peters, "Idjtihād and Taqlīd," 138–143.
11. Muḥammad b. ʿAlī al-Shawkānī, *al-Qawl al-mufīd fī ʿadillat al-ijtihād wa al-taqlīd* (Cairo, 1340 A.H.), 12.
12. Muḥammad b. ʿAlī al-Shawkānī, *Nayl al-awṭār* (Cairo, 1347/1928). ʿAbd al-Salām was the grandfather of the better known Taqī al-dīn Aḥmad b. Taymiyya.
13. Shāh Walī Allāh and Shawkānī were by no means alone in their attitudes toward *taqlīd* and *ijtihād* or in their emphasis on ḥadīth. They are introduced here as representatives of and major contributors to a wider trend which also encompassed numerous other scholars both before and after these two figures. These ideas were given special force by their representation in the Wahhābī movement and in the movement of the *mujāhidīn,* activist heirs of Shāh Walī Allāh in India.
14. For development of this argument see H. A. R. Gibb, *Mohammedanism* (Oxford, 1949), 96; George F. Hourani, "The Basis of Authority of Consensus in Sunnite Islam," *Studia Islamica* 21 (1964): 13–60.
15. A useful discussion of the Ahl-i-Ḥadīth in English is in Barbara Daly Metcalf, *Islamic Revival in British India* (Princeton, 1982), 264–296. See also Aziz Ahmad, *Islamic Modernism in India and Pakistan, 1857–1964* (Oxford, 1967); S. M. Ikrām, *Mawj-i-kawthar* (Lahore, 1962), 66; Abū Yaḥyā Imān Khān Nawshahrawī, *Tarājim-i ʿulamāʾ-yi ḥadīth-i Hind* (Delhi, 1356 A.H.); Muḥammad Ibrāhīm Mīr Siālkōṭī, *Tārīkh-i Ahl-i-ḥadīth* (Lahore, 1952); Abū al-Wafāʾ Thanāʾ Allāh Amritsarī, *Ahl-i-Ḥadīth kā madhhab* (Lahore, 1970).
16. For background see Muhammad Hedayatullah, *Sayyid Ahmad: A Study of the Religious Reform Movement of Sayyid Ahmad of Ra'y Bareli* (Lahore, 1970) and Aziz Ahmad, "Le mouvement des mujāhidīn dans l'Inde au XIXe siècle," *Orient* 4 (1960): 105–116. Many of the leaders of the early Ahl-i-Ḥadīth were students of Sayyid Aḥmad of Rā'ē Barēlī's main disciples. See Metcalf, *Islamic Revival,* 275.

17. Hedayatullah, *Sayyid Ahmad*, 144.
18. Ikrām, *Mawj-i-kawthar*, 65.
19. He was the first to use the term Ahl-i-Ḥadīth, in 1864, and he was called *shaykh al-kull* because almost all lines of the Ahl-i-Ḥadīth in northern India trace from him. See Metcalf, *Islamic Revival*, 272 n. 11.
20. For general biographical information on this important figure see the works listed above in n. 9 and Saeedullah, *The Life and Works of Muhammad Siddiq Hasan Khan, Nawab of Bhopal* (Lahore, 1973).
21. Saeedullah, *Life and Works*, 35.
22. Ikrām, *Mawj-i-kawthar*, 66.
23. Ṣiddīq Ḥasan Khān, *al-Tāj al-mukallal min jawāhir ma'āthir al-ṭirāz al-ākhir wa al-awwal* (Bhopal, 1882; repr. Bombay, 1963) 447, 449–450; Saeedullah, *Life and Works*, 36 n. 58.
24. Ṣiddīq Ḥasan Khān, *Kitāb al-mu'taqad al-muntaqad* (Delhi, 1889), 6–14.
25. *Ibid.*
26. Aziz Ahmad, *Islamic Modernism*, 114–115.
27. *Ibid.*, 114.
28. Ṣiddīq Ḥasan Khān, *'Āqibat al-muttaqīn* (Benares, 1904), 3–13. Aziz Ahmad, *Islamic Modernism*, 117.
29. Aziz Ahmad, *Islamic Modernism*, 117.
30. Henri Laoust, *Essai sur les doctrines sociales et politiques de Takī-d-dīn Aḥmad b. Taymīya* (Cairo, 1939), 535; *EI*[2], s.v. al-Alūsī.
31. The term *salafiyya* is used to describe a complex of individuals and movements in the nineteenth- and twentieth-century Islamic world which share certain doctrines and attitudes. Although the term suggests a coherent movement, in actual fact it refers rather to ideological tendencies which emerged in a wide variety of circles and arose out of diverse influences. For general background see Henri Laoust, "Les vraies origines dogmatiques du Wahhabisme: liste des œuvre de son fondateur," *Revue du Monde Musulman* 36 (1918–1919), 320–328; Laoust, *Essai*; *EI*[2], s.v. Islāḥ (by A. Merad). For later manifestations of *salafī* tendencies, especially in the career of Rashīd Riḍā, see Charles C. Adams, *Islam and Modernism in Egypt* (London, 1933); Hourani, *Arabic Thought*; Malcolm Kerr, *Islamic Reform: The Political and Legal Theories of Muhammad Abduh and Rashid Rida* (Berkeley, 1966); Hamid Enayat, *Modern Islamic Political Thought* (Austin, 1982). For a more recent treatment of the *salafiyya* movement in Syria see David Dean Commins, *Islamic Reform: Politics and Social Change in Late Ottoman Syria* (New York, 1990).
32. David Dean Commins, "Religious Reformers and Arabists in Damascus, 1885–1914," *International Journal of Middle Eastern Studies* 18 (1986): 405.
33. For considerations of the role of the *'ulamā'* in eighteenth- and early nineteenth-century Egypt, see Afaf Lutfi al-Sayyid Marsot, "The Ulama of Cairo in the Eighteenth and Nineteenth Centuries," in Nikki R. Keddie, ed. *Scholars, Saints and Sufis* (Berkeley, 1972), 149–165; Afaf Lutfi al-Sayyid Marsot, "The Role of the 'ulamā' in Egypt during the early Nineteenth Century" in P. M. Holt, ed. *Political and Social Change in Modern Egypt* (London, 1968) 264–280; Afaf Lutfi al-Sayyid Marsot, "The Beginnings of Modernization among the Rectors of Al-Azhar," in William R. Polk and

Richard Chambers, eds. *Beginnings of Modernization in the Middle East*, (Chicago, 1968); Stanford J. Shaw, *Ottoman Egypt in the 18th Century* (Cambridge, Mass., 1962). The standard source for this period of Egyptian history is ʿAbd al-Raḥmān al-Jabartī, *ʿAjāʾib al-āthār fī al-tarājim wa al-akhbār* (Cairo, 1882).

34. *EI²*, s.v. Iṣlāḥ.
35. Jamāl al-Dīn al-Qāsimī, *Qawāʿid al-taḥdīth min funūn muṣṭalaḥ al-ḥadīth* (Damascus, 1935). For background on al-Qāsimī see Commins, "Religious Reformers"; Commins, *Islamic Reform.*
36. For Sayyid Aḥmad Khān's biography see Alṭāf Ḥusayn Hālī, *Ḥayāt-i-jawēd* (Cawnpore, 1901; repr. Lahore, 1966). His major writings are collected in *Maqālāt-i-Sar Sayyid*, Ismāʾīl Pānīpatī (Lahore, 1962–1965). Of the many studies on Sayyid Aḥmad Khān's religious thought, the two most important for our purposes are Christian W. Troll, *Sayyid Ahmad Khan: A Reinterpretation of Muslim Theology* (New Delhi, 1978) and B. A. Dar, *Religious Thought of Sayyid Ahmad Khan* (Lahore, 1957). See also J. M. S. Baljon, *Reforms and Religious Ideas of Sir Sayyid Aḥmad Khān* (Lahore, 1964).
37. Both his mother, ʿAzīz al-Nisā Bēgam, and his father, Sayyid Muḥammad Mīr Muttaqī, were devotees of the Naqshbandī shaykh Shāh Ghulām ʿAlī (d. 1824), who was known for his strict opposition to popular cult practices in Indian Islam. His father also had close connections with another important successor to Shaykh Aḥmad Sirhindī, Mīr Dard (1721–1785). For biographical information on Mīr Dard see Annemarie Schimmel, *Pain and Grace* (Leiden, 1976).
38. Sayyid Aḥmad Khān, *Taṣānīf-i- aḥmadiyya* (Aligarh, 1883), I/1, 3–18.
39. Troll, *Sayyid Ahmad Khan,* 52; Aḥmad Khān, *Maqālāt,* VII, 32.
40. Troll, *Sayyid Ahmad Khan,* xvii.
41. Ikrām, *Mawj-i-kawthar*, 69–70. Citing a letter written in 1895, just three years before his death.
42. The debates that resulted from Pfander's activity were given this label by William Muir. Troll, *Sayyid Ahmad Khan*, 61.
43. Author of the controversial *Life of Mohamet* to which Sayyid Aḥmad Khān replied with *A Series of Essays on the Life of Muhammad and Subjects Subsidiary Thereto* (London, 1870).
44. Troll, *Sayyid Ahmad Khan*, 102. Sprenger's influence was especially important in Sayyid Aḥmad Khān's historical writings, *Athār al-ṣanādīd* (Delhi, 1947; repr. in *Maqālāt,* XVI, 212–284); *Asbāb-i baghāwat-i Hind* (Moradabad, 1858; repr. in *Maqālāt,* IX, 47–124).
45. Sayyid Aḥmad Khān, *Tabyīn al-kalām: The Mohamedan Commentary on the Holy Bible* (Ghazeepore, 1862 and 1865), I, 14.
46. *Ibid.*, I, 16, 22; II, 339 ff., 349.
47. *Ibid.*, I, 14 ff.
48. William Muir, *The Life of Mahomet and the History of Islam to the Era of Hegira* (London, 1861; repr. Osnabruck, 1988), I, xxvii. The emphasis is in the original. Muir's work was first serialized in *Calcutta Review* 19 (January–June, 1853), 1–80. It was written with clear missionary intent and probably grew out of Muir's association with Pfander. (Troll, *Sayyid Ahmad*

Khan, 113.) Muir set out to demonstrate to Muslims the truth about the origins of Islam – origins which he thought would not stand comparison with Christianity. But in taking on this venture he also emphasized the importance of scrupulous fairness and accuracy with regard to sources; otherwise Muslims would reject the work out of hand as prejudiced.

49. *Ibid.*, lxxxvii.
50. *Ibid.*, lxv.
51. *Ibid.*, liii, lv.
52. This was translated into Urdu as *Al-Khuṭbāt al-Aḥmadiyya fī al-ʿArab wa al-sīra al-Muḥammadiyya.*
53. Muḥammad ʿAbduh, *The Theology of Unity*, trans. Kenneth Cragg and Ishaq Masaʿad (London, 1966), 156.
54. *Ibid.*
55. Muḥammad Ḥusayn al-Dhahabī, *al-Tafsīr wa al-mufassirūn* (Cairo, 1961–1962), III, 239. J. J. G. Jansen, *The Interpretation of the Qurʾān in Modern Egypt* (Leiden, 1974), 27.
56. G. H. A. Juynboll, *The Authenticity of the Tradition Literature: Discussions in Modern Egypt* (Leiden, 1969), 18.
57. For general treatments of this movement, see Rāja F. M. Mājid, "Ghulām Jīlānī Barq: A Study in Muslim 'Rationalism'" (M. A. thesis, McGill University, Institute of Islamic Studies, 1962) and Iftikhār Aḥmad Balkhī, *Fitna-i-Inkār-i-ḥadīth kā manẓar-o-pas manẓar* (Karachi, 1955–1960). Brief treatments can be found in Murray Titus, *Indian Islam* (Oxford, 1930) and Aziz Ahmad, *Islamic Modernism*, 120–121.
58. Early adherents of the sect in Lahore came to be known as Chakṟālawīs. The chief biographical source for this figure is in *al-Bayān* (Lahore, March 1952). Mājid, "Ghulām Jīlānī Barq," also provides a brief biographical sketch, based partly on interviews with surviving family members.
59. Khwāja Zia Allāh, *al-Balāgh* (Amritsar, September 1936) claims that this figure was in fact the first to reject ḥadīth and to rely solely on the Qurʾān. Mājid, "Ghulām Jīlānī Barq," 31–34.
60. Mājid, "Ghulām Jīlānī Barq," 31.
61. The book was reportedly translated into Arabic by Muḥammad Aslam Jayrājpūrī as *al-Wirāthāt fī al-Islām* and published in Amritsar.
62. A similar structure may be observed in Ahl-i-Ḥadīth conversion accounts, where the spiritual journey is away from *taqlīd* to pure reliance on ḥadīth. The key element is the shaking off of the restraints of authority and awakening to the truth.
63. Continued as *al-Bayān* after 1937. It continued until 1952 with only a two-year gap following partition (1947–1949), at which time the place of publication moved, with the Anjuman, from Amritsar to Lahore.
64. Murray Titus, *Islam in India and Pakistan* (Calcutta, 1959), 197.
65. Nawshahrawī, *Tarājim*, 314.
66. Muḥammad Ikrām argues that he was not, in fact, a member of the Ahl-i-Qurʾān proper, but simply shared with them certain doctrines (Ikrām, *Mawj-i-kawthar*, 72). However, his associations with the Amritsar group suggest that the connection was more than just a superficial intellectual affinity. We must also allow for the overwhelming tendency in these circles to

claim complete intellectual independence, denying that one's viewpoints are a product of any external influences.

67. Ikrām, *Mawj-i-kawthar*, 70–71.
68. Muḥammad Tawfīq Ṣidqī, "al-Islām huwa al-Qur'ān waḥdahu," *al-Manār* 9 (1906): 515–524. Both the article and the controversy surrounding it are described in Juynboll, *Authenticity*, 23 ff. Biographical information on Ṣidqī may be found in *al-Manār* 21 (1920): 483–495 and in Adams, *Islam and Modernism*, 240.
69. *al-Manār* 9 (1906): 515.
70. This becomes the foundation of the characteristic revivalist approach to sunna, discussed in chapter 5.

3 BOUNDARIES OF REVELATION

1. al-Shāfiʿī, *Risāla*, 223–224.
2. Abū Bakr Muḥammad b. Mūsā b. ʿUthmān b. Ḥazim al-Hamadhānī, *Kitāb al-iʿtibār fi bayān al-nāsikh wa al-mansūkh min al-āthār* (Hyderabad, 1319), 24–25. Cited in Burton, *Collection*, 21.
3. al-Shāfiʿī, *Kitāb al-umm*, VII, 250.
4. Sayyid Aḥmad Khān, *Tafsīr al-Qur'ān* (Aligarh, 1297 A.H.).
5. Sayyid Aḥmad Khān, "Taḥrīr fī uṣūl al-tafsīr" in his *Maqālāt*, II, 197–258.
6. Aḥmad Khān, *Tafsīr*, I, 31–34. Sayyid Aḥmad Khān was by no means strict in the application of this principle, however. While he elevated the Qur'ān above other sources, his approach was that of a speculative rationalist rather than a scripturalist.
7. *Ishāʿat al-Qur'ān* (Lahore, 1921–1925), frontispiece of each issue. The sufficiency of the Qur'ān was a central tenet of the doctrine of the Jamāʿat-i-Ahl-i-Qur'ān, the organization founded by Chakṟālawī. Among the purposes of the organization were the following: "To enlighten the followers of all religions in general, and Muslims in particular, that the Qur'ān alone is a sufficient guide, and that the Book of God does not stand in need of the collections of *ḥadīth* for its interpretation"; and "to proclaim that all books of *tafsīr* fail to interpret the Qur'ān satisfactorily, and that the Qur'ān should be interpreted by its own verses."
8. Muḥammad Aslam Jayrājpūrī, *Taʿlīmāt al-Qur'ān* (Delhi, 1934).
9. ʿInāyat Allāh Khān Mashriqī, *Tadhkira* (Amritsar, 1924), 91. Quoted in Mājid, "Ghulām Jīlānī Barq," 3.
10. ʿAbd Allāh Chakṟālawī, *Tarjumat al-Qur'ān bi āyāt al-furqān* (Lahore, 1906).
11. Jayrājpūrī, *Taʿlīmāt*; Ghulām Aḥmad Parwēz, *Maʿarif al-Qur'ān*. (Karachi, 1949–1958). An important corollary of this approach to Qur'ānic exegesis is the assumption that the Qur'ān does not have a single, fixed meaning. The way is opened, in other words, for a dynamic theory of inspiration according to which the Qur'ān takes on different, yet still authentic, meanings in different circumstances.
12. ʿAbd Allāh Chakṟālawī, *Burhān al-furqān ʿalā ṣalāt al-Qur'ān* (Lahore, n.d.), iii.

13. *Ibid.*, 7–8.
14. *Ibid.*, 292. The square brackets indicating the author's commentary appear in the original. The italics are my own.
15. Mājid, "Ghulām Jīlānī Barq," 34–37 gives a brief biography based on interviews with family members.
16. Mistrī Muḥammad Ramaḍān, *Aqīmū al-ṣalāt* (Gujrānwāla, 1938).
17. Published in Gujrānwāla. In circulation January 1924–December 1926.
18. *Ṭulūʿ-i-Islām* (August 1976): 59.
19. Mawlānā Abū al-Wafāʾ Thanāʾ Allāh Amritsarī, *Dalīl al-furqān bi jawāb Ahl-i-Qurʾān* (Amritsar, 1906).
20. Ṣidqī, "al-Islām huwa al-Qurʾān waḥdahu," 517.
21. Qurʾān 4:101–104.
22. Ṣidqī, "al-Islām huwa al-Qurʾān waḥdahu," 517–520.
23. *Ibid.*, 521–522.
24. The controversy is described in Juynboll, *Authenticity*, 21–32.
25. *al-Manār* 10 (1907): 140.
26. *ʿAqāʾid* (Amritsar, n.d.), 6–9.
27. Ghulām Aḥmad Parwēz, ed., *Maqām-i-ḥadīth* (Karachi, 1965), 355.
28. Quoted in Abū al-Wafāʾ Thanāʾ Allāh Amritsarī, *Burhān al-Qurʾān* (Amritsar, [1923]), 151.
29. Seyyed Hossein Nasr, *Ideals and Realities of Islam* (London, 1966; Boston 1975), 78.
30. Muhammad Ismāʿīl al-Salafī, *Ḥujjiyyat-i-hadīth* (Lahore, n.d.), 178–179.
31. Abū al-ʿAlā Mawdūdī, *Tafhīmāt* (Lahore, 1989), 324.
32. *Ibid.*, 257.
33. S. M. Yusuf, *An essay on the Sunnah* (Lahore, 1966), 5.
34. *Ibid.*, 7.
35. *Ibid.*, 5.
36. Muḥammad Ayyūb Dihlawī, *The Mischief of Rejection of Hadith* (Karachi, n.d.), 19.
37. Mawdūdī, *Tafhīmāt*, 329.
38. Balkhī, *Fitna*, I, 63.
39. *Ibid.*, I, 68.
40. al-Dārimī, Muqaddima, 48; Wensinck, *Handbook*, 223.
41. Abū Muḥammad Ibn Ḥazm, *Kitāb al-iḥkām fī uṣūl al-aḥkām*, ed. Aḥmad Shākir (Cairo, 1322 A.H.), I, 96. Although Ibn Ḥazm was himself a Ẓahirite, this statement accurately reflects the widely accepted orthodox position.
42. al-Ghazālī, *Kitāb al-mustasfā*, I, 125. Cited in Burton, *Collection*, 57.
43. al-Shāfiʿī, *Risāla*, 250.
44. Abū al-ʿAlā Mawdūdī, *Tarjumān al-Qurʾān* 56, 6, Manṣib-i-risālat nambar (1961): 193.
45. Letter to Mawdūdī from one ʿAbd al-Wudūd quoted in *ibid.*
46. Quoted in Amritsarī, *Burhān*, 96.
47. Muslim, Zuhd, 72: "Do not write anything from me except the Qurʾān." Numerous traditions have been cited both favoring and prohibiting the recording of ḥadīth.

48. Maḥmūd Abū Rayya, *ʿAḍwāʾ ʿalā al-sunna al-Muḥammadiyya* (Cairo, 1958; 3rd edn. with foreword by Ṭāhā Husayn, Cairo, n.d.). See chapter 4 for detailed treatment of issues related to the recording of ḥadīth.
49. Ṣidqī, "al-Islām huwa al-Qurʾān waḥdahu," 515. See also Parwēz, ed., *Maqām-i-ḥadīth*, 350.
50. *Ibid.*
51. Parwēz, Ghulām Aḥmad, *Salīm kē nām khuṭūṭ* (Karachi, 1953), II, 122.
52. *Ibid.*, I, 43.
53. Documented in numerous Ahl-i-Qurʾān writings. See for example, Parwēz, ed., *Maqām-i-ḥadīth*, 107–124.
54. Ṣidqī, "Al-Islām huwa al-Qurʾān waḥdahu," 516.
55. Parwēz, ed., *Maqām-i-ḥadīth*, 27. For a scholarly refutation of this argument, see Sayyid Sulaymān Nadvī, "Phīr baḥath-i-sunnat kuch awr ikhtirāʿāt-o-ilzāmāt," *al-Maʿarif* 26 (July 1930): 10–19.
56. Parwēz, *Salīm kē nām*, I, 40–42.
57. ʿAbd al-Ghanī ʿAbd al-Khāliq, *Ḥujjiyyat al-sunna* (Beirut, 1986), 291–308, lists five categories of verses which may be used to support the authority of sunna: (1) verses demanding belief in the Prophet: 4:136, 64:8, 7:158, 24:62; (2) proofs that the Prophet was appointed to explain the Qurʾān: 16:44,16:64, 2:151, 3:164, 62:2, 2:231, 4:113; (3) proofs that the requirement to obey the Prophet is absolute and equates to obeying God: 62:132, 62:32, 8:20–21, 8:46, 47:33, 64:12, 4:59; (4) verses showing the necessity of obeying the Prophet in everything he did and equating obedience to the Prophet with love of God: 3:31, 33:21, 7:156–157, 33:37; (5) verses showing that God charged the Prophet with obedience to all *waḥy*, whether recited or unrecited, and with preaching all that was sent to him: 33:1–2, 6:106, 45:18, 5:48–49, 67, 42:52–53.
58. Qurʾān 16:125; 17:39; 31:12; 33:34; 38:20; 43:53; 54:5; 62:2.
59. al-Shāfiʿī, *Risāla*, 32, 86, 93; Muhammad Rashīd Riḍā, "al-Islām huwa al-Qurʾān wa al-sunna," *al-Manār*, 9 (1906): 925–930; ʿAbd al-Khāliq, *Ḥujjiyyat al-sunna*, 296–7; Abū al-ʿAlā Mawdūdī, *Sunnat kī aʾinī ḥaithiyyat* (Lahore, 1963), 135–139.
60. Muṣṭafā al-Sibāʿī, *al-Sunna wa makānatuhā fī al-tashrīʿ al-Islāmī* (Cairo, 1961; 4th imp., Cairo, 1985), 50–51.
61. Muḥammad Karam Shāh, *Sunnat khayr al-anām* (Karachi, 1373 A.H.), 60–61.
62. Mawdūdī, *Sunnat kī aʾinī ḥaithiyyat*, 135–139.
63. al-Salafī, *Ḥujjiyyat-i-ḥadīth*, 161; Mawdūdī, *Tarjumān al-Qurʾān*, 100.
64. Mawdūdī, *Tarjumān al-Qurʾān*, 100; Dihlawī, *Rejection*, 8–9.
65. Mawdūdī, *Sunnat kī aʾinī ḥaithiyyat*, 79.
66. al-Salafī, *Ḥujjiyyat-i-ḥadīth*, 21; Dihlawī, *Rejection*, 3–8.
67. Mawdūdī responds that the reference to recitation *(tilāwa)* in this verse is generic and should not be confused with the later technical usage.
68. Mawdūdī, *Tarjumān al-Qurʾān*, 199, 203–204.
69. Ghulām Aḥmad Parwēz, *Miʿrāj insāniyyat* (Karachi, 1947), 451.
70. al-Sibāʿī, *al-Sunna wa makānatuhā*, 156–7; Qurʾān 15:9.
71. Mawdūdī, *Tafhīmāt*, 355.
72. Muḥammad Ṣādiq Sīālkōṯī, *Ḍarb-i-ḥadīth* (Gujrānwāla, 1961), 352.

73. al-Salafī, *Ḥujjiyyat-i-ḥadīth*, 161.
74. Mawdūdī, *Sunnat kī aʾīnī ḥaithiyyat*, 41.
75. *Ibid.*, 159.

4 THE NATURE OF PROPHETIC AUTHORITY

1. Ibn Isḥāq, *Sīrat rasūl Allāh: Das Leben Muhammads bearbeitet von ʿAbd el-Malik ibn Hishām*, ed. Ferdinand Wustenfeld (Göttingen, 1858–1860), I, 106; Alfred Guillaume, *The Life of Muhammad: A Translation of Ibn Isḥaq's Sīrat rasūl Allāh* (London, 1970), 72. For background see Annemarie Schimmel, *And Muhammad is His Messenger* (Chapel Hill, 1985), 68; Harris Birkeland, *The Legend of the Opening of Muhammad's Breast* (Oslo, 1955).
2. Schimmel, *And Muhammad is His Messenger*, 56–60. The polemics of al-Baqillānī (d. 1012) show that the doctrine was in wide circulation during the ninth century.
3. *EI²*, s.v. ʿIṣmā. Only some Ḥanbalites remained skeptical on the basis of the apparent inconsistency between the doctrine and certain revealed texts. Even then the later Ḥanbalites, including Ibn Taymiyya and his disciple Ibn Qayyim al-Jawziyya, accepted a limited version of this doctrine.
4. *Ibid.*
5. Muslim, Kitāb al-Faḍāʾil, 31.
6. Muslim, Kitāb al-Ṣayd, 15.
7. al-Ghazālī, *Kitāb al-arbaʿīn fī uṣūl al-Dīn* (Cairo, 1344), 89.
8. Schimmel, *And Muhammad is His Messenger*, 56–60.
9. Goldziher, *The Ẓāhirīs*, 78–79.
10. George Lindbeck, *Infallibility* (Milwaukee, 1972).
11. Aḥmad Khān, *Maqālāt*, II, 383.
12. Aḥmad Khān, *Tafsīr*, III, 19.
13. *Ibid.*, IX, 385.
14. ʿAbduh, *Theology of Unity*, 155.
15. Schimmel, *And Muhammad is His Messenger*, 237.
16. ʿAbduh, *Theology of Unity*, 80.
17. His most important works are: [Chirāgh ʿAlī] Moulavi Cheragh Ali, *Proposed Political Legal and Social Reforms in the Ottoman Empire* (Bombay, 1883) and *A Critical Exposition of the Popular Jihad* (Calcutta, 1885). In addition to these works, views on ḥadīth may be found in Chirāgh ʿAlī, *Rasāʾil* (Hyderabad, 1918–1919).
18. ʿAlī ʿAbd al-Rāziq, "L'Islam et les bases du pouvoir," trans. Leon Bercher, *Revue des Etudes Islamiques* 8 (1934): 209.
19. *Ibid.*
20. *al-Manār* 9:925.
21. *al-Manār* 9:913.
22. *al-Furqān* (Lucknow), Shāh Walī Allāh nambar, 264.
23. ʿAbdullāh Chakrālawī, *Tarjumat al-Qurʾān*, 208–209.
24. *ʿAqāʾid*, 4.
25. Amritsarī, *Burhān*, 95, 151.
26. Parwēz, *Miʿrāj insāniyyat*, 315. Jayrājpūrī, *Taʿlīmāt*, 128. Mawdūdī, *Tafhīmāt*, 257.

27. Qur'ān 5:102.
28. Mawdūdī, *Tafhīmāt*, 260.
29. Parwēz, *Maqām-i-ḥadīth*, 40.
30. Jayrājpūrī, cited in Mawdūdī, *Tafhīmāt*, 264.
31. Ghulām Jīlānī Barq, *Dō Islām* (Lahore, 1950), 343.
32. Parwēz, *Miʿrāj insāniyyat*, 344–345.
33. *Ibid.*, 349.
34. Barq, *Dō Islām*, 344.
35. Ghulām Aḥmad Parwēz, *Shāhkār-i-risālat* (Lahore, 1987).
36. Parwēz, *Miʿrāj insāniyyat*, 436–8.
37. Iqbāl, *Reconstruction*, 126. The emphasis is mine. Similar ideas can also be found in the writings of other modernists. Muḥammad ʿAbduh, for example, writes: "When one has sound training, does one need a mentor; or a guardian when one's mind is fully ripe? Hardly! . . . For this reason, Muḥammad's prophethood brought prophecy to an end" (*Theology of Unity*, 133).
38. Parwēz, *Salīm kē nām,* II, 60.
39. Shāh, *Sunnat khayr al-anām*, 51.
40. al-Salafī, *Ḥujjiyyat-i-ḥadīth*, 188.
41. Dihlawī, *Rejection*, 18–20. This emphasis on the unity of the Prophetic personality and the Prophetic mission does not necessarily imply a rejection of the distinction made by classical jurists between legal and non-legal precedents. Some authors continue to recognize such a distinction, but they refuse to accept the conclusion that non-legal precedents of the Prophet are any less an indication of God's will than legal precedents. The difference, they claim, is merely a formal one based on whether the rule calls for enforcement by the state. Because a rule is not within the boundaries of what the state should enforce does not necessarily mean that its observance is not still incumbent on Muslims. The majority of authors, more concerned with defending the authority of sunna than with sorting out the details of its legal application, choose to ignore this distinction altogether.
42. Shāh, *Sunnat khayr al-anām*, 70–73.
43. *Ibid.*, 194–195.
44. ʿAbduh, *Theology of Unity*, 141.
45. *al-Manār* 9:926.
46. Mawdūdī, *Tafhīmāt*, 327–8.
47. al-Salafī, *Ḥujjiyyat-i-ḥadīth*, 64; Sīālkōṭī, *Ḍarb-i-ḥadīth*, 65.
48. Jaʿfar Shāh Phulwārawī, *Maqām-i-sunnat* (Lahore, 1952), 113–115.
49. Mawdūdī, "Azādī kā Islāmī taṣawwur," in his *Tafhīmāt*, 98–113; "Ittibāʿ wa iṭāʿat-i-Rasūl," *ibid.*, 256–272; "Rasūl kī ḥaithiyyat shakhṣī wa ḥaithiyyat nabawī," *ibid.*, 273–281. All three articles originally appeared in the journal *Tarjumān al-Qur'ān*. The first two also appeared in Arabic translation in *al-Muslimūn* 6, numbers 6, 7, and 8.
50. Mawdūdī, *Tafhīmāt*, 104.
51. Mawdūdī, *Rasā'il-o-masā'il* (Lahore, 1975), I, 308.
52. Mawdūdī, *Tafhīmāt*, 106.
53. *Ibid.*, 261.

54. *Ibid.*, 263.
55. *Ibid.*
56. The article was written in answer to criticism of his views by Syrian *'ulamā'* after his articles were published in Arabic translation.
57. *Ibid.*, 274.
58. *Ibid.*, 279–281.

5 THE AUTHENTICITY OF ḤADITH

1. "As for us, [the Prophet's] statements cannot reach except by the tongue of transmitters, either via *tawātur* or *aḥād* reports" (Al-Ghazālī, *Kitāb al-mustaṣfā*, III, 541).
2. *laysa li ummatin min al-umam isnādun ka asnādihim.* For discussion of the *isnād* as a theme in Islamic civilization see William A. Graham, "Traditionalism in Islam: An Essay in Interpretation," *Journal of Interdisciplinary History* 23 (1993): 495–522.
3. For considerations of this point in early discussions of sunna see my discussion of the *ahl al-kalām* in chapter 1.
4. Pellat, *Le Milieu Baṣrien*, 83; Parwēz, *Maqām-i-ḥadīth*, 30; Abū Rayya, *'Aḍwā'*, 4–6.
5. The possibility of criticism of the content (*matn*) of a tradition was recognized in theory, but the option was seldom systematically exercised. For more detailed discussion of *matn* criticism and attempts to revive it in modern times see the following chapter.
6. See T. Khalidi, "Islamic Biographical Dictionaries: A Preliminary Assessment," *Muslim World* 63 (1973): 53–65. The major dictionaries are: Ibn Sa'd (d. 230/844), *Ṭabaqāt*; Ibn Abī Ḥātim (d. 327/938), *Kitāb al-jarḥ wa al-ta'dīl* (Hyderabad, 1952–1953); Muḥammad b. 'Abd Allāh al-Bukhārī (d. 256/870), *al-Ta'rīkh al-kabīr* (Hyderabad, 1361 A.H.); Ibn Ḥajar (d. 852/1459), *Tahdhīb al-tahdhīb* (Hyderabad, 1325–1327 A.H.).
7. Suyūṭī, *Tadrīb al-rāwī fī sharh taqrīb al-Nawawī*, ed. 'Abd al-Wahhāb 'Abd al-Laṭīf (Cairo, 1963), 108; Juynboll, *Authenticity*, 55. Ibn al-Mubārak adds the following qualifications: he must pray in congregation, avoid drink, and abstain from lying. M. M. Azami, *Studies in Hadith Methodology and Literature* (Indianapolis, 1977), 58. See also *EI*[2], s.v. 'Adl (by E. Tyan).
8. Azami, citing Ibn Ḥajar, lists twelve different grades of scholar. Azami, *Studies in Hadith Methodology*, 59–60.
9. al-Khaṭīb al-Baghdādī (d. 463 A.H.), *al-Kifāya fī 'ilm al-riwāya* (Hyderabad, 1357 A.H.), 46; Quoted in Juynboll, *Muslim Tradition*, 195.
10. Goldziher, *Muslim Studies*, II, 20 n. 5; Alois Sprenger, introductory excursus, "Die Sunna" in his *Das Leben und die Lehre des Mohammad* (Berlin, 1861–1865), lxxvii–civ; Alois Sprenger, "On the Origin of Writing Down Historical Records among the Musulmans," *Journal of the Asiatic Society of Bengal* 25 (1856): 303–329, 375–381.
11. Goldziher, *Muslim Studies*, II, 19. (*Muhammedanische Studien*, II, 5).
12. See the works of Juynboll and Azami listed in the bibliography. Perhaps the most significant challenge to Schacht's general conclusions may be found in Motzki, "Muṣannaf."

13. Goldziher has had perhaps the most impact, through refutations, partial translations into Arabic, and plagiarization of his work. e.g. Sibāʿī's refutation in *al-Sunna wa makānatuhā*, 364–420. Sibāʿī reports an Arabic summary of Goldziher prepared by his teacher, ʿAlī Ḥasan ʿAbd al-Qādir. As Juynboll points out, ʿAbd al-Qādir's later work, *Naẓra ʿāmma fī taʾrīkh al-fiqh al-Islāmī* (Cairo, 1956) contains large sections plagiarized from Goldziher. Schacht has remained largely unknown and inaccessible among Arab writers, but his work has evoked important and creative responses from Pakistani scholars.
14. Azami, *Studies in Hadith Methodology*, 58. For an attempt to trace the origins of this doctrine see Juynboll, *Muslim Tradition*, 190–206. Modern discussions of this issue in Egypt have been dealt with in detail by Juynboll, *Authenticity*, 55–99.
15. ʿAbd al-Munʿim Ṣāliḥ al-ʿIzzī, *Difāʿ ʿan Abī Hurayra* (Baghdad, 1973), 488; cited by Juynboll, *Muslim Tradition*, 191.
16. Bukhārī, ʿIlm, 38; throughout in all collections. For detailed discussion of this tradition see Juynboll, *Muslim Tradition*, 96–133.
17. Muḥammad Aslam Jayrājpūrī, *ʿIlm-i-ḥadīth* (Lahore, n.d.), 2.
18. Aḥmad Amīn, *Fajr al-Islām* (Cairo, 1933), 216.
19. *Ibid.*; Abū Rayya, *Aḍwāʾ*, 29; Jayrājpūrī, *ʿIlm-i-ḥadīth*, 3.
20. Criticism of Abū Hurayra is not a modern phenomenon, as Juynboll points out. He theorizes that "it was the emergence of critical appraisals of Abū Hurayra in particular, which, through the rijāl critics' efforts to exonerate him, eventually led to the formulation of the collective *taʿdīl* of all of Muḥammad's Companions." Juynboll, *Muslim Tradition*, 192.
21. Jayrājpūrī, *ʿIlm-i-ḥadīth*, 6.
22. Especially Abū Rayya, whose central project is to discredit Abū Hurayra. See Juynboll, *Authenticity*, 62–99.
23. Mawdūdī, *Tafhīmāt*, 359.
24. All of Mawdūdī's examples are from Ibn ʿAbd al-Barr, *Jāmiʿ*.
25. See, for example, the *fatwā* of Amjad al-Zahāwī quoted by Juynboll, *Muslim Tradition*, 191.
26. Sayyid Nūr al-Ḥasan Bukhārī, *Aṣḥāb-i-rasūl par ʿadilānah difāʿ* (Lahore, 1387 A.H.); Sayyid Amīn al-Ḥaqq, *Mawdūdī maslak par naqd-ō-naẓar: Saḥābah miʿyār-i-ḥaqq hēn* (Lahore, 1383 A.H.); Mawlana Aḥmad ʿAlī, *Ḥaqq parast ʿulamāʾ kī Mawdūdiyyat sē nārāẓgī kē asbāb* (Lahore, n.d.); Mihr Muḥammad Miyānvalvī, *Adālat-i hazrat-i ṣaḥabah-i kirām* (Karachi, [1972]); Muftī Muḥammad Shafīʿ, *Maqām-i-Ṣaḥābah* (Karachi, 1971).
27. ʿAbd al-Razzāq Ḥamza, *Ẓulumāt Abī Rayya imām aḍwāʾ al-sunna [sic] al-muḥammadiyya* (Cairo, 1959); Muḥammad ʿAjjāj al-Khaṭīb, *Abū Hurayra rāwiyyat al-Islām* (Cairo, 1962); al-Sibāʿī, *al-Sunna wa makānatuhā;* Muḥammad Muḥammad al-Samāḥī, *Abū Hurayra fī al-mīzān* (Cairo, 1958); al-ʿIzzī, *Difāʿ*.
28. Muḥammad Idrīs Kandehlavī, *Ḥujjiyyat-i-ḥadīth* (Lahore, n.d.), 145–148; Sibāʿī, *al-Sunna wa makānatuhā*, 15–18.
29. Sibāʿī, *al-Sunna wa makānatuhā*, 264.
30. Sibāʿī, for example, dismisses the *man kadhaba* tradition by reading it as predictive of the future. The Prophet is predicting the lies that will be told about

him in the future: "Whoever *will* lie about me will earn hell fire" (*ibid.*, 238–239). In answer to the report that ʿUmar confined three Companions to Medina to prevent them from spreading traditions, Abū Shuhba points out that Ibn Ḥazm, the source of this tradition, considers it inauthentic (Abū Shuhba, "Naqd Kitāb aḍwāʾ ʿalā al-sunna al-Muḥammadiyya," *Majallat al-Azhar* 30 (1959): 267. Ibn Ḥazm, *Kitāb al-iḥkām fī uṣūl al-aḥkām*, II, 139).

31. This tradition still continues. A true *muḥaddith* must receive his knowledge directly from another transmitter. On the connection between legal testimony and ḥadīth transmission see al-Shāfiʿī, *Risāla*, 241–250.
32. Aḥmad Khān, *Maqālāt*, II, 190. This is a telling reversal of al-Shāfiʿī's argument that precision in words is not to be trusted unless we can be sure that the transmitter understands the meaning of what they transmit. For al-Shāfiʿī understanding the intent rather than precise memory is the key to accuracy; Sayyid Aḥmad, along with most modern authors, insists that having the exact words is preferable.
33. *Ibid.*, 187.
34. Ṣidqī, "Al-Islām huwa al-Qurʾān waḥdahu," 9: 515.
35. Muḥammad Tawfīq Ṣidqī, "Kalimāt fī al-naskh wa al-tawātur wa akhbār al-āḥād wa al-sunna," *al-Manār* 11 (1908): 594–598, 688–696, 771–780, at 693.
36. *Ibid.*
37. Amīn, *Fajr al-Islām*, 210.
38. Jayrājpūrī, *ʿIlm-i-ḥadīth*, 27–29.
39. Abū Rayya, *Aḍwāʾ*, 10.
40. *Ibid.*, 8.
41. *Ibid.*, 10.
42. Juynboll, *Authenticity*, 115; Abū Rayya, *Aḍwāʾ*, 54–63.
43. Barq, *Dō Islām*, 39–40.
44. *Ibid.*, 122.
45. Cited in J. M. S. Baljon, "Pakistani Views of Hadith," *Die Welt des Islams*, n.s. 5 (1958): 222.
46. Muḥammad Fahīm ʿUthmānī, *Ḥifāzat-ō-ḥujjiyyat-i-ḥadīth* (Lahore, 1979), 133; Mawdūdī, *Sunnat kī aʾīnī ḥaithiyyat*, 159. See also my discussion of Mawdūdī's views on this question in the previous chapter.
47. Rafīq Bey al-ʿAẓm, "al-Tadwīn fī al-Islām," *al-Manār* 10 (1907): 930; M. M. Azami, *Studies in Early Hadith Literature* (Beirut, 1968; repr Indianapolis, 1978), 20; Mawdūdī, *Tafhīmāt*, 333; Mawdūdī, *Tarjumān al-Qurʾān* 331; Muftī Muḥammad Rafīʿ ʿUthmānī, *Kitābat-i-ḥadīth ʿahd-i-risālat-ō-ʿahd-i-Ṣaḥāba mēn* (Karachi, 1985), 34; Muḥammad Fahīm ʿUthmānī, *Ḥifāzat-ō-ḥujjiyyat-i-ḥadīth*, 90.
48. The two arguments are not viewed as mutually exclusive and are often combined. E.g., Muḥammad Fahīm ʿUthmānī, *Ḥifāzat-ō-ḥujjiyyat-i-ḥadīth*, 85–190.
49. Nabia Abbott, *Studies in Arabic Literary Papyri*, (Chicago 1967), II: *Qurʾanic Commentary and Tradition*; Azami, *Studies in Early Hadith Literature*, trans. into Arabic as Muḥammad Muṣṭafā al-Aʿẓamī, *Dirāsāt fī al-ḥadīth al-nabawī wa taʾrīkh tadwīnihā* (Riyāḍ, 1976); Fuad Sezgin, "Hadiṯ." in his *Geschichte des arabischen Schrifttums* (Leiden, 1967–), I, 53–84.
50. al-ʿAẓm, "al-Tadwīn."

51. In Urdu: Sayyid Minnat Allāh Raḥmānī, *Kitābat-i-ḥadīth, ya'nī ḥadīthōn kī tartīb-ō-tadwīn kī tārikh par ēk mukhtaṣar aur jāmī' maqāla* (Lahore, 1370 A.H.); Muftī Muḥammad Rafī' 'Uthmānī, *Kitābat-i-ḥadīth*; Sayyid Murtaḍā Ḥusayn, *Tārikh-i-tadwīn-i-ḥadīth* (Rawalpindi, n.d.); Sayyid Manāẓir Aḥsan Gīlānī, *Tadwīn-i-ḥadīth* (Karachi, 1956); Khālid Alvī, *Hifāẓat-i-ḥadīth* (Lahore, 1971); Muḥammad Fahīm 'Uthmānī, *Ḥifāzat-ō-ḥujjiyyat-i-ḥadīth*; Muḥammad Khālid Sayf, *Kitābat-i-ḥadīth tā 'ahd-tābi'īn* (Lyallpur, n.d.); Abū Bakr Ghaznawī, *Kitābat-i-ḥadīth 'ahd-i-nabawī mēn* (Lahore, n.d.); 'Alī Taqī Lakhnawī, *Tadwīn-i-ḥadīth* (Hyderabad [Deccan], 1354 A.H.). Ghulām Jīlānī Barq, *Tārīkh-i-ḥadīth* (Lahore, 1988). This last contribution represents a complete reversal of Barq's earlier views on ḥadīth. In Arabic: 'Abd al-Mun'im Nimr, *Āḥādīth rasūl Allāh kayfa waṣalat ilaynā* (Cairo, 1987); Muḥammad 'Ajjāj al-Khaṭīb, *Uṣūl al-ḥadīth* (Beirut, 1967); Abū al-Yaqẓān 'Aṭiyya al-Jabūrī, *Mabāḥith fī tadwīn al-sunna al-muṭahhara* (Cairo, 1972).
52. Aḥmad Dīn Amritsārī, cited in Balkhī, *Fitna*, 93.
53. Parwēz, *Salīm kē nām*, III, 217. Similar arguments are made by Aslam Jayrājpūrī, Ghulām Jīlānī Barq, Muḥammad Tawfīq Ṣidqī, Aḥmad Amīn, Muḥammad Ḥusayn Haykal, and Maḥmūd Abū Rayya.
54. Bukhārī, 'Ilm, 39; Abū Dā'ūd, 'Ilm, 3; Dārimī, Muqaddima, 43; cited in Azami, *Studies in Early Hadith Literature*, 43.
55. Bukhārī, Luqṭa, 7; Tirmidhī, 'Ilm, 12; Azami, *Studies in Early Hadith Literature*, 40, 50.
56. *al-Manār* 10 (1907): 752–768.
57. 'Abd al-'Azīz al-Khūlī, *Miftāḥ al-sunna aw ta'rīkh funūn al-ḥadīth*, 2nd imp. (Cairo, 1928); Muḥammad Muḥammad Abū Zahw, *al-Ḥadīth wa al-muḥaddithūn* (Cairo, 1958), 122; Muḥammad 'Ajjāj al-Khaṭīb, *al-Sunna qabla al-tadwīn* (Cairo, 1963), 306; Mawdūdī, *Tarjumān al-Qur'ān*, 329–330. Deniers of ḥadīth portray this argument as a cynical attempt to avoid the prohibition, e.g., *Maqām-i-ḥadīth*, (Lahore, 1986), I, 116.
58. Azami, *Studies in Early Hadith Literature*, 23.
59. al-Sibā'ī, *al-Sunna wa makānatuhā*, 71–75.
60. Juynboll, *Authenticity*, 108–111.
61. Ibn Sa'd, *Ṭabaqāt*, II, ii, 135. Cited in Azami, *Studies in Early Hadith Literature*, 285.
62. See the citations in Azami, *Studies in Early Hadith Literature*, 18 n. 1–5.
63. Amīn, *Fajr al-Islām*, 221.
64. Azami, *Studies in Early Hadith Literature*, 284.
65. *Ibid.*, 34–182; Abbott, *Studies*, 11; Muḥammad Fahīm 'Uthmānī, *Ḥifāzat ō ḥujjiyyat-i-ḥadīth*, 76–90; Muftī Muḥammad Rafī' 'Uthmānī, *Kitābat-i-ḥadīth*, 65–119.
66. Azami, *Studies in Early Hadith Literature*, 34–60.
67. For early use of the *isnād* see Azami, *Studies in Early Hadith Literature*, 212–247 and James Robson, "The Isnād in Muslim Tradition," *Glasgow University Oriental Society Transactions* 15 (1955): 15–26. At the other extreme, Schacht argues that *isnāds* were not systematically used before the early second century A.H. Schacht, *Origins*, 36–37. For a middle position see Juynboll, *Muslim Tradition*, 9–23.

68. James Robson, "Ibn Isḥāq's use of the Isnād," *Bulletin of the John Rylands Library* 38 (1956): 449–465.
69. Aḥmad b. Ḥanbal (d. 241/855), *Musnad* (Cairo, 1312–1313 A.H.).
70. The major collections are: Muḥammad b. ʿAbd Allāh al-Bukhārī (d. 256 A.H.), *al-Jāmiʿ al- ṣaḥīḥ*; Muslim b. al-Ḥajjāj (d. 261), *al-Jāmiʿ al- ṣaḥīḥ*; Abū Dā'ūd (d. 275), *Kitāb al-sunan*; al-Tirmidhī (d. 279), *al-Jāmiʿ al-ṣaḥīḥ*; al-Nasā'ī (d. 303), *Kitāb al-sunan*; Ibn Mājah (d. 273), *Kitāb al-sunan*; al-Dārimī (d. 225), *Kitāb al-sunan*.
71. The critical position of the *isnād* as the bridge between the argument for the early recording of ḥadīth and the argument for the authenticity of ḥadīth is vividly demonstrated in Azami, *Studies in Early Hadith Literature*, 212–247.
72. *lawlā al-isnādu la qāla man shā'a mā shā'a*. Cited in Alfred Guillaume, *The Traditions of Islam: An Introduction to the Study of Hadith Literature* (Oxford, 1924), 84.
73. Khwāja Aḥmad Dīn's conversion is described in Majid, "Ghulām Jīlānī Barq," 32.
74. Barq, *Dō Islām*, 203.
75. Juynboll, *Authenticity*, 41. The tradition appears in all the major collections.
76. Barq, *Dō Islām*, 162–196. Certain categories of traditions have been especially vulnerable to such attacks, for example *faḍā'il* traditions (traditions praising particular people or places): traditions dealing with the coming of the *Mahdī*, traditions about the *abdāl* (a special category of saints), and traditions connected with the *isrā'īliyyāt*. Juynboll, *Authenticity*, 102–103.
77. al-Salafi, *Ḥujjiyyat-i-ḥadīth*, 75–76.
78. Sidqī, "Kalimāt fī al-naskh," 694.
79. Jayrājpūrī, *'Ilm-i-ḥadīth*, 14.
80. *Ibid.*, 15.
81. *Ibid.*
82. Rashida Begum v. Shahab Din, *All Pakistan Legal Decisions* (1960) Lahore, 1167. Figures vary widely in different sources.
83. Jayrājpūrī, *'Ilm-i-ḥadīth*, 16.
84. *Ibid.*, 18.
85. Chirāgh ʿAlī, *Aʿẓam al-kalām* (Agra, 1910), 19; Jayrājpūrī, *'Ilm-i-ḥadīth*, 15, 20.
86. Mawdūdī, *Tafhīmāt*, 360.
87. Aḥmad Khān, *Maqālāt*, XI, 419.
88. Chirāgh ʿAlī, *Aʿẓam al-kalām*, 20; Aḥmad Khān, *Maqālāt*, I, 27–28; Amīn, *Fajr al-Islām*, 217; Abū Rayya, *Aḍwā'*, 4–6.
89. Jayrājpūrī, *'Ilm-i-ḥadīth*, 22.
90. See chapter 5 for more discussion of proposed methods for scrutinizing the content of traditions.
91. Aḥmad Khān, *Maqālāt*, I, 27–28.
92. Mawdūdī, *Tafhīmāt*, 357.
93. Ṣidqī, "Kalimāt fī al-naskh," 692.
94. Jayrājpūrī, *'Ilm-i-ḥadīth*, 22–23.
95. Ṣidqī, "Kalimāt fī al-naskh," 693. For a western scholarly critique of the biographical literature see Juynboll, *Muslim Tradition*, 134–160.
96. Jayrājpūrī, *'Ilm-i-ḥadīth*, 22–23.

97. *Ibid.*, 26.
98. Sibāʿī, *al-Sunna wa makānatuhā*, 75–79.
99. Salafī, *Ḥujjiyyat-i-ḥadīth*, 80–82.
100. Sibāʿī, *al-Sunna wa makānatuhā*, 90–97; Azami, *Studies in Hadith Methodology*, 48.
101. Salafī, *Ḥujjiyyat-i-ḥadīth*, 74.
102. *Ibid.*, 72; Sibāʿī, *al-Sunna wa makānatuhā*, 271–272.
103. Salafī, *Ḥujjiyyat-i-ḥadīth*, 71–72. Sibāʿī, *al-Sunna wa makānatuhā*, 90.
104. Mawdūdī, *Sunnat kī aʾinī ḥaithiyyat*, 58.
105. Salafī, *Ḥujjiyyat-i-ḥadīth*, 83–84.
106. Jayrājpūrī, *ʿIlm-i-ḥadīth*, 22–23.
107. Yusuf, *Essay on Sunnah*. See also Phulwārawī, *Maqām-i-Sunnat*.
108. Yusuf, *Essay on Sunnah*, 24.
109. *Ibid.*, 31.
110. *Ibid.*, 33.
111. *Ibid.*, 40.
112. al-Shāfiʿī, *Umm*, vii, 242.
113. Fazlur Rahman, "Concepts Sunnah, Ijtihad and Ijmāʿ in the Early Period," *Islamic Studies* 1, 1 (1962): 5–21; "Sunna and Ḥadīth," *Islamic Studies* 1, 2 (1962): 1–36; "Post-formative Developments in Islam," *Islamic Studies* 1, 4 (1962): 1–23. These articles were collected and published separately as *Islamic Methodology in History* (Karachi, 1965). They were subsequently published in both Urdu and Arabic. By his own account he was responding through these articles to two quite separate, although interrelated, controversies. He was responding, first of all, to the immediate controversy in Pakistan aroused by Parwēz's radical rejection of sunna. But he was also responding to the ongoing international scholarly debate about Joseph Schacht's skeptical views on the authenticity of ḥadīth which had been published some years earlier in his *Origins of Muhammadan Jurisprudence*.
114. Rahman, *Methodology*, 11–12.
115. *Ibid.*, 19.
116. *Ibid.*, 6, 18.
117. *Ibid.*, 27.
118. *Ibid.*, 29.
119. *Ibid.*, 12.
120. *Ibid.*, 13–14.
121. *Ibid.*, 33.
122. *Ibid.*
123. *Ibid.*, 67.
124. *Ibid.*, 80.
125. *Ibid.*, 44.
126. *Ibid.*, 73.
127. *Ibid.*, 74.
128. *Ibid.*, 71.
129. *Ibid.*, 75.
130. *Ibid.*, 69–70.
131. *Ibid.*, 76.

132. *Ibid.*
133. *Ibid.*, 81. The preference for historical reports over ḥadīth, and as a judge of ḥadīth, echoes the work of Shiblī Nuʿmānī.
134. *Ibid.*, 77.
135. *Ibid.*, 76.
136. *Ibid.*, 77.
137. E.g., especially his attitude toward certain aspects of ṣūfism: *ibid.*, 102 ff.

6 SUNNA AND ISLAMIC REVIVALISM

1. *al-Sunna al-nabawiyya bayna ahl al-fiqh wa ahl al-ḥadīth* (Cairo, 1989; 2nd edn., 1990). All references refer to the 2nd edn. Ghazālī, a prominent religious figure and a prolific and popular writer on religious topics, was at one time an active publicist for the Ikhwān al-Muslimīn. He was involved with the Brotherhood for sixteen years, ending in 1953 when he was expelled on charges of collaborating with the regime.
2. Fahmī Huwaydī, "Berestruika Islāmiyya!" *Al-Ahrām* (January 31, 1989).
3. Jamāl Sulṭān, *Azmat al-ḥiwār al-dīnī, naqd kitāb al-sunna al-nabawiyya bayna ahl al-fiqh wa ahl al-ḥadīth* (Cairo, 1990); Ṣāliḥ b. ʿAbd al-ʿAzīz b. Muḥammad Āl al-Shaykh, *al-Miʿyār li ʿilm al-Ghazālī fī kitābihi "al-sunna al-nabawiyya"* (Cairo, 1990); Ashraf b. ʿAbd al-Maqṣūd b. ʿAbd al-Raḥīm, *Jināyat al-Shaykh Muḥammad al-Ghazālī ʿalā al-ḥadīth wa ahlihi* (Ismailia, 1989); Muḥammad Jalāl Kishk, *al-Shaykh Muḥammad al-Ghazālī bayna al-naqd al-ʿātib wa-al-madḥ al-shāmit* (Cairo, 1990); Rabīʿ ibn Hādi ʿUmayr Madkhalī, *Kashf mawqif al-Ghazālī min al-sunna wa-ahliha wa-naqd baʿḍ ārāʾih.* (Medina, 1989); Aḥmad Ḥijāzī Aḥmad Saqqā, *Dafʿ al-shubhāt ʿan al-shaykh Muḥammad al-Ghazālī* (Cairo, 1990).
4. al-Ghazālī, *al-Sunna al-nabawiyya*, 7.
5. Muḥammad ʿAjjāj al-Khaṭīb, *Uṣūl al-ḥadīth*, 305. There is significant disagreement among scholars on the interpretation of these rules.
6. Some interpret *ʿilla qādiḥa* to signify defects in the *matn* of a tradition rather than in the *sanad.*
7. Aron Zysow, "Agreement and Authenticity in Islamic legal theory," MESA, 1991. Ibn ʿAbd al-Barr and al-Nawāwī are free in their criticism of ḥadīth contrary to reason, or the dignity of the Prophet, even though these are canonical. Guillaume, *Traditions of Islam*, 94. Ibn al-Qayyim al-Jawziyya lists more than a hundred examples of sound traditions that are rejected by Ḥanafī jurists.
8. As I have noted in chapter 1, they distinguished between binding and non-binding sunna, i.e. not everything that looks like a command is, in fact, a command.
9. The subordination of the concerns of *ʿilm al-ḥadīth* to practical concerns of legal application is perhaps best exemplified in the work of the Mālikī jurist al-Shāṭibī, a figure who has provided important inspiration for some modern Muslim thinkers. Shāṭibī is most celebrated for his discussion of the *maqāṣid al-sharīʿa* and his emphasis on *maṣlaḥa* as the central principle of Islamic law. For background on this important figure and his influence on modern Islamic legal thought, see Muhammad Khalid Masud, *Islamic Legal*

Philosophy: A Study of Abū Isḥāq al-Shāṭibī's Life and Thought (Islamabad, 1977).

10. The extent to which Muslim scholars have come to accept the need to reassess ḥadīth may be illustrated by ongoing attempts, even among conservative *ʿulamāʾ*, to put together new collections of sound and spurious traditions. E.g., in 1941 the council of *ʿulamāʾ* at al-Azhar approved a proposal to put together such a collection by critically reexamining medieval collections and commentaries. H. A. R. Gibb, *Modern Trends in Islam* (Chicago, 1947), 50.
11. Islamic revivalist writers seek to characterize their position on ḥadīth as centrist – balanced, moderate, and avoiding extremes; e.g., Mawdūdī's essay on sunna, entitled "Maslak-i-iʿtidāl" (the middle way) in his *Tafhīmāt*, 350–370.
12. *Ibid.*, 354.
13. While the *ʿulamāʾ* placed special emphasis on the *sanad*, they did in fact examine the content of traditions as well. Sibāʿī lists fifteen standards for *matn* criticism cited in works on ḥadīth. Ḥadīth reports must not conflict with fundamental principles of reason, general principles of wisdom and morality, facts known by direct observation, or fundamental principles of medicine. They must not contain absurd statements or statements contrary to the teaching of more authoritative sources (i.e., the Qurʾān). They should coincide with historical conditions during the time of the Prophet, and reports of events that have been widely known should be rejected if only a single witness reports them. Finally, they should not encourage vice, contradict reason, or promise large rewards or grave punishments for insignificant acts. Sibāʿī, *al-Sunna wa makānatuhā*, 271–272.
14. We have no adequate biography of Shiblī in English, although there are several excellent works in Urdu. Certain aspects of Shiblī's biography, especially his relationship with Sayyid Aḥmad Khān and his controversial romantic involvements, have been the subject of lively exchanges among historians in the Subcontinent. See Shaykh Muḥammad Ikrām, *Yādgār-i-Shiblī* (Lahore, 1971) and the same author's earlier and less sympathetic *Shiblī Nāmah* (Lucknow, n.d.). For a less critical account by one of his chief disciples, see Sayyid Sulaymān Nadvī, *Ḥayāt-i-Shiblī* (Azamgarh, 1943). For a general treatment in English, see Aziz Ahmad, *Islamic Modernism*, 77–86. Ahmad's portrayal typifies the common judgment of historians that Shiblī was out of touch with the main currents in Indian Muslim thought of his time. For a contrasting treatment see Mehr Afrōz Murād, *Intellectual Modernism of Shiblī Nuʿmānī: An Exposition of his Religious and Political Ideas* (Lahore, 1976). For a discussion of one of Shiblī's most important involvements, the Nadwat al-ʿulamāʾ, see Metcalf, *Islamic Revival*, 335–347.
15. In his youth he was deeply influenced by two scholars, Muḥammad Fārūq Charyākōṭī and Irshād Ḥusayn Rampūrī, who were active polemicists against the Ahl-i-Ḥadīth on behalf of a reinvigorated Ḥanafism. Shiblī's approach to ḥadīth emerged from a blend of this strong Ḥanafī influence and his exposure to the influence of Sayyid Aḥmad Khān. We have two main sources for his views on ḥadīth. The first is his biography of Abū Ḥanīfa, *Sīrat al-Nuʿmān* (Lahore, n.d.), trans. Muhammad Tayyab Bakhsh Badauni

as *Method of Sifting Prophetic Tradition* (Karachi, 1966), the second his biography of Muḥammad (*Sīrat al-Nabī* [Lahore, n.d.]). In the former, Shiblī was concerned primarily with defending Abū Ḥanīfa's record on ḥadīth against the attacks of the traditionists; in the latter he was concerned with establishing rules for the use of ḥadīth as a historical source. In both works Shiblī deals extensively with the question of how traditions should be scrutinized.

16. Shiblī, *Sirat al-Nu'mān,* 196.
17. *Ibid.*, 195–196.
18. That Shiblī does not consider the *ṣaḥīḥ* collections immune from criticism is clear from the examples he cites, see *Sīrat al-Nabī*, 73–80. His editor, Sayyid Sulaymān Nadvī, tries to conceal this position (see n. 1, p. 10) as does his English translator, who excises the whole section. See *Method of Sifting Prophetic Tradition*.
19. Shiblī, *Sīrat al-Nu'mān*, 155.
20. *Ibid.*, 156
21. *Ibid.*, 179.
22. *Ibid.*, 180–182.
23. *Ibid.*, 193–194.
24. *Ibid.*, 195–196.
25. *Ibid.*, 198. For authority Shiblī turns to Ibn al-Jawzī, who outlines ten different characteristics that discredit a tradition without regard for its transmission. This list appears repeatedly in modern literature on ḥadīth although it is used for different purposes. Shiblī uses it here to argue for a more critical, rational approach to ḥadīth. By contrast, Muṣṭafā al-Sibā'ī repeats the same list to argue that the traditionists did actually apply rational criticism and that their work must be accepted.
26. Mawdūdī, *Tafhīmāt*, 356.
27. *Ibid.*, 362.
28. *Ibid.*
29. *Ibid.*, 360
30. *al-Manār* 29 (1928): 40; cited in Juynboll, *Authenticity*, 139.
31. al-Ghazālī, *al-Sunna al-nabawiyya*, 21.
32. *Ibid.*, 19.
33. *Ibid.*
34. *Ibid.*, 21.
35. *Ibid.*, 32.
36. *Ibid.*, 19. *Qad yasiḥḥ al-ḥadīth sanadan wa yaḍa'if matnan ba'd iktishāf al-fuqahā' li 'illa kāmina fīhi.*
37. *Ibid.*, 32.
38. *Ibid.*, 8–9.
39. *Ibid.*, 24.
40. *Ibid.* 33.
41. Bukhari, Janā'iz, 32, 33, 44; Qur'ān 6:164.
42. al-Ghazālī, *al-Sunna al-nabawiyya*, 21–22.
43. *Ibid.*, 25.
44. *Ibid.*, 20–21.
45. Qur'ān 5:45; al-Ghazālī, *al-Sunna al-nabawiyya*, 24–25.

46. al-Ghazālī, *al-Sunna al-nabawiyya*, 25.
47. *Ibid.*, 13.
48. Ibn ʿAbd al-Raḥīm, *Jināyat*, 115.
49. *Ibid.*, 125–136.
50. *Ibid.*, 130–134. The author lists seven different solutions to this particular problem.
51. *Ibid.*, 156.
52. The connection and similarity between the work of these two prominent revivalists is not coincidental. Qaraḍāwī's work, like Ghazālī's, was sponsored and promoted by the International Institute for Islamic Thought (al-Maʿhad al ʿālamī li'l fikr al-Islamī) based in Herndon, Virginia. Since the late 1980s the institute has become a major catalyst for the publication of revivalist views on sunna. In the institute's stated program of placing modern Islamic thought on a solid foundation, the place of the sunna is of vital importance. Other publications on sunna include *Nadwat al-sunna al-nabawiyya wa manhajihā fī binā' al-maʿarifa wa al-haḍāra* (Amman, 1991) and ʿAbd al-Khāliq, *Ḥujjiyyat al-sunna*.
53. Yūsuf al-Qaraḍāwī, *Kayfa nataʿāmalu maʿ al-sunna al-nabawiyya* (El-Mansura, 1990), 23.
54. *Ibid.*, 27.
55. *Ibid.*, 23.
56. *Ibid.*, 24.
57. *Ibid.*, 25.
58. *Ibid.*, 57.
59. *Ibid.*, 93.
60. *Ibid.*, 99.
61. *Ibid.*, 100–102.
62. *al-Manār* 12 (1911): 693–99; cited in Juynboll, *Authenticity*, 30.
63. *al-Manār* 27 (1926): 616; cited in Juynboll, *Authenticity*, 22–23.
64. Ṭāḥā Ḥusayn, *Muraʿat al-Islām* (Cairo, 1959), 236–238; Muḥammad Ḥusayn Haykal, *Hayāt Muḥammad* (Cairo, 1954), 46–50.
65. Richard P. Mitchell, *Society of the Muslim Brothers* (London, 1969), 238.
66. *Ibid.*
67. *Ibid.*
68. al-Ghazālī, *al-Sunna al-nabawiyya*, 43–70.
69. *Ibid.*, 160–167.
70. *Ibid.*
71. *Ibid.*, 25.
72. *Ibid.*, 27.
73. Shiblī, *Sirat al-Nuʿmān*, 190–192.
74. *Ibid.*, 192.
75. Shiblī, *Method of Sifting Prophetic Tradition*, 66–67.
76. Shiblī, *Sirat al-Nuʿmān*, 193.
77. *Ibid.*, 194.
78. Mawdūdī, *Tafhīmāt*, 360–361.
79. Qaraḍāwī, *Kayfa nataʿāmalu maʿ al-sunna*, 33–34.
80. *Ibid.*, 55–57.
81. *Ibid.*, 113.

82. Mawdūdī, *Tafhīmāt*, 374.
83. *Ibid.*, 362.
84. *Ibid.*, 361.
85. *Ibid.*, 362.
86. For detailed discussion of this aspect of Mawdūdī's thought, see Charles J. Adams, "The Authority of the Prophetic Hadith in the Eyes of Some Modern Muslims," in Donald P. Little, ed. *Essays on Islamic Civilization Presented to Niyazi Berkes* (Leiden, 1976), 42–45.
87. Mawdūdī, *Tafhīmāt*, 362.
88. Adams, "The Authority of Prophetic Hadith," 43–44.
89. Aḥmad Khān, *Maqālāt*, I, 29.
90. Mājid, "Ghulām Jīlānī Barq," 6.
91. "Ḥadīth kē bārē mēn mērā mawqaf," *Chatan*, Lahore, January 9, 1956; cited by Mājid, "Ghulām Jīlānī Barq," 80.
92. Barq, *Dō Islām*, 347.
93. Barq, *Tārikh-i-ḥadīth.*
94. Sibāʿī, *al-Sunna wa makānatuhā*, 280.
95. *Ibid.*, 242–245; Juynboll, *Authenticity*, 60.
96. Sibāʿī,*al-Sunna wa makānatuhā*, 276–277.
97. *Ibid.*, 278–279.
98. *Majallat al-Azhar* 30 (1959): 149; cited in Juynboll, *Authenticity*, 140.
99. Ibn Khaldūn, *Muqaddima* (Cairo, 1274 A.H.), 412; Goldziher, *The Ẓāhirīs*, 78.
100. Salafī, *Ḥujjiyyat-i-ḥadīth*, 71.
101. Ibn ʿAbd al-Rahīm, *Jināyat*, 53–84.
102. Shiblī, *Sirat al-Nuʿmān*, 47–48, 200.
103. Salafī, *Ḥujjiyyat-i-ḥadīth*, 151.
104. ʿAbduh, *Theology of Unity*, 155.
105. *Ibid.*, 107.
106. Riḍā, *al-Manār* 19 (1918): 529–533; Muslim, Imān, 263.
107. Bukhārī, Bad' al-khalq, 4.
108. Juynboll, *Authenticity*, 145–146; *al-Manār* 30 (1929): 261–272, 361–376.
109. Bukhārī, Tibb, 58.
110. Juynboll, *Authenticity*, 142–143; *al-Manār* 29 (1928): 48.
111. Juynboll, *Authenticity*, 102–103; *al-Manār* 27 (1926): 748–754; Abū Rayya, *Aḍwāʾ*, 94–99.

7 CONCLUSION: THE SPECTRUM OF CHANGE

1. E.g., the massive *fatwā*, carrying the signatures of more than a thousand *ʿulamāʾ*, declaring that Parwēz was a *kāfir*.
2. Rashida Begum v. Shahab Din. *All Pakistan Legal Decisions* (1960) Lahore, 1162.
3. *Ibid.*, 1165.
4. *Ibid.*, 1150.
5. *Ibid.*, 1153.
6. The program began with *ad hoc* measures: encouraging prayer in government offices, strict enforcement of the *Ramaḍān* fast, the introduction of

flogging and amputation as penalties for criminal offenses. After 1979 this *ad hoc* approach began to give way to reliance on institutions designed to supervise more systematically the enactment and application of Islamic laws. Among the most important of these was a system of Shariat (*Sharīʿa*) courts. The first of these courts were merely separate benches appended to each of Pakistan's superior courts. But in May 1980, due to duplication of cases and the strain on the already overextended superior courts, the four Shariat benches of the High Courts at Karachi, Lahore, Rawalpindi, and Peshawar were consolidated into a single Federal Shariat Court. A Shariat bench of the Supreme Court of Pakistan remained the highest court of appeal for *Sharīʿa* matters.

7. The record of the FSC as a criminal appellate court has been analyzed by Charles Kennedy, "The Implementation of the Hudood Ordinances in Pakistan," *Islamic Studies* 26 (1987): 307–319.
8. Constitution of Pakistan, 1973, Article 203(d). Inserted by Constitution (Amendment) Order 1 of 1980.
9. Constitution of Pakistan, 1973, Article 31(1) and Article 227(1).
10. Hazoor Baksh vs. Federation of Pakistan, *All Pakistan Legal Decisions* (1981), FSC.
11. *Ibid.*, 207.
12. *Ibid.*, 206.
13. President's Order 5 of 1981. Effective April 13, 1981: "The Court shall have the power to review any decision or order made by it."

Bibliography

Abbott, Nabia. *Studies in Arabic Literary Papyri*, vol. II: *Qur'anic Commentary and Tradition*. Chicago, 1967.

"Hadith Literature: Collection and Transmission of Hadith." In *Arabic Literature to the End of the Umayyad Period*, ed. A. F. L. Beeston, et al., 289–298. Cambridge, 1983.

ʿAbd al-Khāliq, ʿAbd al-Ghanī. *Ḥujjiyyat al-sunna*. Beirut, 1986.

ʿAbd al-Qādir, ʿAlī Ḥasan. *Naẓara ʿāmma fī taʾrīkh al-fiqh al-Islāmī*. Cairo, 1956.

ʿAbd al Rāziq, ʿAlī. *Al-Islām wa uṣul al-ḥukm*. Cairo, 1925. Trans. Leon Bercher as "L'Islam et les bases du pouvoir," in *Revue Des Etudes Islamiques* 7, (1933): 353–391; 8 (1934): 163–222.

ʿAbduh, Muḥammad. *The Theology of Unity*. Trans. Kenneth Cragg and Ishaq Masaʿad. London, 1966.

Abdul Rauf, Muhammad. "Hadith Literature: The Development of the Science of Hadith." In *Arabic Literature to the End of the Umayyad Period*, ed. A. F. L. Beeston, et. al., 271–288. Cambridge, 1983.

Abū Ḥanīfa. *Risāla* of Abū Hanīfa addressed to ʿUthmān al-Batti. In *Kitāb al-ʿālim wa'l-mutaʿallim*, ed. M. Z. al-Kawthari. Cairo, 1368 A.H., 34–38.

Abū Rayya, Maḥmūd. *ʾAḍwāʾ ʿalā al-sunna al-Muḥammadiyya*. Cairo, 1958; 3rd edn. with foreword by Tāhā Ḥusayn, Cairo, n.d.

Abū Shuhba, Muḥammad Muḥammad. "Naqd kitāb aḍwāʾ ʿalā al-sunna al-Muḥammadiyya." *Majallat al-Azhar* 30 (1959): 55–59, 146–151, 264–271, 321–329, 426–431, 522–527, 660–665.

Abū Yūsuf, al-Qāḍī. *Kitāb al-Kharāj*. Cairo, 1302 A.H.

Abū Zahra, Muhammad. "An Analytical Study of Dr. Schacht's Illusions." *Journal of Islamic Studies* 1 (1968): 24–44.

Abū Zahw, Muḥammad Muḥammad. *al-Ḥadīth wa al-muḥaddithūn*. Cairo, 1958.

Adams, Charles C. *Islam and Modernism in Egypt*. London, 1933.

Adams, Charles J. "The Authority of Prophetic Hadith in the Eyes of some Modern Muslims." In *Essays on Islamic Civilization Presented to Niyazi Berkes*, ed. Donald P. Little, 25–47. Leiden, 1976.

Aḥmad Khān, Sir Sayyid. *Asbāb-i baghāwat-i Hind*. Moradabad, 1858; repr. in *Maqālāt*, IX, 47–124.

Athār al-ṣanādīd. 1st edn. Delhi, 1947; repr. in *Maqālāt*, XVI, 212–284.

Maqālāt-i Sir Sayyid, 16 vols. Ed. Ismāʿīl Pānīpatī. Lahore, 1962–1965.

A Series of Essays on the Life of Muhammad and Subjects Subsidiary Thereto. London, 1870. Trans. into Urdu as *al-Khuṭubāt al-aḥmadiyya fī al-ʿarab wa al-sīra al-Muḥammadiyya*.

Tabyīn al-kalām: The Mohamedan Commentary on the Holy Bible, 2 vols. Ghazeepore, 1862 and 1865.

Tafsīr al-Qur'ān, 6 vols. Aligarh, 1297 A.H.

Tahzib al-akhlāq [collected reprint]. Lahore, n.d.

Taṣānīf-i aḥmadiyya, 2 vols. Aligarh, 1883.

Ahmed, Munir-ud-din. "Hadith in Ahmadiyya Theology." In *Actes du XXIXe Congrès International des Orientalistes Etudes Arabes et Islamiques*. Paris, 1975.

Āl al-Shaykh, Ṣāliḥ b. ʿAbd al-ʿAzīz b. Muḥammad. *al-Miʿyār li ʿilm al-Ghazālī fī kitābihi "al-sunna al-nabawiyya."* Cairo, 1990.

ʿAlī Mawlana, Aḥmad. *Ḥaqq parast ʿulamāʾ kī Mawdūdiyyat sē nārāẓgī kē asbāb*. Lahore, n.d.

Alvī, Khālid. *Fayḍ al-khāṭir*. Cairo, 1966.

Ḥifāẓat-i-ḥadīth. Lahore, 1971.

Yawm al-Islām. Cairo, 1952; 2nd edn., Cairo, 1958.

Amīn, Aḥmad. *Fajr al-Islām*. Cairo, 1933; 14th imp. Cairo, n.d.

al-ʿAmrī, Ḥusayn b. ʿAbdullah. *The Yemen in the 18th and 19th Centuries: A Political and Intellectual History*. London, 1985.

Amritsarī, Abū al-Wafāʾ Thanāʾ Allāh. *Ahl-i-Ḥadīth kā madhhab*. Lahore, 1970.

Burhān al-Qurān. Amritsar, [1923].

Dalīl al-furqān bi jawāb ahl-i-Qur'ān. Amritsar, 1906.

Ansari, Zafar Ishaq. "The Authenticity of Traditions – a Critique of Joseph Schacht's Argument E. Silentio," *Hamdard Islamicus* 7 (1984): 51–61.

"Islamic Juristic Terminology before Safi'i: A Semantic Analysis with Special Reference to Kufa," *Arabica* 19 (1972): 255–300.

ʿAqāʾid. Amritsar, n.d.

al-Athārī, Muḥammad Bahja. *Aʿlām al-Irāq fī tarīkh bayt al-Alūsī*. Baghdad, n.d.

Azami, M. M. *Studies in Early Hadith Literature*. Beirut, 1968; repr. Indianapolis, 1978. Trans. into Arabic as Muḥammad Muṣṭafā al-Aʿẓamī, *Dirāsāt fī al-ḥadīth al-nabawī wa taʾrīkh tadwīnihā*. Riyadh, 1976.

Studies in Hadith Methodology and Literature. Indianapolis, 1977.

Aziz Ahmad. *Islamic Modernism in India and Pakistan, 1857–1964*. Oxford, 1967.

"Le mouvement des mujāhidīn dans l'Inde au XIXe siècle," *Orient* 4 (1960): 105–116.

Studies in Islamic Culture in the Indian Environment. London, 1964.

al-ʿAẓm, Rafiq Bey, "al-Tadwīn fī al-Islām," *al-Manār* 10 (1907): 930.

Baljon, J. M. S. "Pakistani Views of Hadith," *Die Welt Des Islams*, n.s. 5 (1958): 219–227.

Reforms and Religious Ideas of Sir Sayyid Aḥmad Khān. Lahore, 1964.

Religion and Thought of Shāh Walī Allāh Dihlawī, 1703–1762. Leiden, 1986.

Balkhī, Iftikhār Aḥmad. *Fitna-i-Inkār-i-ḥadīth kā manẓar-o-pas manẓar*, 3 vols. Karachi, 1955–1960.

Barq, Ghulām Jīlānī. *Dō Islām*. Lahore, 1950.

"Ḥadīth kē bārē mēn mērā mawqaf," *Chatan*, Lahore. January 9, 1956.

Tārīkh-i-ḥadīth. Lahore, 1988.

al-Bayān. Lahore, 1939–1947, 1949–1952.

al-Bāz, Aḥmad Manṣūr. *al-Manār* 9 (1906): 610–614.

Binder, Leonard. *Islamic Liberalism*. Chicago, 1988.
Birkeland, Harris. *The Legend of the Opening of Muhammad's Breast*. Oslo, 1955.
al-Bishrī, Shaykh Ṭāhā. "al-Dīn wa al-ʿaql," *al-Manār* 9 (1906): 771–781.
"Uṣūl al-Islām," *al-Manār* 9 (1906): 699–711.
Bravmann, M. M. *The Spiritual Background of Early Islam: Studies in Ancient Arab Concepts*. Leiden, 1972.
Bukhārī, Sayyid Nūr al-Ḥasan. *Aṣḥāb-i-rasūl par ʿadilānah difāʿ*. Lahore, 1387 A.H.
al-Bukhārī, Muḥammad b. ʿAbd Allāh. *al-Taʾrīkh al-kabīr.* Hyderabad [Deccan], 1361 A.H.
Burton, John. *The Collection of the Qur'an*. Cambridge and New York, 1977.
"Notes Toward a Fresh Perspective on the Islamic Sunna," *British Society of Middle Eastern Studies Bulletin* 11 (1984): 3–17.
The Sources of Islamic Law. Edinburgh, 1990.
Butler, R. A. "Penseurs Musulmans contemporains III: Influences non-Arabes et purification de l'Islam selon le Pakistanais Ghulam Ahmad Parwez." *IBLA* (Tunis) 38 (1975): 136.
Camaroff, Jean. "Missionaries and Mechanical Clocks," *Journal of Religion* 71 (1991): 1–17.
Chakṟālawī, ʿAbd Allāh. *Burhān al-furqān ʿalā ṣalāt al-Qurʾān*. Lahore, n.d.
Ishāʿat al-Qurʾān. Lahore, 1902.
Tarjumat al-Qurʾān bi āyāt al-furqān. Lahore, 1906.
[Chirāgh ʿAlī] Moulavi Cheragh Ali. *Aʿzam al-kalām*. Agra, 1910.
A Critical Exposition of the Popular Jihad. Calcutta, 1885.
Proposed Political Legal and Social Reforms in the Ottoman Empire. Bombay, 1883.
Rasāʾil. Hyderabad [Deccan], 1918–1919.
Commins, David Dean. *Islamic Reform: Politics and Social Change in Late Ottoman Syria*. New York, 1990.
"Religious Reformers and Arabists in Damascus, 1885–1914." *International Journal of Middle Eastern Studies* 18 (1986): 405–435.
Cook, Michael. *Early Muslim Dogma*. Cambridge, 1981.
Cook, Michael and Patricia Crone. *Hagarism: The Making of the Islamic World.* Cambridge and New York, 1977.
Coulson, Noel. "European Criticism of Hadith Literature." In *Arabic Literature to the End of the Umayyad Period*, ed. A. F. L. Beeston, et. al. Cambridge, 1983.
A History of Islamic Law. Edinburgh, 1964; 1978.
Crone, Patricia and Martin Hinds. *God's Caliph: Religious Authority in the First Centuries of Islam*. Cambridge, 1986.
Dar, B. A. [Bashīr Aḥmad]. *Religious Thought of Sayyid Ahmad Khan.* Lahore, 1957.
Dhahabī, Muḥammad Ḥusayn. *al-Tafsīr wa al-mufassirūn*, 3 vols. Cairo, 1961–1962.
Difāʿ ʿan al-ḥadīth al-nabawī wa-tafnīd shubahāt khuṣūmihi. Cairo, 1958.
Dihlawī, Muḥammad Ayyūb. *The Mischief of Rejection of Hadith*. Karachi, n.d.
Enayat, Hamid Enayat. *Modern Islamic Political Thought.* Austin, 1982.
Encyclopaedia of Islam. 1st edn. 9 vols. Ed. D. B. MacDonald. Leiden, 1913–1938 (EI^1); 2nd edn. Ed. H. A. R. Gibb et al. Leiden, 1960– (EI^2).

Escovitz, Joseph H. "'He was the Muḥammad ʿAbduh of Syria': A Study of Tahir al-Jaza'iri and His Influence," *International Journal of Middle Eastern Studies* 18 (1986): 293–310.

Ess, Josef van. "The Kitāb al-Irǧāʾof al-Ḥasan b. Muḥammad b. al-Ḥanafiya," *Arabica* 21 (1974): 20–52.

"ʿUmar II and his Epistle against the Qadariyya," *Abr Nahrain* 1 (1971–1972): 20 ff.

Zwischen Hadit und Theologie: Studien zum Entstehen pradestinatianischer Überlieferung. Berlin, 1975.

al-Ghazālī, Abū Ḥāmid. *Kitāb al-arbaʿīn fī uṣūl al-dīn.* Cairo, 1344.

Kitāb al-mustaṣfā, 2 vols. Cairo, 1322 A.H.

al-Ghazālī, Muḥammad. *al-Sunna al-nabawiyya bayna ahl al-fiqh wa ahl al-ḥadīth.* Cairo, 1989; 2nd edn., 1990.

Ghaznawī, Abū Bakr. *Kitābat-i-ḥadīth ʿahd-i-nabawī mēn.* Lahore, n.d.

Gibb, H. A. R. *Modern Trends in Islam.* Chicago, 1947.

Mohammedanism. Oxford, 1949.

Gīlānī, Sayyid Manāẓir Aḥsan. *Tadwīn-i-ḥadīth.* Karachi, 1956.

Goldziher, Ignaz. *Introduction to Islamic Theology and Law.* Trans. Andras and Ruth Hamori. Princeton, 1981.

Muhammedanische Studien, 2 vols. Leiden, 1896. Trans. S. M. Stern as *Muslim Studies*, 2 vols. London, 1967.

The Ẓāhirīs: Their Doctrine and their History. Ed. and trans. Wolfgang Behn. Leiden, 1971.

Graham, William. *Divine Word and Prophetic Word in Early Islam: A Reconsideration of the Sources with Special Reference to the Divine Saying or Hadith Qudsi.* The Hague, 1977.

"Traditionalism in Islam: An Essay in Interpretation," *Journal of Interdisciplinary History* 23 (1993): 495–522.

Guillaume, Alfred. *The Life of Muhammad: A Translation of Ibn Isḥaq's Sīrat rasūl Allāh.* London, 1970.

The Traditions of Islam: An Introduction to the study of Hadith Literature. Oxford, 1924.

Hālī, Alṭāf Ḥusayn. *Hayāt-i-jawēd.* 1st edn. Cawnpore, 1901; rep. Lahore, 1966.

Hallaq, Wael B. "Was al-Shāfiʿī the Master Architect of Islamic Jurisprudence?" *International Journal of Middle East Studies* 25 (1993): 587–605.

al-Hamadhānī, Abū Bakr Muḥammad b. Mūsā b. ʿUthmān b. Ḥazim. *Kitāb al-iʿtibār fī al-nāsikh wa al-mansūkh min bayān al-āthār.* Hyderabad [Deccan], 1319.

Ḥamza, ʿAbd al-Razzāq. *Ẓulumāt Abī Rayya imām aḍwāʾ al-sunna [sic] al-muḥammadiyya.* Cairo, 1959.

Ḥaqīqat al-Islām wa uṣūl al-ḥukm. Cairo, 1344 A.H.

al-Ḥaqq, Sayyid Amīn. *Mawdūdī maslak par naqd-ō-naẓar: saḥāba miʿyār-i-ḥaqq hēn.* Lahore, 1383 A.H.

Haykal, Muḥammad Ḥusayn. *Hayāt Muḥammad.* 2nd imp. Cairo, 1954.

Hedayatulla, Muhammad. *Sayyid Ahmad: A Study of the Religious Reform Movement of Sayyid Ahmad of Raʾy Bareli.* Lahore, 1970.

Hermansen, Marcia K. "Shāh Walī Allāh's Theory of Religion in *Ḥujjat Allāh al-Bāligha*." 2 vols. Ph.D. Thesis, University of Chicago, 1982.

Hinds, Martin. "The Siffin Arbitration Agreement," *Journal of Semitic Studies* 17 (1972): 93–129.
Hodgson, Marshall. *The Venture of Islam*, 3 vols. Chicago, 1974.
Hourani, Albert. *Arabic Thought in the Liberal Age, 1798–1939*. Oxford, 1962.
Hourani, George F. "The Basis of Authority of Consensus in Sunnite Islam," *Studia Islamica* 21 (1964): 13–60.
Ḥukm hay'at al-ʿulama' fī al-kitāb al-Islām wa uṣūl al-ḥukm. Cairo, 1344 A.H.
Ḥusayn, Sayyid Murtaḍā. *Tārikh-i-tadwīn-i-ḥadīth*. Rawalpindi, n.d.
Ḥusayn, Ṭāḥā. *Muraʿat al-Islām*. Cairo, 1959.
Huwaydī, Fahmī. "Berestruika Islamiyya!" *Al-Ahrām*. January 31, 1989.
Ibn ʿAbd al-Barr. *Jamīʿ*, 2 vols. Cairo, 1346 A.H.
Ibn ʿAbd al-Rahīm, Ashraf b. ʿAbd al-Maqṣūd, *Jināyat al-Shaykh Muḥammad al-Ghazālī ʿalā al-ḥadīth wa ahlihi*. Ismailia, 1989.
Ibn Abī Ḥātim. *Kitāb al-jarḥ wa al-taʿdīl*, 8 vols. Hyderabad [Deccan], 1952–1953.
Ibn Ḥajar. *Tahdhīb al-tahdhīb*. Hyderabad [Deccan], 1325–1327 A.H.
Ibn Ḥanbal, Aḥmad. *Musnad*, 6 vols. Cairo, 1312–1313 A.H.
Ibn Ḥazm, Abū Muḥammad. *Kitāb al-iḥkām fī uṣūl al-aḥkām*, 4 vols. Ed. Aḥmad Shākir. Cairo, 1322 A.H.
Ibn Isḥaq. *Sīrat rasūl Allāh: Das Leben Muhammads bearbeitet von ʿAbd el-Malik ibn Hisham*. Ed. Ferdinand Wustenfeld, 2 vols. in 3. Göttingen, 1858–1860.
Ibn Khaldūn. *Muqaddima*. Cairo, 1274 A.H.
Ibn Manzūr. *Lisān al-ʿArab*, 20 vols. Cairo, 1300–1308 A.H.
Ibn Qutayba. *Kitāb ta'wīl mukhtalif al-ḥadīth*. Trans. Gerard Lecomte as *Le Traité des Divergences du Hadīt d'Ibn Qutayba*. Damascus, 1962.
Ibn Saʿd, Muḥammad. *Kitāb al-ṭabaqāt al-kabīr*, 9 vols. Ed. E. Sachau. Leiden, 1904–1940.
Ikrām, S. M. [Shaykh Muḥammad]. *Mawj-i-kawthar*. Lahore, 1962.
Rūd-i-kawthar. Lahore, 1968.
Shiblī Nāma. Lucknow, n.d.
Yadgār-i-Shiblī. Lahore, 1971.
Iqbal, Mohammed. *The Reconstruction of Religious Thought in Islam*. London, 1934; repr. Lahore, 1965.
Ishāʿat al-Qur'ān. Lahore, 1921–1925.
al-ʿIzzī, ʿAbd al-Munʿim Ṣāliḥ. *Difāʿ ʿan Abī Hurayra*. Baghdad, 1973.
al-Jabartī, ʿAbd al-Raḥmān. *ʿAjā'ib al-athār fī al-tarājim wa al-akhbār*. Cairo, 1882.
al-Jabūrī, Abū al-Yaqẓān ʿAṭiyya. *Mabāḥith fī tadwīn al-sunna al-muṭahhara*. Cairo, 1972.
Jalbani, G. N. *Life of Shah Waliyullah*. Lahore, 1978.
Jansen, J. J. G. *The Interpretation of the Qur'ān in Modern Egypt*. Leiden, 1974.
Jayrājpūrī, Muḥammad Aslam. *ʿIlm-i-ḥadīth*. Lahore, n.d.
Taʿlīmāt al-Qur'ān. Delhi, 1934.
Tarīkh al-ummat, 8 vols. 2nd edn. Lahore, 1953–1960.
al-Wirāthāt fī al-Islām. Amritsar, n.d.
al-Jurjānī, *Kitāb al-taʿrīfāt*. Cairo, 1321 A.H.
Juynboll, G. H. A. *The Authenticity of the Tradition Literature: Discussions in Modern Egypt*. Leiden, 1969.

Muslim Tradition: Studies in Chronology, Provenance and Authorship of Early Hadith. Cambridge, 1983.

"Some New Ideas on the Development of Sunna as a Technical Term in Early Islam," *Jerusalem Studies in Arabic and Islam* 10 (1987): 108.

Kandehlavī, Muḥammad Idrīs. *Ḥujjiyyat-i-ḥadīth.* Lahore, n.d.

Keddie, Nikki R., ed. *Scholars, Saints and Sufis.* Berkeley, 1972.

Kedourie, Elie. *Afghani and 'Abduh: An Essay on Religious Unbelief and Political Activism in Modern Islam.* London, 1966.

Kennedy, Charles. "The Implementation of the Hudood Ordinances in Pakistan," *Islamic Studies* 26 (1987): 307–319.

Kerr, Malcolm. *Islamic Reform: The Political and Legal Theories of Muhammad Abduh and Rashid Rida.* Berkeley, 1966.

Khālid, Khālid Muḥammad. *Min hunā nabdaʾ.* Cairo, 1950. Trans. Isma'il R. el Faruqi as *From Here We Start.* Washington, 1953.

Khalidi, T. "Islamic Biographical Dictionaries: A Preliminary Assessment," *Muslim World* 63 (1973): 53–65.

Khān, Ṣiddīq Ḥasan. *ʿĀqibat al-muttaqīn.* Benares, 1904.

Kitāb al-muʿtaqad al-muntaqad. Delhi, 1889.

al-Tāj al-mukallal min jawāhir maʾāthir al-ṭirāz al-ākhir wa al-awwal. 1st edn. Bhopal, 1882; repr. Bombay, 1963.

al-Khaṭīb al-Baghdādī (d. 463 A.H.). *al-Kifāya fī ʿilm al-riwāya.* Hyderabad [Deccan], 1357 A.H.

al-Khaṭīb, Muḥammad ʿAjjāj. *Abū Hurayra rāwiyyat al-Islām.* Cairo, 1962.

al-Sunna qabla al-tadwīn. Cairo, 1963.

Uṣūl al-ḥadīth. Beirut, 1967.

al-Khūlī, ʿAbd al-ʿAzīz. *Miftāḥ al-sunna aw taʾrīkh funūn al-ḥadīth.* 2nd imp. Cairo, 1928.

Kishk, Muḥammad Jalāl. *al-Shaykh Muḥammad al-Ghazālī bayna al-naqd al-ʿātib wa-al-madḥ al-shāmit.* Cairo, 1990.

Lakhnawī, ʿAlī Taqī. *Tadwīn-i-ḥadīth.* Hyderabad [Deccan], 1354 A.H.

Laoust, Henri. *Essai sur les doctrines sociales et politiques de Takī-d-dīn Aḥmad b. Taymīya.* Cairo, 1939.

"Les vraies origines dogmatiques du Wahhabisme: liste des œuvre de son fondateur," *Revue du Monde Musulman* 36 (1918–1919): 320–328.

Librande, Leonard. "Contrast in the Two Earliest Manuals of Ulum al-Hadith – The Beginning of the Genre." Ph.D. thesis, McGill University, Institute of Islamic Studies, 1976.

Lindbeck, George. *Infallibility.* Milwaukee, 1972.

Madkhalī, Rabīʿ ibn Hādi ʿUmayr. *Kashf mawqif al-Ghazālī min al-sunna wa-ahliha wa-naqd baʿḍ ārāʾih.* Medina, 1989.

Mājid, Rāja F. M. "Ghulām Jīlānī Barq: A Study in Muslim 'Rationalism.'" M.A. thesis, McGill University, Institute of Islamic Studies, 1962.

Maqām-i-ḥadīth, 4th edn., 2 vols. Lahore, 1986.

Margoliouth, D. S. *The Early Development of Muhammedanism.* New York, 1914.

"Omar's Instructions to the Kadi," *Journal of the Royal Asiatic Society* (1910): 307–326.

Marsot, Afaf Lutfi al-Sayyid. "The Beginnings of Modernization among the

Rectors of Al-Azhar." In *Beginnings of Modernization in the Middle East,* ed. William R. Polk and Richard Chambers. Chicago, 1968.

"The Role of the ʿulamāʾ in Egypt during the early Nineteenth Century." In *Political and Social Change in Modern Egypt,* ed. P. M. Holt, 264–80. London, 1968.

"The Ulama of Cairo in the Eighteenth and Nineteenth Centuries." In *Scholars, Saints and Sufis,* ed. Keddie, 149–165.

Mashriqī, Ināyat Allāh Khān. *Tadhkira.* Amritsar, 1924.

Masud, Muhammad Khalid. *Islamic Legal Philosophy: A Study of Abū Isḥāq al-Shāṭibī's Life and Thought.* Islamabad, 1977.

Mawdūdī, Abū al-ʿAlā. "Hadīth awr Qur'ân", *Tarjumān al-Qur'ān* (June 1934); repr. in *Tafhīmāt,* 318–349.

"Muftarijāt li al-dustūr al-Islāmī," *al-Muslimūn* 1 (1953–1954): 499–501; 576–578; 679–680.

Rasāʾil-o-masāʾil, 4 vols. Lahore, 1975.

Sunnat kī aʾīnī ḥaithiyyat. Lahore, 1963.

Tafhīmāt, 16th edn. Lahore, 1989.

Tarjumān al-Qurʾān, 56, no. 6 *Manṣib-i risālat nambar* (1961).

McDonough, Sheila. *The Authority of the Past: A Study of three Muslim Modernists.* Chambersburg, Pa., 1970.

"An Ideology for Pakistan: A Study of the Works of Ghulām Aḥmad Parwiz." Ph.D. thesis, McGill University, Montreal, 1963.

Merad, A. *Le Reformisme Musulman en Algerie de 1925 à 1940.* Paris, 1967.

Metcalf, Barbara Daly. *Islamic Revival in British India.* Princeton, 1982.

Mitchell, Richard P. *Society of the Muslim Brothers.* London, 1969.

Mīyānvalvī, Mihr Muḥammad. *ʿAdālat-i hazrat-i ṣaḥaba-i kirām.* Karachi, [1972].

Motzki, Harald. "The Muṣannaf of ʿAbd al-Razzāq al-Sanʿānī as a Source of Authentic Aḥadīth of the First Century A.H.," *Journal of Near Eastern Studies* 50 (1991): 21.

Muir, William. *The Life of Mahomet and the History of Islam to the Era of Hegira,* 4 vols. London, 1861; repr. Osnabruck, 1988. First serialized in *Calcutta Review* 19 (January–June, 1853): 1–80.

Murād, Mehr Afrōz. *Intellectual Modernism of Shiblī Nuʿmānī: An Exposition of his Religious and Political Ideas.* Lahore, 1976.

Muslim Students' Association of the U.S. and Canada. *The Place of Hadith in Islam: Proceedings of the Seminar on Hadith to Celebrate the 1200th Anniversary of the Great Muhaddith Imam Bukhari.* Plainfield, Ind., 1977.

Nadvī, Sayyid Sulaymān. *Hayāt-i-Shiblī.* Azamgarh, 1943.

"Phīr bahath-i-sunnat kuch awr ikhtirāʿāt-o-Ilzāmāt," *al-Maʿarif* 26 (July 1930): 10–19.

"Sunnat," *al-Maʿarif* 24 (1929): 84–96.

Nadwat al-sunna al-nabawiyya wa manhajihā fī bināʾ al-maʿarifa wa al-haḍāra, 4 vols. ʿAmman, 1991.

Nasr, Seyyed Hossein. *Ideals and Realities of Islam.* London, 1966; Boston, 1975.

Nawshahrawī, Abū Yaḥyā Imān Khān. *Tarājim-i ʿulamāʾ-yi ḥadīth-i Hind.* Delhi, 1356 A.H.

Nimr, ʿAbd al-Muniʿm. *Aḥādīth Rasūl Allāh kayfa waṣalat ilaynā.* Cairo, 1987.

al-Sunna wa al-tashrīʿ. Cairo, n.d.

Obermann, Julian. "On Muslim Tradition," *Muslim World* 2 (1912): 113–121.
"Political Theology in Early Islam," *Journal of the American Oriental Society* 55 (1925): 138–162.
Parwēz, Ghulām Aḥmad. *Ma'arif al-Qur'ān*, 7 vols. Karachi, 1949–1958.
Mafhūm al-Qur'ān. Lahore, 1961.
Maqām-i- ḥadīth. 2nd edn. Karachi, 1965.
Mi'rāj insāniyyat. Karachi, 1949.
Salīm kē nām khuṭūṭ, 3 vols. Karachi, 1953.
Shāhkār-i-risālat. 4th edn. Lahore, 1987.
Pellat, Charles. *Le Milieu Baṣrien et la formation de Ǧāḥiẓ*. Paris, 1953.
Peters, Rudolph. "Idjtihād and Taqlīd in 18th and 19th Century Islam," *Die Welt Des Islams* 20 (1980): 131–145.
Phulwārawī, Muḥammad Ja'far Shāh. *Maqām-i-sunnat*. Lahore, 1952.
al-Qaraḍāwī, Yūsuf. *Kayfa nata'āmalu ma' al-sunna al-nabawiyya*. El-Mansur, 1990.
al-Qāsimī, Jamāl al-Dīn. *Qawā'id al-taḥdīth min funūn muṣṭalaḥ al-ḥadīth*. Damascus, 1935.
Rahbar, Mohammad Daud. "Shah Wali Ullah and Ijtihad," *Muslim World* 45 (1955): 44–48.
Rahman, Fazlur [Faẓl al-Raḥmān]. "Concepts Sunnah, Ijtihad and Ijmā' in the Early Period," *Islamic Studies* 1, 1 (1962): 5–21.
Islam. 2nd edn. Chicago, 1979.
Islamic Methodology in History. Karachi, 1965.
"Post-formative Developments in Islam," *Islamic Studies* 1, 4 (1962): 1–23.
"Sunna and Ḥadīth," *Islamic Studies* 1, 2 (1962): 1–36.
Raḥmānī, Sayyid Minnat Allāh. *Kitābat-i-ḥadīth, ya'nī ḥadīthōn kī tartīb ō tadwīn kī tārikh par ēk mukhtaṣar awr jāmī' maqāla*. Lahore, 1370 A.H.
Ramaḍān, Mistrī Muḥammad. *Aqīmū al-Ṣalāt*. Gujrānwāla, 1938.
"al-Naskh wa-al-akhbār al-āḥād," *al-Manār* 12 (1910): 693–699.
Tārīkh al-ustādh al-imām al-Shaykh Muḥammad 'Abduh, 2 vols. Cairo, 1907–1908.
Riḍā, Muḥammad Rashīd. "al-Islām huwa al-Qur'ān wa al-sunna," *al-Manār* 9 (1906): 925–930.
Ritter, H. "Studien zur Geschichte der islamischen Frömmigkeit," *Der Islam* 21 (1933): 1–83.
Rizvi, S. A. A. *Shāh Walī Allāh and His Times*. Canberra, 1980.
Robson, James. "The Form of Muslim Tradition," *Glasgow University Oriental Society Transactions* 16 (1957): 38–50.
"Ibn Isḥāq's Use of the Isnād," *Bulletin of the John Rylands Library* 38 (1956): 449–465.
"The Isnād in Muslim Tradition," *Glasgow University Oriental Society Transactions* 15 (1955): 15–26.
"The Material of Tradition," *Muslim World* 41 (1951): 166–180; 257–270.
"Standards Applied by Muslim Traditionists," *Bulletin of the John Rylands Library* 43 (1961): 459–479.
"Tradition–Investigation and Classification," *Muslim World* 41 (1951): 98–112.
"Varieties of the Hasan Tradition," *Journal of Semitic Studies* 6 (1961): 47–61.

Saeedullah. *The Life and Works of Muhammad Siddiq Hasan Khan, Nawab of Bhopal*. Lahore, 1973.
al-Salafi, Muhammad Ismāʿīl. *Hujjiyyat-i-ḥadīth*. Lahore, n.d.
al-Samāḥī, Muḥammad Muḥammad. *Abū Hurayra fī al-mīzān*. Cairo, 1958.
Saqqā, Aḥmad Ḥijāzī Aḥmad. *Dafʿ al-shubhāt ʿan al-shaykh Muḥammad al-Ghazālī*. Cairo, 1990.
Sayf, Muḥammad Khālid. *Kitābat-i-ḥadīth tā ʿahd-i-tābiʿīn*. Lyallpur, n.d.
Scarcia, Gianroberto. "Scambio," *Annali Dell'Istituto Universitario Orientale di Napoli* n.s. 14 (1964): 623–645.
Schacht, Joseph. *Introduction to Islamic Law*. Oxford, 1964.
The Origins of Muhammadan Jurisprudence. Oxford, 1950; repr. 1964.
"Sur l'expression 'Sunna du Prophet,'" in *Mélanges d'orientalisme offerts à Henri Masse*. Teheran, 1963, 361–365.
Schimmel, Annemarie. *And Muhammad is His Messenger*. Chapel Hill, 1985.
Pain and Grace. Leiden, 1976.
Schuon, F. "Remarks on the Sunnah," *Studies in Comparative Religion* 6 (1972): 194–199.
Sezgin, Fuad. "Hadiṯ." In Fuad Sezgin, *Geschichte des arabischen Schrifttums*, 9 vols.: vol. I, 53–84. Leiden, 1967.
Shafīʿ, Justice Muḥammad. "Rashida Begum v. Shahab Din," *All Pakistan Legal Decisions* (1960) Lahore.
Shafīʿ, Muftī Muḥammad. *Maqām-i-Ṣaḥābah*. Karachi, 1971.
al-Shāfiʿī, Muḥammad b. Idrīs. *Kitāb al-risāla*. Ed. Muhammad Shākir. Cairo, 1940.
Kitāb al-umm, 7 vols. Cairo, 1321–1325 A.H.
Shāh, Muḥammad Karam. *Sunnat khayr al-ānām*. Karachi, 1373 A.H.
Shaw, Stanford J. *Ottoman Egypt in the 18th Century*. Cambridge, Mass., 1962.
Shawkānī, Muḥammad b. ʿAlī. *Nayl al-awṭār*. Cairo, 1928.
al-Qawl al-mufīd fī adillat al-ijtihād wa al-taqlīd. Cairo, 1340 A.H.
al-Shaybānī, Muḥammad b. al-Ḥasan, *Kitāb al-siyār al-kabīr*, 4 vols. Hyderabad [Deccan], 1335–1336 A.H.
al-Shiblī. *Sīrat al-Nabī*. Lahore, n.d.
Sirat al-Nuʿmān. Lahore, n.d. Trans. Muhammad Tayyab Bakhsh Badauni as *Method of Sifting Prophetic Tradition*. Karachi, 1966.
Siālkōṭī, Muḥammad Ibrāhīm Mīr. *Tārīkh-i Ahl-i-Ḥadīth*. Lahore, 1952.
Siālkōṭī, Muḥammad Ṣādiq. *Ḍarb-i-ḥadīth*. Gujrānwāla, 1961.
al-Sibāʿī, Muṣṭafā, *al-Sunna wa makānatuhā fī al-tashrīʿ al-Islāmī*. Cairo, 1961; 4th imp. Cairo, 1985.
Siddiqi, Muhammad Zubayr. *Hadith Literature: Its Origin, Development, Special Features and Criticism*. Calcutta, 1961.
Ṣidqī, Muḥammad Tawfiq. "al-Islām huwa al-Qurʾān waḥdahu," *al-Manār* 9 (1906): 515–524.
"al-Islām huwa al-Qurʾān waḥdahu: radd li-radd," *al-Manār* 9 (1906): 906–925.
[recantation of views] *al-Manār* 10 (1907): 140.
"Kalimāt fī al-naskh wa al-tawātur wa akhbār al-āḥād wa al-sunna," *al-Manār* 11 (1908): 594–598, 688–696, 771–780.
Smith, Wilfred Cantwell. *Islam in Modern History*. Princeton, 1957.

Modern Islam in India. London, 1946.

Sprenger, Alois. "On the Origin of Writing Down Historical Records among the Musulmans," *Journal of the Asiatic Society of Bengal* 25 (1856): 303–329, 375–381.

"Die Sunna." in Alois Sprenger, *Das Leben und die Lehre des Mohammad*, lxxvii–civ. Berlin, 1861–1865.

Sulṭān, Jamāl. *Azmat al-ḥiwār al-dīnī, naqd kitāb al-sunna al-nabawiyya bayna ahl al-fiqh wa ahl al-ḥadīth.* Cairo, 1990.

Suyūṭī. *Tadrīb al-rāwī fī sharh taqrīb al-Nawāwī*. Ed. ʿAbd al-Wahhāb ʿAbd al-Laṭīf, 2 vols. Cairo, 1963.

al-Ṭabarī, Muḥammad b. Jarīr, *Annales* [*Taʾrīkh al-rusul wa al-mulūk*], 15 vols. Ed. M. J. de Goeje. Leiden, 1879–1901.

Titus, Murray. *Indian Islam*. Oxford, 1930.

Islam in India and Pakistan. Calcutta, 1959.

Troll, Christian W. *Sayyid Ahmad Khan: A Reinterpretation of Muslim Theology*. Delhi, 1978.

Tyan, E. EI^2 s. v. ʿAdl.

ʿUthmānī, Muftī Muḥammad Rafīʿ. *Kitābat-i-ḥadīth ʿahd-i-risālat ō ʿahd-i-Ṣaḥāba mēn*. Karachi, 1985.

ʿUthmānī, Muḥammad Fahīm. *Ḥifāẓat-ō-ḥujjiyyat-i-ḥadīth*. Lahore, 1979.

Voll, John Obert. "Hadith Scholars and Tariqahs: An Ulama Group in the 18th Century Haramayn and their Impact in the Islamic World," *Journal of Asian and African Studies* 15 (1980): 264–273.

Islam: Continuity and Change in the Modern World. Boulder, 1982.

Waldman, Marilyn Robinson. "Tradition as a Modality of Change: Islamic Examples," *History of Religions* 25 (1986): 318–340.

Walī Allāh, Shāh. *Ḥujjat Allāh al-Bāligha*, 2 vols. Delhi, 1954.

Izālat al-khafāʾ ʿan khilāfat al-khulafāʾ. Bareli, 1869.

Wansbrough, John. *Qurʾanic Studies*. Oxford, 1977.

The Sectarian Milieu: Content and Composition of Islamic Salvation History. Oxford, 1978.

Welch, A. T. "The Ḳur'ān in Muslim Life and Thought." In EI^2, s. v. Ḳur'ān.

Wensinck, A. J. *A Handbook of Early Muhammadan Tradition, Alphabetically Arranged*. Leiden, 1927; repr. 1960, 1971.

al-Yāfiʿī, Ṣāliḥ b. ʿAlī. "al-Sunan wa al-aḥādīth al-nabawiyya," *al-Manār* 11 (1908): 141–144, 214–220, 292–302, 371–375, 454–463, 521–527.

al-Yamānī, ʿAbd al-Raḥmān b. Yaḥyā al-Muʿallimī. *al-Anwār al-kāshifa li-mā fī kitāb aḍwāʾ ʿalā al-sunna min al-zalal wa al-taḍlīl wa al-mujāzafa*. Cairo, 1959.

Yusuf, S. M. *An Essay on the Sunnah*. Lahore, 1966.

"Sunna – its Transmission, Development and Revision," *Islamic Quarterly* 37 (1964): 271–282; 38 (1964): 15–25.

Zubayrī, Muḥammad Amīn. *Hayāt-i-muḥsin*. Aligarh, 1934.

Zysow, Aron. "Agreement and Authenticity in Islamic Legal Theory," Middle East Studies Association, 1991.

Index

God
purposes of, 59
sovereignty of, 76
Goldziher, Ignaz, 12, 84, 100, 130, 158 n.13

ḥadīth qudsī, 53, 75
Hadood Ordinances, 135
Hammām b. Munnabih, Ṣaḥīfah of, 94
Ḥanafī school of law, 29, 39, 112, 123, 132
law of *diya*, 123
Ḥanbalī school of law, 18, 20, 22, 30, 111, 155 n.3
see also Ibn Ḥanbal, Ibn Taymiyya.
Ḥaramayn (Mecca and Medina), as center of reformist movements, 147 n.1
Ḥasan b. ʿAlī, 86
Ḥasan al-Baṣrī, 11
Ḥasan b. Muḥammad b. al-Ḥanafiyya, 11
Haykal, Muḥammad Ḥusayn, 120
Ḥijāz, 7, 23
ḥikma (Qurʾānic term), 55, 56, 57
Hinds, Martin, 11
Hishām, Caliph, 92
Hourani, Albert, 4
ḥudūd (crimes for which Islamic law requires a fixed penalty)
consumption of alcohol, 55
women's evidence in cases of, 121, 122
ḥujja (proof), 50
Ḥusayn, Ṭāḥā, 120

ʿibādāt, 63
Ibn ʿAbbās, 86
Ibn ʿAbd al-Wahhāb, 29, 148
Ibn Ḥanbal, 20
Ibn Ḥazm, ʿAlī b. Aḥmad, 51, 159
Ibn Ibād, 11
Ibn al-Jawzī, 165 n.25
Ibn Khaldūn, 129
Ibn Qayyim al-Jawziyya, Muḥammad ibn Abī Bakr, 163 n.7
Ibn Qutayba, 15, 16, 81
on non-binding sunna, 18
Ibn al-Ṣalāḥ, 114
Ibn Taymiyya, ʿAbd al-Salām, 26
Ibn Taymiyya, Taqī al-dīn Aḥmad, 2, 30, 155 n.3
Ibn ʿUmar, 86, 123
Ibn al-Zubayr, 86
Idāra-yi Tulūʿ-i-Islām, 140
iḥyāʾ al-sunna, 22
iʿjāz al-Qurʾān, *see* Qurʾān, inimitability of
ijmāʿ (consensus), 20, 26, 28, 44, 103, 104–105, 118, 133
traditions concerning, 105
ijtihād (the use of personal effort to decide a point of law), 20, 24, 25, 26, 30, 41, 52, 69, 70, 75, 77
Ikhwān al-Muslimīn, 120–121, 163
Ikrām, Shaykh Muḥammad, 40
ikthār al-ḥadīth, 86
ilhām (inspiration), 35, 142 n.3
ʿilla qādiḥa (corrupting defects), 110, 115
ʿilm al-rijāl, 82, 97–98
imitatio Muḥammadi, 1, 33
imām
in Parwēz's thought, 69
Shīʿī, 25, 60–61
India, 21, 23, 27, 30, 47, 65, 66
infallibility, doctrines of
challenges to, 63–64
Christian, 61, 63
general function, 61
Muslim, *see ʿiṣma*
insān al-kāmil, 63
inspiration, Prophetic
see waḥy, ilhām
Institute for Islamic Culture, Lahore, 75, 101
intellectual history, 2, 4
International Institute of Islamic Thought, 166 n.52
Iqbāl, Muḥammad, 25, 72
Iran, Islamic revolution, 2, 4
Iraq, early school of jurisprudence in, 7
Iṣlāḥī, Amīn Aḥsan, 130
Islam in Modern History, 2
Islamic criminal laws, 108
Islamic jurisprudence, 12
use of ḥadīth in, 17–20
Islamic law
formative phase of, 6
modern revival of, 111–112
role of sunna in, 119
Islamic state, 138
Islamization, 137
ʿiṣma (infallibility)
challenges to, 64, 66, 70, 72, 78–80
defense of, 73
definition of, 60–61
jurists' doctrine of, 61–63
Prophetic, 60–61, 85
Shīʿite doctrine of, 60
ṣūfī doctrine of, 63
see also infallibility
isnād (chain of transmission),
backward growth of, 84–85, 103
earliest use, 12, 160 n.67
forgery of, 98
function of, 81–82, 157 n.2